BEING PRESENT

Being Present

GROWING
UP IN
HITLER'S
GERMANY

WILLY
SCHUMANN

THE KENT
STATE
UNIVERSITY
PRESS
KENT, OHIO,
AND
LONDON, ENGLAND

© 1991 by the Kent State University Press, Kent, Ohio 44242
ALL RIGHTS RESERVED
Library of Congress Catalog Card Number 91-9996
ISBN 0-87338-447-4
ISBN 0-87338-493-8 (pbk.)
Manufactured in the United States of America

Second printing and first paperback issue, 1993

Library of Congress Cataloging-in-Publication Data

Schumann, Willy, 1927–
    Being present : growing up in Hitler's Germany / Willy Schumann.
      p. cm.
    Includes index.
    ISBN 0-87338-447-4 (cloth : alk. paper) (alk.) ∞
    ISBN 0-87338-493-8 (pbk. : alk.) ∞
    1. Schumann, Willy, 1927– . 2. National socialism.
    3. Germany—History—1933–1945. 4. Children—Germany—Biography.
    5. Youth—Germany—Biography. I. Title.
    DD247.S384A3 1991
    943.086'092—dc20
    [B]   91–9996

British Library Cataloging-in-Publication data are available.

To the memory of my mother and father

Contents

Preface

*I*t is common knowledge among responsible writers that they at all times keep their audience in mind, the people they want to address. The readership I had in mind during the two years when this book was taking shape was not composed of the specialists, the Germanists and Central European historians, but rather the younger generations of Americans for whom the Third Reich and the Second World War is merely the history of more than four decades ago. I know that many have an avid interest in the events of the 1930s and 1940s. They ask questions: What led to the second global war in our century? How did a divided Europe come about? In other words, I am thinking of my students and others who cannot have firsthand knowledge of the events, but who have the intellectual curiosity and the desire to learn *wie es eigentlich gewesen*, "as it actually happened" (Leopold von Ranke).

Above the main entrance of the university library in Boulder, Colorado, are chiseled in stone the words: "Who knows only his own generation remains always a child." The well-known quotation by George Santayana points in a similar direction: "Those who cannot remember the past are condemned to fulfil it." I fully subscribe to these views and I am convinced that a society without historical consciousness is a society without a future. In innumerable discussions and conversations with students, colleagues, friends, and my three children, it has become clear to me in more than forty years how fragmentary, sporadic, and one-sided the real knowledge in this country is about the events that led to the founding of the Third Reich, how little is known of the mentality, the inner attitudes, the thinking and feeling of a people who, because of their central geographical location, were destined to play a major role in history.

It was not my intention to write another history book presenting the course of events from 1930 to 1950. What I do want to convey to a larger general audience is to what extent the minds of the young, their thinking and feelings, were formed by the events of the day. In 1933, the year of Hitler's seizure of power, I was six years old. I have tried to reproduce an eye- and-ear-witness account of the twelve years of the National Socialist regime from the point of view of a young person—*aus der Froschperspektive,* "from a worm's eye view." I am, of course, aware that more than forty years have passed since then, and I also recognize the fallibility of human memory, which is often colored by later events. Therefore I was particularly careful and scrupulous about reporting only those reactions, feelings, and attitudes in those years of which I am absolutely certain. When I had doubts about the accuracy and reliability of my memory, I have said so.

My writing of the last three chapters, covering the years 1945 to 1950, is an attempt to show how long it took us to change some of our most basic concepts of politics, history, and social and moral issues and what the main contributing factors for this gradual transformation were: the influence of parents, teachers, and older friends; the intensive study of literature and history; and, in my own case, two immensely valuable and eye-opening stays abroad, three months in England and eleven months in the United States, months of true reeducation.

If there is one all-encompassing motivation for writing this book it is to show young Americans how easy it is, given the right historical and political circumstances, to form, control, and manipulate a whole nation—especially its young people. Today I cannot imagine a generation in the history of Germany less susceptible to political extremism than my own, one less prone to adventurism in the area of foreign policy. The lessons of the past are too gruesome, the consequences too catastrophic.

It is with great pleasure and a deeply felt sense of gratitude that I record the invaluable assistance and support my wife, Marianne Morrell-Schumann, provided from the inception of the project to the final sentence. She was instrumental first of all in her strong encouragement to undertake the endeavor. Secondly, she was the patient audience as I read to her week after week the results of my efforts. She was always ready with constructive criticism about what would be of interest to an American readership and what should be eliminated. Thirdly, she was, as a first-rate editor, to a large extent responsible for the readability of the manuscript. She saw to it that the book would not read like a translation.

A special note of thanks goes to Lillian N. Kezerian for her skill and patience in preparing the manuscript, for always being ready to do yet another draft. It helped greatly that she became fascinated by the evolving story. She was part of the first tiny audience of *Being Present.*

Ministerialrat Walter Fehling, a long-time friend, and the Landeszentrale für politische Bildung Nordrhein-Westfalen, Düsseldorf, helped me greatly by researching in Germany and acquiring permission for photographic material.

I wish also to mention my colleagues and friends at Smith College, who showed interest in the project and made valuable suggestions. My friends at the Hampshire Regional YMCA provided me with some of the specific English vocabulary with which I was not familiar, especially that of a military and maritime nature.

The Board of Trustees of Smith College, President Mary Maples Dunn, and Dean of the Faculty Robert B. Merritt generously approved the year's sabbatical which allowed me to give my full attention to the writing of this book.

I wish to express my appreciation to the Kent State University Press and especially to its director, Dr. John T. Hubbell, whose interest encouraged me through the completion of the text. His able editorial staff provided cogent suggestions; for their assistance I am most grateful.

1
Bread
and
games

In the annals of Western history, 1927 is not a spectacular year. Today's historians do not consider it a significant turning point in any respect—not politically, economically, militarily, socially, or culturally. Perhaps only in the history of aeronautics could an event of the first magnitude be recorded in 1927: Charles A. Lindbergh's first west-east crossing of the Atlantic in July.

The year 1927 cannot be compared to the year 1914, which initiated the end of an epoch, the Wilhelmian-Victorian age, and when "the lamps went out all over Europe." Indeed there are some historians who see the first days of August 1914 as the end of the nineteenth century, rather than December 31, 1899. Nineteen twenty-seven also cannot be compared with the year 1929, which signifies for many people "Black Friday," the beginning of the collapse of the New York Stock Exchange and the ensuing Great Depression and all its consequences. And most certainly 1927 cannot be measured with 1939—the outbreak of World War II, with all its profound and often horrendous effects on individuals and nations alike and the new power groupings in world politics.

Nineteen twenty-seven was relatively calm and uneventful. In German history—that is to say, in the history of the Weimar Republic—it was the time when one could hope for the gradual convalescence and strengthening of the "unloved republic."[1] The confused, chaotic, and often bloody beginning for the republic was in the past. It had become history. The transition from monarchy to a parliamentary democracy had been seemingly successful. The German people remembered very clearly the civil wars of 1918–19, the political assassinations, the Ruhr occupation, the catastrophic inflation of 1923, the various putsches from the extreme political Left and Right— but they were all memories. Things seemed better in 1927. The situation

appeared to have stabilized, especially politically, economically, and culturally. There were enough indications to justify the friends of the republic speaking of a first flourishing of Weimar culture: in the previous year Germany
had been asked to join the League of Nations in Geneva, thus ending the
pariah status of the republic; the "Spirit of Locarno" seemed to prevail with
the conclusion of a mutual security treaty between the two archenemies, Germany and France; the reparation demands of the 1919 Treaty of Versailles
were being cut back and, piece by piece, eliminated. In literature, the arts,
the theater, and the new film medium there was much adventurous mobility
and an irrepressible drive to experiment. Expressionism, the German contri-
bution to the development of modernism, became internationally recognized.

In this year, 1927, I was born. I am a member of *Jahrgang* 1927.[2] It is the
Jahrgang of the *dickgewordenen Flakhelfer*, "the antiaircraft gunners grown
fat," as we were called a few years ago in a rather acerbic German newspaper
column. It is also the last "nonwhite" Jahrgang whose members had to pay
with their health or with their lives for the insane "German war," World War
II. Too many in our "class" did not come back from this last big war. The
"white Jahrgänge" are the age groups born in 1928 and thereafter.

On January 30, 1933, my Jahrgang was five or six years old. It was the day
of *Machtergreifung*, "seizure of power," the day on which the aging, second
president of the republic, Paul von Hindenburg, entrusted the leader of the
National Socialist German Workers Party (NSDAP), Adolf Hitler, to form a
new cabinet. It was the beginning of the Third Reich, which was supposed to
last "a thousand years." In reality it came to a catastrophic end after just twelve
years. But in this short time in history, the Third Reich caused unspeakable
suffering for the people of the world and brought about radical changes in the
global constellation of power.

What do I remember of the years of my earliest childhood, of the time
before the ominous date of January 30, 1933? There are three scenes that
even today, more than fifty years later, are clearly etched in my memory like
short but well-defined action clips from a movie. All three have a common
denominator.

The first memory is a children's scene. My childhood friend, Helmut D.
and I were playing on a sandpile left over from minor road repairs made on
our street. We flattened the sand and with small sticks drew figures and faces
into the smooth surface. One was a swastika. We quickly looked around and
then whispered to each other, "And now, when a Communist goes by, we will
quickly draw four lines, and then it is a window." Like this:

The implication of this seemingly banal children's scene is not hard to de-
tect. Even in the limited view of four-year-olds from the bourgeois milieu,

2

Portrait of my siblings and me ca. 1930. I was three years old. *Left to right*: Rudolf, Hans-Heinrich, Willy, Lieselotte.

Communists were threatening and somewhat sinister people. Our families were very middle class. Our fathers were pilots, former captains in the merchant marine who now had qualified as highly specialized navigational experts on specific and difficult navigable waters, which in Brunsbüttel, our hometown, meant the Elbe estuary, the approach to the Kiel Canal locks, and the canal itself. We lived in the *Beamtenviertel*, the civil servants' quarter, which in our little town was considered a very desirable residential area. It was unthinkable that real Communists lived in our neighborhood. I cannot even remember neighbors who sympathized with the Social Democratic Party (SPD), the *Sozis*. Virtually all our friends and neighbors were World War I veterans who, because of their profession, had served in the Imperial Navy. Basically, my parents were apolitical. If I should classify them in modern political terminology, they probably stood slightly to the right of center. It stands to reason that their views strongly affected those of their children.

The second scene is also only very short and fleeting. My mother and I were waiting at the ferry to cross the Kiel Canal, which divides our town in

Aerial view of my hometown of Brunsbüttel. The estuary of the Elbe River, the canal locks, and part of the Kiel Canal are clearly visible.

two parts, the north side and the south side. Brunsbüttel is by European standards a young town. It was built at the end of the nineteenth century as part of the gigantic construction project of the Kiel Canal, the link of the Baltic and the North Sea.

As we were standing by the ferry gate, we heard from afar a strangely alien squeaking noise. When the band came closer the noise turned out to be the music of a Communist marching band approaching the ferry ramp. I can still see the twenty or thirty young musicians in their gray windbreakers, gray peaked caps, and red neckerchieves. What was so unusual about them was their music. It was a shawm band; its slightly nasal and shrill sound impressed me as very alien, almost exotic. Many years later, as a student of history, I learned why the political Left before and after the First World War revived the shawm, this obsolete and almost forgotten musical instrument from the late Middle Ages. It was a conscious gesture, a counterreaction to Prussian military music, the regimental bands playing their stirring military marches

4

with their snare drums and big drums, their trumpets and trombones. This kind of music, with its sharply accentuated beat, I knew even as a five-year-old, and I loved the simple melodies and marching rhythms. With its mixture of wafting, lyrical, and at times shrill sounds, the Communist shawm band appeared to me not only different and strange, but also, in an undefinable manner, threatening. My mother must have had similar feelings, because she said when the ferry arrived, "Let's go to the other side of the boat."

The third memory of my earliest childhood has to do with the flag, the official colors of the republic. We lived in a relatively spacious six-room apartment, in one of the houses built in the civil servants' quarter. The houses had been designed, financed, and constructed with federal money for the employees working on the widening of the Kiel Canal, a project finished in 1914. Each of the apartment houses had a tall flagpole in the front yard. It was customary at the time, and was probably recommended by the government, that on Sundays and on national holidays the national flag be flown in order to give the area a more festive appearance. I remember how happy I was when I was allowed to help my father or my older brother when it was our turn to fasten the flag to the rope and hoist it.

It is often pointed out in the relevant historical literature of the Weimar Republic that the initial insecurity and unpopularity of the first German republic is reflected in its controversial choice of the national colors. Many, but not all, of the responsible founding fathers wanted to show that they no longer identified with the Kaiser's empire, the Second Reich. Instead of black-white-red, they selected the colors of the *Jena Burschenschaft* and the *Lützow Jäger* during the wars of liberation from the Napoleonic hegemony, 1812–15: black-red-gold.[3] In 1848–49 the democratic and republican forces had attempted to create a progressive constitutional state and had gathered under this flag. But they failed. And when in 1870–71 the German unification came *von oben*— by governmental decree from the various German state cabinets, not by the efforts of the people—the new color combination of black-white-red was chosen: black and white, the old Prussian colors, plus red, the dominant color of the Hanseatic cities, representatives of the North German Alliance.

Black-red-gold were then the official national colors from 1919 to 1933. Nothing shows the feeling of inferiority of the "unloved republic" better than the merchant flag. The German merchant fleet sailed as before under the black-white-red flag with a black-red-gold *Gösch*, a small, hardly visible inset in the upper left corner of the flag.

As a five-year-old I did not know all this, but we children clearly felt how unpopular the republican flag was, at least in our part of town. Most people longed for the good old days, the splendor and pride of the imperial days and the old imperial colors, though in the historical sense they were not old at all. Black-white-red had been the colors for less than fifty years. In the early thirties

5

we children spoke often of the black-red-gold national flag as "black-red-mustard," and we were quite aware of the derisive connotation of this phrase.

The common denominator of these short memories of my early childhood is that they clearly show the deep-seated resentment and fear of the political Left harbored by the middle classes, of which we young children were representative members.

I do not remember much about the events of January 30, 1933, a day that changed the course of world history. My parents had purchased a good and rather expensive radio set, a small sensation for us children, and I seem to recollect endless broadcasts from Berlin, radio reporters who were close to tears with enthusiasm, the unending roar of approval of the masses in the capital, and, above all, the almost continuous strains of martial music and the hard, sharply accentuated rhythm of the marching columns celebrating their newly appointed chancellor with torchlight processions. But it is quite possible that my memory is playing tricks on me, for in the following years and decades I have seen and heard innumerable films and recordings of these parades and perhaps am projecting in reverse.

What I do remember very clearly, however, is an evening in our house in March 1933. My father, usually calm, sober, and levelheaded, came home very upset. My mother started crying. Neighbors and friends came and went. My father left again for a while. There was a mood of severe crisis. What had happened? Mr. H., a neighbor and friend of the family, chairman of the Pilots Brotherhood, their professional organization, had informed my father that he, Mr. H., had been forced to resign from his office. He was a member of the *Deutsche Volkspartei*, a moderate political party in the system that was no longer acceptable to the NSDAP in power. The National Socialists had gained 44 percent of the votes in the parliamentary elections of March 5, 1933. That was not the majority in the *Reichstag*, but they now had enough self-confidence to put pressure on all other parties and organizations in public life and force them to adjust to the new political realities and conform, "or else." This "or else" meant, according to Mr. H., dismissal from the pilot profession, thus unemployment. The NS functionary had not been timid or squeamish in his conversation with Mr. H. Among other things, the man had said that he could well imagine that at least half of the pilots—there were about 110 to 115 at that time in our town—would be replaced by candidates sympathetic and true to the party line.

Unemployment was the fear and horror for millions of people of the industrial nations all over the world during the Great Depression. The real or potential loss of one's job was felt by most people as an almost palpable threat. In later years I often heard my father proudly say that he had never in his whole life been unemployed, not for a single day, not even during the bad times immediately after the lost war. After four years of practically uninter-

My father in 1918, a warrant officer in the Imperial Navy. He wears the Iron Cross First Class, *right*, and the Turkish Star, *left*, high decorations for his World War I service.

rupted war service on submarines, he had come home. There were at that time thousands of sailors in every German port city who were laid up, who had no jobs and, what was worse, apparently had no chance for gainful employment in the foreseeable future, all because there were no ships. One

7

of the decrees of the hated Treaty of Versailles was the confiscation of the entire German merchant fleet, all vessels above a certain tonnage, and delivery to the Allies.

In these critical days, my father, without a moment's hesitation, changed his profession. He either purchased or rented a small fishing boat together with his future brother-in-law, my Uncle Louis, and for the next two or three years he and my uncle earned their living as fishermen. The work ethic of his generation was very much intact, and he was proud of it.

Now, after he had succeeded through competence, connections, and probably some luck in achieving the dream profession of every sailor, that of pilot, he was faced with the very real threat of losing his job, of dismissal for political reasons beyond his control. He was almost forty-six years old and was married with four children, all still of school age.

Many years later, when I was an adult myself, he described the following scene to me: he had decided to join the NSDAP, to become a party member, in order to save his job. The highest party functionary in our town at that time was Mr. R. T., whom nobody had taken very seriously until then. He was the owner of a disreputable pub and he had gone bankrupt at least once. Mr. T., now *Standartenführer* T.,[4] lived on the third floor of an apartment house on the Koogstrasse, the main street of our town. My father reported that he had climbed the stairs three times before he found the courage to ring the doorbell. Again and again he had said to himself in his beloved Low German language, *Hein Schümann, dat kanns du doch nich mooken,* "Hein Schümann, you can't do that." But he finally did do it and became a member of the NSDAP.

At that time my father probably knew little about the character and the aims of the NS party. I am certain that he had not read Hitler's book *Mein Kampf* or the official party platform, the *Parteiprogramm*, with its twenty-five points. There were, however, certain themes of the new regime that continued to be proclaimed loudly and repeatedly and with which he wholeheartedly did agree. These were the sharp attacks on the Versailles treaty of 1919, which he and probably most Germans considered to be humiliating, dishonorable, discriminating, and unfair. (The harsh peace treaty of Brest-Litovsk of 1918, which was forced upon Russia by imperial Germany and which was often mentioned by the defenders of the Versailles treaty as a valid parallel, was virtually unknown.) My father was also angered by the Allied war and postwar propaganda. In particular he took quite personally the false and distorted presentation of the German submarine warfare, and the deliberate lies in connection with the sinking of the *Lusitania* in 1915 were examples he often mentioned.[5]

Why it was so difficult for my father to join the party and why he was later so ashamed of it, and remained ashamed to the end of his life, can be found in the style of the new state party, now also his party—their noisy and vulgar bragging, their lack of tolerance, the shady and questionable background of the new power elite on the local as well as the national level. The aforementioned Standartenführer R. T. is a good example of the NSDAP style. I like to believe that it was also the flagrant anti-Semitism of the National Socialists that repelled him. I certainly never heard a single anti-Semitic remark from my father or my mother. That simply was not done in our family. But that is how my father became a *Märzgefallener*, "one who had fallen in March," as he and hundreds of thousands of Germans were soon called in grim, vernacular humor. They were the citizens who, out of fear or calculation or opportunism, joined the NSDAP after the parliamentary elections of March 1933.

It was strongly recommended to the new members—perhaps they were even ordered—that they join one of the paramilitary organizations of the party. For my father and his seafaring colleagues, the Marine-SA was the appropriate unit, a special branch of the general SA in which the members were trained and instructed in maritime skills. Thus my father appeared one day in his newly acquired brown shirt with navy-blue tie, navy-blue riding breeches, shiny riding boots, and navy-blue peaked cap. He wore all his war medals, of which he had quite a few, including the EK I, the Iron Cross First Class. He wanted to show "those people," as he phrased it, the NS people, *dat we ook wat mookt hebt*, "that we also had accomplished something." Despite his sartorial spendor, the new SA man appeared even to me, the six-year-old, as being inappropriately disguised. That was not the father I knew. He made a number of ironic remarks about his new uniform; for example, about his navy-blue riding breeches, a type of floppy jodhpurs, he said, *Seelüd un Peer, wie passt dat tosomen*, "sailors and horses, how do they go together?" My mother also was quite amused about his new costume. All this did not help to convince us children of the authenticity of the new Storm Trooper.

His career as such did not last long and came to an abrupt halt. I do not think I saw him more than three or four times in uniform. One evening he came home from a Marine-SA meeting in an angry mood, but we children felt the concealed laughter behind his apparent indignation. His unit, the SA-Sturm, consisted of forty to fifty men, more than half of whom were experienced merchant marine masters, highly trained navigational experts. The subject of the meeting was how to use a sextant and other navigational instruments. And who was the "instructor"? Mr. Max V., a town buffoon who had tried his hand at a dozen different jobs, among them patchwork tailoring and poster hanging, thus his nickname *Klebemaxe*, "Sticker Max." He was now SA-*Scharführer* V., and their instructor.[6] That was too much for my father and his colleagues. They felt insulted and simply stayed away from any more meetings. The totally irregular and unpredictable work schedule of harbor and canal pilots served as a convenient and acceptable excuse. The uniform was put in a closet, and I never saw it again.

The first big change in my life occurred in the spring of 1933: I started school. I became an *Osterküken*, an "Easter chick," as first graders even today are called. (Easter was for more than a hundred years the traditional beginning of the school year.) Nursery school and kindergartens in the modern American sense did not exist. I liked school; learning was easy for me. As a four- or five-year-old I had taught myself how to read; thus I had a considerable jump on my classmates and always brought home good grades. For the next four years I went to school every morning, including Saturdays, from eight in the morning to twelve or one o'clock in the afternoon. The elementary school was located about twenty-five minutes by foot from my home. School buses did not exist in Germany in the early thirties. There were about twenty-five to thirty children in our class. We remained for four years in the same building and changed classrooms only once. Our teacher, Miss A., was a splendid pedagogue, a warm, outgoing person, and a dedicated professional. She had the reputation in town of being an excellent teacher; when people asked me who my homeroom teacher was, and I replied, "Miss A.," the almost inevitable comment was "you lucky boy."

Our classroom was large and bright with five big windows, and a huge iron coal stove, which was serviced by our janitor during the winter months, stood in one corner. The room was quite austere. There were no decorations and only one picture, a fairly large engraving of the Battle of Hemmingstedt in the year 1500, an important historical event of the region. One day, in second or third grade (1935), a new picture was added. It was a print depicting the heads of four prominent figures in German history. They were idealized portraits, and they looked firmly and admonishingly at the onlooker. The first portrait was of Frederick I, called "Barbarossa," emperor of the Holy Roman Empire in the High Middle Ages. Next to him was the well-known face of Frederick II of Hohenzollern, Frederick the Great, with his three-cornered hat and curved nose—the *Alte Fritz* who two hundred years ago had made Prussia one of the five major European powers.[7] The third head was that of Otto von Bismarck, founder of the Second Reich and its first chancellor, with his famous bald head, big drooping mustache, and square jaw. The last portrait, on the extreme right, was that of the new leader, *Führer und Reichskanzler* Adolf Hitler, a youthful-looking man with somewhat piercing blue eyes, who for the next two or three years looked at us schoolchildren with a serious but friendly face.

The intention of this picture, which hung in every German classroom, was obvious: every hour of every day of the school year we were to see the Führer as the youngest representative in an unbroken chain of great and heroic men in the history of Germany, as the person who had finally fulfilled the thousand-year-old dream of a new united empire, the Third Reich. That was a special kind of historical worldview promoted consciously and systematically by the new NS educational policy. We small children, of course, were not aware of this; but later, in my years at the *Gymnasium*,[8] this teleological interpretation of history—seeing the entire history of a nation as moving toward a specific goal—was heavily stressed. It took many years before I could liberate myself from this one-sided and basically fraudulent way of looking at historical events and developments in German history.

I do not remember any direct ideological slant in our daily lessons. Miss A., who taught almost all our school subjects, must have joined the NS-*Lehrerbund* like all teachers, a kind of newly created teachers union that was completely loyal to the party line. Since she was a friend of my parents, I assume that she also shared their political views. Her opposition to the Versailles treaty was based on very personal reasons. She was born and raised in Flensburg, the northernmost German city on the German-Danish border. There had been plans to add the city to Northern Schleswig, a province separated from Germany by the Versailles treaty, and there was a good possibility that Flensburg might become Danish. Miss A. told us sometimes how she and her friends as young students had stood in the railroad station of Flensburg for hours singing, "until our voices were hoarse," the Schleswig-Holstein hymn and other German folk songs to shake up the citizens and encourage them to vote for Flensburg to remain part of Germany.[9] Miss A. certainly was a nationalist, but hardly a National Socialist.

There was a severe shortage of instructional aids. To be sure, we had the necessary readers and arithmetic books, but in the history and geography lessons the teachers at that time had to rely on their own knowledge and imagination. Once in a while they were able to hang up a map of the county, the province, or the country, but there existed only three or four maps in the whole school, and they were moved from classroom to classroom. This situation improved gradually. Eventually new schoolbooks appeared on the market which had to be bought by the parents of each pupil. We had no school library.

There was one exception to the relatively ideology-free instruction, and it came in one of the new primers. It was a very sentimentalized narrative of a family with several children. The father had been unemployed for several years; the children had no shoes and often had to go to bed hungry, crying themselves to sleep. But then came the big turning point. Adolf Hitler became Reichskanzler, and one of his first measures was large-scale creation of jobs. In the final scene of the story, the father was working happily and diligently together with many other formerly unemployed men at an *Autobahn* construction site. The Führer drove by in his big, black, open Mercedes limousine, and the workers waved to him enthusiastically "with profound

11

gratitude in their hearts." All this was illustrated with many colored drawings, and at the end it showed the famous photograph of Hitler breaking ground for the building of the first Autobahn segment.

The term "brainwashing" had not yet been coined, but it is clear that the collage of historical portraits hung in thousands of German classrooms and the Autobahn story were examples of unsubtle ideological propaganda. Undoubtedly there were other examples of this, but I do not remember them. In a later chapter about my years in the Gymnasium, I will provide more examples of flagrant, and in one case diabolical and perfidious, instances of this kind of mind-control, of the influencing of young and uncritical children.

We children took little notice of the important historical events of the 1930s, and, of course, we were not aware of their significance: the burning of the Reichstag in 1933; the "Enabling Act" of 1933; Germany's withdrawal from the League of Nations in 1933; President von Hindenburg's death and the combining of the offices of *Reichspräsident* and Reichskanzler into one in 1934; the return of the Saar region to the Reich in 1935; the Nuremberg laws of 1935; the Olympic Games of 1936; and the remilitarization of the Rhineland in 1936. At the time of the Saarland plebiscite, I remember the continuously repeated singing and playing on the radio of the song *Deutsch ist die Saar*, "The Saar is German," an old and traditional miners' song with a new patriotic text. I can still sing all the stanzas even today, more than fifty years later.

The olympiad in August 1936 was a great festival for us children. In the newspapers and magazines, in the radio broadcasts, and later in the famous olympiad films made by director Leni Riefenstahl, two ideas were emphasized again and again: the Olympic Games was a peace festival for the youth of the world conducted by the New Germany as host nation; and secondly, the German team performed splendidly in almost all competitions. Special news bulletins were issued several times a day over the radio and were heralded by a special Olympic fanfare followed by the announcement of another triumphant victory of a German athlete, team, or crew. With great enthusiasm we children counted the gold, silver, and bronze medals won by Germany. We felt proud, and the same was probably true for the majority of the German people.

Thirty years later the saying *wir sind wieder wer*, "we are somebody again," meaning we once again have a national identity, became a political slogan in the sixties. It certainly can be applied to the mood and attitude in Germany in August 1936. The NS government knew, as did such Roman emperors as Nero and Caligula, that feeding the masses and entertaining them with circus games were eminently useful tools to gain their support—*panem et circensem*, bread and games. That had been, after all, one of the main mo-

Hitler at a widely publicized ceremony turning the first spade at an *Autobahn* construction site. It was one of many attempts to give the Führer exclusive credit for the creation of new jobs. Courtesy of the Bundesarchiv Koblenz.

tivations for the new regime to invest millions of *Reichsmarks* in the games and to initiate so many acclaimed innovations in organizing them.

For the first time in the olympiad's history, the construction of a special super stadium took place; a separate Olympic village was built, and there young athletes from all over the world could freely mingle and become acquainted; and the tradition of lighting the Olympic fire in a grove at Olympia in Greece and carrying the flame from there to the site of the new olympiad was created, as were many other ideas and symbols. The fact that a non-Aryan, the American Jesse Owens, became the most successful athlete of the games by winning four gold medals did not bother us at all. Hitler's alleged refusal to shake hands with Owens was also played down in German news reports. In our children's games of playing the roles of the great athletes and reenacting their victories, everybody wanted to be Jesse Owens (though naturally we pronounced his name "Yesse Ovens").

Many historians today consider these years, the mid-thirties, as the high point of amicable and harmonious relations between the Third Reich and the rest of the world. Many Germans at the time shared this opinion. There seemed to be visible progress in all areas. People were regaining some of their self-respect, self-confidence, and pride. It was fun again to be a German. All this was a natural and understandably human reaction to my parents' generation, which lived through three shattering catastrophes in one decade: the lost war, the horrendous inflation, and the Great Depression.

This psychological lift of the people was one of the main goals during the first governing years of the NS leadership, which was made up of men who were indeed master psychologists. The other goal was the immediate and tangible improvement of living conditions. That too was accomplished. Even we children could see and feel it. The long lines of job seekers outside the official employment agencies disappeared. There were no more beer hall brawls, and the street fighting between the political extremists on the Right and the Left that had upset so many citizens in the past ceased. There was more money. Houses were freshly painted. The people wore better and newer clothes. The improvement of the world economy had a direct and positive effect on the shipping traffic on the Kiel Canal. The number of ships increased from year to year, and thus my father's income also grew.

For the Schümann family it meant, among other things, the purchase of an electric stove and of modern furniture for our living room. The master painter, Mr. S., a friend of the family who painted our living room and who thought of himself as an interior decorator, had convinced my parents that only one color for the window sills could go with the new furniture, the new carpet, and the new wallpaper—pink. Pink window sills! That was considered most progressive—almost radical—in our neighborhood. For weeks friends and neighbors who had never been in our apartment before came for a visit to see "Frau Schümann's pink window sills." My father suggested to my mother that she charge a small visitor's fee, an attempt at humor that did not sit well with her.

The general mood in the family, in the neighborhood, in our town, and in the entire country was optimistic and upbeat. We young people and, I am sure, the great majority of the adults did not realize that behind the new attractive and colorful facade and the many encouraging signs that pointed to a better and happier future there were serious, dangerous signals. Who at that time could imagine that a new war, World War II, called by some modern historians the second European civil war, lay only three years ahead? We also could not know that many of the so-called economic achievements of the regime were a direct result of gigantic and rapid rearmament. To be sure, unemployment was radically reduced, but at the same time an enormous national debt piled up and seriously endangered the economic stability of the nation. Some historians believe that for this reason alone Hitler needed a new war. We also did not know that the economic recovery was by no means a German phenomenon; the Great Depression was subsiding all over the world. In Germany, however, the NS government took sole and full credit for the country's general improvement, and that was constantly announced and emphasized by the information media now closely guided and supervised from Berlin.

2

Young people must be guided by young people

Us far as their formal education was concerned, neither of my parents had attended school for more than the required minimum number of years. They spent those eight school years in Prerow, Pomerania, their home village. After working for several years as an able seaman, my father, through diligence, tenacity, and talent, was then admitted to the merchant marine school for two years and graduated with the A5 diploma, a mate's license. A few years later he returned to the same school and after nine months passed the examination for the A6 license, the master's license. But neither my father nor my mother had the opportunity for a *humanistische Bildung*, a liberal arts education with its considerable emphasis on classical languages and literatures. They had only the vaguest concept of this ideal that played such an important role in the nineteenth and twentieth centuries in German educational philosophy. Like most parents of their social class, however, they were ambitious for their children. We were to achieve and enjoy what had been denied them. We were to have a better starting position for a later career, to achieve a higher and more prestigious position in society.

Thus, after four years of elementary school they sent my three older siblings to the *Mittelschule*, where they were to stay for six years and attain a better and more thorough education than in the *Volksschule's* four-year program. For me they had even higher aspirations. Since learning was easy for me—I always brought home good marks on my report cards and was usually class valedictorian—they were determined to send me to the Gymnasium, which meant I would be the first member of our whole family to attend this elite school. At that time the Gymnasien were much more exclusive than they are today. Only about 5 percent of all German students graduated from them. My parents' decision was made easier for them by the fact that in the third grade I was diagnosed as severely myopic, thus the traditional

16

family seafaring career was out of the question for me. Sailors had to have 20/20 vision, which is still the case today.

At this point there developed a complication. My teacher, Miss A., suggested that my parents apply for me to take the admission test at a *Napola,* a vernacular abbreviation of *Nationalpolitische Erziehungsanstalt.* They were boarding schools, many of which had previously been Prussian military academies, *Kadettenanstalten.* In the 1930s these Napolas were the educational institutions for training the new National Socialist leadership elite. They were not party schools in the narrower sense; the cadres of future NS functionaries were trained in the *Adolf-Hitler-Schulen* established a few years later. In the Napolas ideological instruction, physical education, and premilitary training were also emphasized (students and teachers always wore uniforms), but the intellectual level of the curriculum was high, discipline was strict, and the teachers were selected according to ideological *and* pedagogical and scholarly qualifications. The Napolas had an excellent reputation. The one closest to my hometown was in Plön, and it was the only Napola in the entire province of Schleswig-Holstein. Plön also had been the site of a former Prussian military academy that many of the high aristocracy of Prussia had attended, including several sons of the last German emperor, Wilhelm II.

Napola Plön was the school to which I was to apply. Undoubtedly Miss A.'s motivation for suggesting that I graduate from a Napola was that it would open up splendid career opportunities for me. How could she know that eight years later the entire NS regime would be history? I have no way of knowing how difficult it was for my parents to turn down my teacher's suggestion. On the one hand my father must have agreed with Miss A. that a Napola degree would be a great advantage for me in any future career now that the NS regime seemed to have consolidated and be firmly and safely in control. On the other hand there was his innate aversion to the NSDAP and its leaders, his skepticism about their political goals and about Germany's geopolitical role. Because of his profession, he had been in many countries, including the United States, and had sailed on ships of several different nationalities, and he knew the world. He was anything but provincial in his outlook.

It must have been at this time that more and more often in conversations with friends and neighbors he expressed his concern about the German rearmament policy and the rapid buildup of the *Wehrmacht,* the armed forces. He was a veteran who knew the war in all its abominable manifestations. His war years had been traumatic, and a repetition of 1914–18 was just about the last thing that he and most members of his generation desired. He summarized his worries in the proverb: *Wer ne Pistool het, de wil ook scheitn,* "He who has a pistol, wants to use it." I heard him repeat this sentence many times in those last years of peace before September 1939. Many of his conversation partners probably did not take him seriously. Most certainly we children did not. We

17

knew that among his colleagues and friends he had the reputation of being a congenital alarmist—*Hein Schümann, der Schwarzseher von Beruf,* "Hein Schümann, the professional pessimist"—and we attributed his "defect" to that.

It is quite possible that my father's skepticism and pessimistic foresight as to the future of a National Socialist Germany were the determining factors in his refusal to let me go to the Napola. I am certain that my mother was only too glad that she did not have to send her youngest son so far away. To be sure, Plön was only eighty kilometers from Brunsbüttel, but the prospect of not seeing me for months must have been a small nightmare for her. After all, I was only ten years old. The tradition of the English public school education, the boarding school system generally accepted by all members of the middle and upper classes in Great Britain, did not, with very few exceptions, exist in Germany. It was difficult enough for my mother to see me in a school world which was unfamiliar to her, where very soon she would be unable to supervise my homework and perhaps even unable to help in such academic subjects as mathematics, English, Latin, and the natural sciences.

Brunsbüttel at that time did not have a Gymnasium. Thus my father and I traveled to Marne, twelve kilometers away, so that I could prove, in a rather demanding entrance examination, that I was qualified for the Marne Gymnasium. I passed the various tests and, together with four other pupils of our former elementary school class, became a Gymnasium student. I was proud and now quite aware of belonging to a privileged group.

The only flaw in this was that shortly before this big event in my life, the traditional *Schülermützen,* the caps for middle school and Gymnasium students, had been banned by governmental decree. For more than a century it had been customary in German society to identify the students who attended schools other than the Volksschulen by special peaked caps. Every grade had a special color, and I had been looking forward to wearing the gray cap for *Sextaner* (fifth grade), blue the following year for *Quinta* (sixth grade), and so on. But these Schülermützen, symbols of the traditional class division, were now officially abolished "to create a more equal classless society." At least that was the official explanation. It was one of many attempts of a large-scale process of egalitarianism. But there was more to it. We know now of the deep and almost innate distrust of the NS regime vis-à-vis all intellectuals, the breeding place of whom were, of course, the Gymnasien. There were other measures that proved this anti-intellectualism in the following years, and some of them had a direct impact on my own education.

At any rate, I was denied the privilege of wearing this symbol of my new student status. But this disappointment was largely compensated by the fact that I then became a *Pimpf,*[1] a member of the *Deutsches Jungvolk* (DJ), the branch of the Hitler Youth for boys aged ten to fourteen. Thus for the first time in my life I was allowed to wear a brown shirt with a black neckerchief, black corduroy shorts with a belt, and a shoulder strap. On the left sleeve and on the shirt pockets we wore the various insignia to identify our units and, later, a host of different merit badges. It was handsome attire, we thought, and enough to make me forget the Gymnasium school caps. The uniforms had to be purchased by our parents, which was a financial burden; but since membership in the DJ was mandatory from 1937 on, there was nothing they could do about it. I do remember, however, that there were always some boys in our units who appeared at our meetings in civilian clothes. We considered them eyesores in our marching columns, and the boys themselves were embarrassed when in parades they were put in the middle of the column to be out of sight. Their excuses were always that their parents could not afford a uniform. All of these boys, however, came from working-class families, most likely on the political Left, and I suspect that they did not want to have NS uniforms in their homes.

The next two years, from 1937 to 1939, my life moved on two tracks: school and Deutsches Jungvolk. By far the most demanding and time-consuming part was school. We attended six days a week, five or six hours per day, from 8:00 in the morning to 1:00 or 2:00 in the afternoon. Three to four hours of homework every day was the norm, and later there was even more. The curriculum was demanding: German, mathematics, and English were the main subjects, given five hours per week; history, geography, biology, religion, music, art, and physical education were the minor subjects, given each two hours per week. Later, in the higher grades, Latin, physics, and chemistry were added. Art, music, and especially religion we did not take very seriously. All members of our class were nominally Lutheran, with one exception. Horst R. was Roman Catholic and was exempt from religious education in school. During our lesson he had to move to the back of the room, ostensibly to do his homework. He also had to bring a written statement from his priest certifying that he participated regularly in private religious lessons after school in his chapel. Horst R. was one of the many members of his Jahrgang 1926 who did not return from the eastern front.

We were commuter students, and it was a question of honor to get to school by bicycle and to use bus or train only in the middle of winter. This was a considerable physical hardship, given the variable, often cold, wet, and windy climate of our northern coastal area; but to go by bus or train in spring, summer, and fall was considered "sissy," and nobody did that.

The lessons were considerably more difficult than they had been in elementary school. Competition was much keener. For every subject we now had a special teacher. There were about twenty students per class, all boys. Not until two years later did our school become coeducational. We twelve-year-olds considered the arrival of the first three girls in our class an undesirable intrusion, and to be ordered to share a desk with one of them was

19

My childhood friend and I as novice members of the Hitler Youth (1937), proudly wearing our brown shirts and black shorts for the first time.

seen as punishment. It goes without saying that this prepubescent attitude changed quickly in later years.

Most of my teachers in these first years were very good instructors, well-educated and devoted pedagogues. Some of them had become NS party members and wore the NSDAP badge on the lapel of their suits or on their dresses. Every lesson began with the Hitler salute. We got up when the teacher entered the classroom; he raised his right arm and greeted us with *Heil Hitler!* and we returned the salute. But I do not remember that any of these professional pedagogues went out of their way to infect us with NS ideology. They tried to the best of their ability to convey to us their knowledge, the facts and figures in their respective disciplines, as they had been trained at their universities. I was most fortunate to have outstanding teachers in the subjects that interested me most and in which I excelled—German, English, and history. My entire later career was profoundly influenced by three splendid pedagogues: Miss J., Mrs. U., and Mr. W. Their enthusiasm for their subjects was infectious. I was spared exposure to any of the caricature-like teacher types that appear frequently in German literature, such as the miniature tyrants and incompetents in Thomas Mann's *Tonio Kröger* and *Buddenbrooks* and in Heinrich Mann's *Professor Unrat*.[2]

There were curriculum changes, but at this time they were still minor and superficial. For example, the Latin terminology in grammar lessons was Germanized. Instead of *Substantive, Verb, Comma, Present Tense*, we now had to use *Hauptwort, Zeitwort, Beistrich, Gegenwartsform*. It did not bother us at all. We also welcomed the introduction of the daily physical education hour, even though this had to be done at the expense of academic disciplines.

Much more serious was another educational reform, although it did not directly concern us beginners. By decree of the Reichs education minister, a whole year, the thirteenth grade, at that time still called *Oberprima*, was eliminated. Instead of the traditional nine years, only eight years were required to obtain the *Abitur* diploma. The radical cut of the educational requirement together with the strong emphasis on physical education and the reduction of daily homework in favor of Hitler Youth service have led some historians to the conclusion that conscious and systematic *Volksverdummung*, "national stupefaction," was intended. Undoubtedly, the explanation for this tendency in NS educational policy is found in the anti-intellectualism of the NSDAP. The fact that the number of German students matriculated into German universities declined from 110,000 in 1928 to 56,000 in 1938 is just another example of the NSDAP's *geistfeindliche*, "anti-intellectual," policies. The party distrusted the *Geist*, "intellect," and was afraid of it.

Very clear in my memory are the many school ceremonies. They were held either outdoors or in the *Aula*, the large auditorium on the third floor of our main building. They proceeded according to a definite pattern. The principal opened the events with a short introduction filled with standard nationalistic phrases.[3] Then followed a longer speech, given by either a member of the faculty or an outside speaker, elaborating on the significance of the given day: the seizure of power, January 30, 1933; Adolf Hitler's birthday, April 20, 1889; the Munich putsch, November 9, 1923; the Battle of Langemarck, November 11, 1914; and others. After the speech we sang the national anthems with our right arms raised. This part of the ceremony seemed to us boys especially endless, because in addition to the traditional "Deutschland, Deutschland über alles," we had to sing the second anthem, the *Horst-Wessel-Lied*. During this long singing it was a popular joke to rest one's arm on the shoulder of the person in front of you, which inevitably led to horseplay and mock

21

fights among us ten- and eleven-year-olds, sometimes disturbing the solemn character of the ceremony considerably.

Our auditorium was a large, attractive hall decorated with dark wood panels and stained-glass windows. Behind the speaker's platform there were more than eighty plaques on the wall with the names and dates of the former students of our school who had been killed in the World War. The lower grades always sat in the front rows; thus we could study closely all the names during the lengthy speeches. Many well-known battlefields were represented more than once: Verdun, Marne, Cambrai, Somme, the Skagerrak, Langemarck. For us there was a mythical aura about these names. Certainly there was not one among us—and only a few among our more thoughtful teachers—who could foresee that ten years later there would be almost two hundred additional plaques with the names of students who were just then sitting next to us or behind us. The battlefields would then be Stalingrad, Leningrad, Kursk, Normandie, the Atlantic.

In addition to school and family activities, it was the service in the Deutsches Jungvolk that occupied our days. We were almost without exception enthusiastic Pimpfe. The girls in the *Hitler Jugend* were called *Jungmädel* (JM). Our meetings were held regularly Wednesday and Saturday afternoons from three to five o'clock. Sometimes there were additional meetings in the evening and even on Sundays, an example of which was the *Jugendfilmstunde*, "youth film hour." On Sunday mornings at eleven o'clock we had to view a movie with an especially strong ideological message. Churches protested mildly against the Jugendfilmstunde at that hour because it interfered with the usual worship services. But the protest was to no avail.

Even our conscientious teachers had to make adjustments to accommodate the DJ. They had been ordered by governmental decree—for all teachers in Germany were, and still are, civil servants—to reduce considerably the rather heavy homework load on Wednesdays and Saturdays. I remember clearly many a classroom situation when, on one of these days, a teacher absentmindedly began to dictate the list of homework assignments and we howled triumphantly in unison: *Heute ist Dienst,* "Today we have meetings."[4]

The two main activities at the DJ-Dienst were the premilitary and ideological training called *Weltanschauliche Schulung* (WS). In military activity, close-order drills ranked high. The drills involved a great deal of marching, almost always accompanied by marching songs, and the execution of standard military orders. This has been customary for two hundred years in all military forces the world over as a form of disciplinary exercise. The special aspect here was the fact that the order-taking units consisted of ten- and eleven-year-old children, and the order-giving DJ leaders were not much older.

I was promoted after one year to the rank of *Jungenschaftsführer* and later to *Jungzugführer*. It meant that I was in charge of about twelve Pimpfe, later about forty in number. Thus we DJ leaders stood twice a week for thirty minutes on the drill ground (most of the time our soccer field) in our uniforms decorated with the insignia of our respective ranks—red-white cords and green, green-black, or green-white aiguillettes—barking out our orders: "Attention!"; "Forward march!"; "Column left!"; "Unit halt!"; and dozens of other commands that we could have recited in our sleep. Our units soon executed our orders in acceptable fashion. This was indeed premilitary training; the commands and their executions were identical with those of the German army. We DJ leaders felt very much like regular army noncommissioned and commissioned officers, and we liked this role. It was my first taste of having power—a heady wine for a twelve-year-old boy.

We, the young people, knew the military and its traditions and rituals from innumerable books and films, and we consciously tried to imitate them as authentically as possible. It goes without saying that these books and films were one-sided glorifications of soldiery and military traditions. The other side—the loss of humanity, the degradation of the individual, the senselessness of the phenomenon of war—was the main topic of the pacifist literature of the 1920s, which was unknown to us because such books were forbidden. During my family's annual vacation in my grandmother's house on the Baltic coast, I discovered some of the forbidden books in my Uncle Louis's bookcase. They were well hidden in the second row behind "safer" volumes. I read one of them, Erich Maria Remarque's international best-seller *Im Westen nichts Neues* (*All Quiet on the Western Front*) and did not like it. It was not heroic enough and ended with the hero's death. It did not occur to me to compare myself as a would-be officer with some of the repulsive barrack types in the book, such as the stupid and vicious drill instructor Corporal Himmelstoss, whose greatest pleasure in life was to torment and degrade his recruits. We were idealists and firmly believed in the value of our service for the glorious future of the New Germany.

The question of why the premilitary and ideological training of the young was entrusted to adolescents can be easily answered. One of the most frequently used slogans of NS youth policy was *Jugend muss von Jugend geführt werden*, "young people must be guided by young people." Thus the NS regime skillfully exploited the instinctual rebellion of teenagers against the adult world, especially teachers and parents. We were searching for our identity and individuality, and we believed to have found it as DJ leaders.

Physical fitness was also strongly emphasized. We often went on *Gepäckmärsche*, marching with full backpacks distances that became longer, and the exercise more strenuous, every year as we grew older and stronger. In sports, simple track-and-field disciplines—running, jumping, and throwing—were stressed for the young boys. For older boys the throwing discipline was especially revealing; it was not javelin and discus throwing that was practiced, but the throwing of stick grenades that were in weight and shape exact replicas of army grenades. At the frequently held sports festivals this discipline was officially called *Handgranatenwerfen*. The premilitary aspect of our training was especially noticeable in our rifle training on the firing range. For the younger boys, air rifles were used; for the older ones, small-bore rifles. These *Kleinkalibergewehre* which closely resembled the standard weapon of the German infantry, the carbine 98k. Various badges for outstanding achievements were awarded, the highest of which, the silver marksman's badge, *silbernes Scharfschützenabzeichen*, we wore with special pride because it was not awarded often.

Much of our time was spent *im Gelände,* in undeveloped outdoor areas. We learned camouflage and how to write combat messages (when, where, who, how), use a compass, and read maps. These exercises culminated a few times a year in the so-called *grosse Geländespiele*: several larger units of hundreds of boys, often from different towns, moved around in open areas on reconnaissance patrols sent out to find the "enemy" and scout for an advantageous terrain suitable for ambush. It all ended in a final "battle" of large groups of boys clashing in a splendid free-for-all scuffle.

Premilitary training was one main activity for the Hitler Youth, ideological instruction the other. At least once a week for thirty or forty minutes—on rainy days for longer and more often—we sat in our DJ center with our units and played the role of teachers, although we were only twelve or thirteen years old. These sessions were not particularly popular with our boys nor with us. We preferred to "play" outdoors, and, besides, they reminded everybody too much of school. Instructional materials were the NS *Schulungsbriefe*, the training manuals we received once a month from the Hitler Youth offices in our county seat, Meldorf, or in the provincial capital, Kiel.

The main subjects of these Schulungsbriefe were the history of the NSDAP, the life history of Adolf Hitler, the Treaty of Versailles, the music and songs of the party, and the party's racial theory. In the history lessons, the party was portrayed as the liberating force saving the nation from the swamp of a corrupt and decadent political regime, the Weimar Republic. In the life history of the Führer, his humble origin was stressed, as well as his courageous service as a front-line soldier, his various decorations, and his personal contributions to undermining, and finally toppling, the Weimar "system."[5] This glorification of Hitler's life took on messianic features. Many a sentence from *Mein Kampf* and from Hitler's speeches had to be memorized like scripture and became familiar quotations, for example, "I, however, decided to become a politician," or "the German youth must become quick like greyhounds, tough like leather, and hard like Krupp steel."

Part of our instruction was on the Versailles treaty of 1919, which was always referred to as a dictate and a treaty of disgrace. We memorized paragraph 231, the "guilt paragraph," according to which Germany was solely responsible for the catastrophe of the World War. It was considered especially unfair and obnoxious. With the help of special maps we learned the names and sizes of the "lost territories" of Alsace-Lorraine, eastern Upper Silesia, the Polish Corridor,[6] Northern Schleswig, and others.

Anybody who tries to understand and get a feel of these years, especially concerning the mood and spirit of the young, will fail if they disregard the importance of music and songs. I have seen innumerable television and film documentaries about the Third Reich in which black-and-white film clips of party rallies, military parades, and similar mass gatherings are always used. My reaction always—and without exception—is "No. That is not the way it was." One of the main reasons for this is that the producers of these documentaries ignored or grossly underestimated the hypnotic effect that certain kinds of music and songs had on the large masses of people. Most of the time in these documentaries some background music is provided, consisting of a few discordant measures of "Deutschland, Deutschland über alles" and military marching songs and some fragments of Wagnerian music. In reality it was very different, and the component music played an important part in the intoxication of the masses at these events.

A few years ago I had the opportunity to watch a telecast of an international youth festival in East Berlin conducted by the *Freie Deutsche Jugend* (FDJ), the official youth organization of the German Democratic Republic. I was deeply disturbed by it from the very beginning—it lasted about four hours—because I was immediately reminded of the many NS rallies I knew so well: the same mass choreography; similar uniforms for the young (only the color was different, blue instead of brown); the same enthusiasm on the faces of these children and teenagers; the same continuous accompaniment of stirring marches and songs, some of which were identical to the ones we had sung hundreds of times. The rally culminated in a moving rendition of Beethoven's *Ode to Joy* performed by a huge orchestra and hundreds of singers. It was a masterfully arranged rally to affect the minds and emotions of the uncritical young.

All our Hitler Youth meetings began and ended with a song. We also had to have a fairly sizable repertoire for our close-order drills and for our parades through town. Naturally, the songs had to be memorized, and we spent much time learning many stanzas. Some of them were new NS songs, but the great majority were popular songs, often folksongs of previous centuries rediscovered and revived by the Youth Movement. At Christmastime traditional German carols like "Silent Night, Holy Night" or "Oh, Christmas Tree, Oh,

25

Christmas Tree" were sung at our Advent and Christmas parties. I remember only one new carol, "Hohe Nacht der klaren Sterne," "Festive Night with Bright Stars." Its text, naturally, had nothing to do with Jesus Christ's birth, but with the winter solstice and the reawakening of nature.

One of the new marching songs deserves to be singled out here. It is the infamous *"Es zittern die morschen Knochen,"* an aggressive fighting song of the SA from the 1920s.[7] It was popular, easy to learn, and easy to sing. What intrigued us especially were the last two lines of the first stanza: *Denn heute da hört uns Deutschland / Und morgen die ganze Welt*, "Today Germany listens to us / Tomorrow the whole world." We liked to make a small change in the text. Enthusiastically and defiantly we shouted: *Denn heute gehört uns Deutschland / Und morgen die ganze Welt*, "Today Germany is ours / Tomorrow the whole world." It is an example of unofficial indoctrination of children and teenagers with plans for global conquest.

One of the least popular instructional topics was the racial theory of the NSDAP. We were supposed to convince our boys that the Nordic, Aryan race was superior to all others in the world. Our training manuals proclaimed and attempted to prove, with the help of many illustrations and a very lopsided retelling of world history, first that the Nordic people—blond, blue-eyed, tall with narrow facial features—were aesthetically the most attractive of all races. Second, the Nordic people, because of their innate qualities of courage, imagination, initiative, and prowess in battle, were destined to rule. Even the European nations were classified according to ethnicity; the Celtic, Slavic, Romanic, and all other races were demonstrably inferior, non-Nordic European groups. Some of these pseudoscientific anthropological theories later even found their way into our biology textbooks. The whole world today knows the horrendous consequences of this extreme racism of NS ideology. The saddest and most painful chapter in the history of Germany is the fate of the Jews under the Third Reich. It has tainted the German image in world history probably forever.

In many conversations with friends and acquaintances and in frequent discussions with my students in the United States, I have been asked one question over and over: How was it possible that a civilized nation with a thousand-year-old, splendid cultural history could in the twentieth century choose a road that led from initially conventional anti-Semitism to officially sanctioned Jew baiting to organized genocide? How does classical Weimar, once considered the "capital of European *Geist*" (Coleridge), fit in with the extermination camps of Auschwitz and Mauthausen? How does one pair Goethe and Himmler, the Bamberg Rider and the gas chambers of Dachau, Beethoven's Ninth Symphony and the *Horst-Wessel-Lied?*

As to the installation of *Konzentrationslager* (KZ), "concentration camps," our reaction at the time is not difficult to explain. We heard and read many times that these were planned to separate the *Staatsfeinde,* "enemies of the state," from the population, and we believed it. The KZs were needed to isolate the enemy that tried to block the German people's road to a new and better future. Communists, Social Democrats, Jews, Gypsies, homosexuals, Freemasons, and Jehovah's Witnesses were all grouped together as one evil force. Of the latter four categories, we did not even know exactly who they were and what they stood for. In its attempts to justify the concentration camps, the NS propaganda did not forget to mention frequently that this type of camp was not a German but a British invention during the Boer War.

"Jews" and "Jewry" were rather nebulous terms for us DJ members. We had almost no close personal Jewish acquaintances. There was only one Jewish family in our whole town, and there were no Jewish students in our classes. The one exception was Herr T. He was a businessman who owned a store for men's and boys' clothing, the Haus T. on the Koogstrasse, the main street of our town. My parents liked to shop there because of the high quality of the merchandise and the reasonable prices. Besides, Herr and Frau T. belonged to the same social club, the *Verein Mecklenburger und Pommern,* a flourishing and very active club in town for people who originally came from the provinces of Mecklenburg or Pomerania. Most, but not all, of the members were sailors, captains, and pilots who felt rather uprooted in Schleswig-Holstein far away from their home provinces. They had joined together to cultivate their own special Low German language, their songs, and their regional literature. Herr T. was born in Stettin and thus was a legitimate club member. Their daughter Edith was my sister's age, and they were classmates and friends. Frau T. was not Jewish.

I remember the time my mother and I went to Haus T. to purchase a pair of short pants for me. It must have been some time before the infamous *Kristallnacht* in November 1938.[8] As we approached the store we saw two young SA troopers in their yellowish-brown uniforms, high black riding boots, and peaked caps with chin straps in place. They had posted themselves to the left and right of the main entrance and were holding writing pads and pencils in their hands, quite obviously for the purpose of writing down the names of all customers entering the store. My mother hesitated briefly but then went in anyway, and we were not harassed by the SA men. The brightly lighted main business room was completely empty. Frau T. herself served us. When my mother asked a question about the lack of customers, she replied, *Ach, es kommt ja niemand mehr,* "Nobody comes in anymore," and then she cried. On our way home, my mother was very quiet. After she had told my father about our experience, I remember that the mood in our house was of depression, and probably fear. It was the last time that any of my family went shopping in the Haus T.

I clearly remember November 9, 1938, the day after the Crystal Night. During the previous night SA raiding squads had smashed the plate glass of the three large display windows of Haus T. They had also, with red oil paint, marked on the asphalt two large Stars of David, the word *Jude*, "Jew," and massive arrows pointing toward Herr and Frau T.'s store and house. The people in our neighborhood whispered to one another that at five o'clock in the morning Frau T. had tried to scrub the pavement and remove the scrawls, but without success. For weeks the sad work of the state graffiti artists was there for all to see.

We know today that these unofficial pogroms were not condoned by the majority of the population and that the damage inflicted on the German image abroad was immense. I remember that even Frau E., our neighbor and the most dedicated National Socialist on our street—she was a member of the NS-*Frauenschaft*, the party organization for women—shook her head in a conversation with my mother and said: *Mein Gott, das war doch nicht nötig,* "For heaven's sake, that was not necessary." This remark of Frau E.'s may sound naive today in our post-Holocaust age, but who among these decent citizens who all their lives had been accustomed to law and order could have imagined at that time the ghastly plans and projects growing in the minds of the NS leadership? The word *Endlösung*, "final solution," was in 1938 only a mathematical term. The word *Vernichtungslager*, "extermination camp," did not exist at all. Auschwitz, Theresienstadt, Bergen-Belsen, Buchenwald were names of villages and towns that nobody knew.

And we young people? How did we react to the never-ceasing anti-Semitic propaganda in the news media, in films, textbooks, and in some of the contemporary works of literature? I am very certain that in re-creating these times my memory does not fail me when I state that the impact this part of the NS propaganda had on us was relatively insignificant. Of all the aspects of the party's mind-control machinery, otherwise so successful, these attempts at brainwashing were not effective. The image of "the Jew" remained strangely vague to us young people. Of course we heard and read the constantly repeated contention that German society was threatened by the growing *Verjudung*, "Jewification," especially in the social and natural sciences, medicine, jurisprudence, the arts, theater, and certain branches of the world of business and finance. "The Jew" was said to be a calculating, cold-hearted individual—a Shylock only interested in personal profit and power at the expense of all other races. The Jews would always remain parasites in the German people's community, *Volksgemeinschaft*.

The many Jewish war veterans and fallen comrades of the Jewish faith during the World War were completely ignored. After all, "the Jew" was considered a nonsoldier. He was stereotyped as nothing but a haggler and peddler by nature. It is worth pointing out here that the NS anti-Semitic campaign always stressed the alleged inferiority and perniciousness of the Jewish *race*, not the religion. Traditional anti-Semitism in Europe, in part based on the perception of the Jews as Christ-murderers, was called "misguided" by the National Socialists. One of the reasons for this shift of emphasis in their anti-Semitic ravings was their ambiguous and uncertain perception of the historical figure of Jesus. In later years I often tried to analyze the relative failure and ineffectiveness of the NS propaganda to turn us young people into rabid anti-Semites.[9] I arrived at four major reasons, which, at least partially, explain this phenomenon as it applied to my family, my circle of friends, and myself.

The first is that the attempts to vilify the entire Jewish people were so exaggerated that they were unconvincing. An example was the inflammatory weekly journal *Der Stürmer*, published by Julius Streicher. We sometimes read the front page, especially the cartoon, because it was displayed in a showcase outside a stationery and book store which served as a kind of meeting place for us young people. The tone and the message of the journal were so shrill, crude, and vulgar that even we children found them repulsive. I know of no person or family in our town who subscribed to *Der Stürmer*.

There were also glaring contradictions in the whole racial theory which even our uncritical minds perceived. On the one hand we were constantly bombarded on paper and in films with the depiction of the ideal type of the Nordic *Herrenmensch*, "member of the master race": his body tall, slender, and broad shouldered, his blue eyes alert and boldly observant, his face narrow but with a square and strong chin, his hair blond. In reality we were very much aware of the appearance of the NS leadership types—Hitler, Goebbels, Himmler, Streicher, and many others. They looked anything but Nordic, and there were plenty of jokes about it.

Furthermore, in the propaganda conspiracy against the Jewish world (for example, the faked *Protocols of the Learned Elders of Zion*), it was stated on the one hand that Western capitalism, prodded by Wall Street Jews, attempted to dominate the world. On the other hand there were leading Communists, also Jews, like Trotsky, Kamenev, or Zinoniev, in Moscow who had similar plans. This was such a conspicuous contradiction that some of my more thoughtful friends and I recognized it, especially as we became older, more knowledgeable, and more critical. I remember many a discussion on this very subject. Wall Street and the Kremlin both dominated by Jews? It made little sense.

The last and perhaps most important reason we did not take the NS racial theory seriously is because the influence of our parents and teachers had a strong effect on us. I have mentioned previously that anti-Semitism did not exist in our family. It was a taboo subject. In our classes in school there was virtually no anti-Semitic emphasis in any subject. To be sure, there were omissions: in the songbook we used in our music classes, Heinrich Heine's "Die Lorelei" appeared with the notation *Verfasser unbekannt*, "lyrics author unknown," and our music teacher did not have the courage to correct this. Gotthold Ephraim Lessing's drama *Nathan the Wise* was deleted from our reading list in our German literature classes. It is a play of religious tolerance from the Enlightenment in which a Jew is the central figure. I read it privately upon recommendation of my literature teacher. And in biology class there was a whole chapter on racial theory in our textbook, but for our teacher, an old and conservative man, these theories were so newfangled and strange that he did not even bother to assign the chapter.

Thus we were almost completely spared this especially odious aspect of NS ideology in our school. Yet I do remember one class—it was already wartime, perhaps 1941—in which our history teacher lectured on the exodus of many Jewish scientists and artists from Germany. He said in his soft Thuringian dialect, "It is stupid and immoral to drive people like Einstein and hundreds of other intellectuals into exile. The justification *Wo gehobelt wird, da fallen Späne* [You can't make an omelet without breaking eggs] is even more fatuous. Someday we may have to pay for it." These were courageous and, although Herr W. could not know it, prophetic words.

3
The flag
rates higher
than death

In his first great work of fiction, the family novel *Buddenbrooks*, Thomas Mann tells at great length—and with many details of and acute insights into the psyche of child and adolescent—about the annual vacation stay of young Hanno in Travemünde, a resort town outside Lübeck. This Hanno chapter, which is autobiographical and affects the reader as being especially convincing, is one of my favorite parts of the novel, and I always look forward to reading and discussing it with my students. One reason for this is the fact that every year my family and I were privileged to enjoy similarly glorious vacations on the Baltic Sea. The last summers prior to the outbreak of the new war were halcyon days for us young people.

My grandmother lived in Prerow, a fishing village on the peninsula Darss, also called Fischland, jutting into the Baltic. Oma Scharnberg lived in a house where my mother and her eight siblings and my brothers, sister, and I were born. It belonged legally to my Uncle Louis, who, as a ship's captain and a bachelor, was financially in the best position to pay the tax bills and maintain the property. It was a big sprawling house, more than a hundred years old, with fifteen rooms, stables for horses and cows (though not used anymore), a very large garden in the back, and a sizable meadow in the front which was rented out to a neighbor and on which cows grazed. Every summer this house became the holiday residence for the extended Scharnberg-Schümann family during the six or seven weeks of school vacation. It was a matter of course for us to go to Prerow as soon as school was over. We did not have to pay rent. We could visit with my grandmother, uncles, aunts, and cousins, and we felt very fortunate to be able to spend almost two months every summer in one of the garden spots of northern Germany.

Prerow in the 1930s was only just beginning to be discovered as a spa for vacationers, especially from Berlin, which was only three or four hours away by train. Every year more summer visitors came to enjoy the magnificent snow-white sandy beaches, the spectacular dunes, and the large Darss forest. The forest was so dense and relatively wild that Hermann Göring had a herd of bison imported and released into the "wilderness." After all, among his many functions and titles, he was also *Reichsjägermeister*, "Reich master of the hunt." After the war these animals ended up in the cooking pots of the starving population.

For us children it was truly a vacation paradise, and I remember how my friends envied us because they usually could only afford to spend two or three weeks in some impersonal resort hotel. Most of our days were spent on the beach. The water of the Baltic was unpolluted. It was a quiet beach, and only the sound of wind and water and the shouts of playing children could be heard. Transistor radios had not been invented. There was a daily routine. After breakfast, we would spend three or four hours swimming, playing ball in and out of the water, and building sand castles, followed by the noontime meal at home. My grandmother's house was located not very close to the water, but the two or three kilometers we had to walk were considered insignificant. In fact, the distance increased our expectation and our thrill each time we crossed the last dune and saw nothing but the immense blue ocean in front of us. After lunch we headed back to the family cabana and more playing and basking in the sun. At four in the afternoon, at the *Kaffeestunde*, the adults arrived, my mother, grandmother, uncles, and aunts, bringing cake or sandwiches with them. Supper was taken at home again after the sun went down.

After the evening meal, all of us, often twelve to fifteen adults and children, gathered on the large veranda, and the conversations and storytelling began: news and gossip about friends, neighbors, and absent family members; incidents in our family history; stories from the war and the inflation years. How often did I hear, and never tire of, the strange and unexplainable details surrounding the death of my uncle who was killed on the western front just before the armistice. The whole family reported hearing a loud crashing sound at the actual day and time of Uncle Richard's death, a noise only they—no neighbors—had heard. Then there was the reliving of the 1923 inflation, the time when my mother rushed to the grocery store as soon as she had received my father's salary by telegraph from Hamburg, because on the next day the money might be worth only half as much. And there were many, many other stories. Two of my uncles were born storytellers, and when my father joined us—he was able to take off only two or three weeks per year from his job—these family gatherings with the storytelling of the three sailors provided thrilling and unsurpassable entertainment for us children.

We were never bored those summers. Even on rainy days there was much to do and discover in the big house filled with memorabilia of three genera-

Beach scene in our vacation paradise, Prerow on the Baltic Sea. The adults in the cabana are my mother, *left*, and her oldest sister, my Aunt Elisabeth, *right*.

tions of sailors, old furniture, photographs, paintings, and ship models. Sometimes after supper we went to visit other relatives in the village; after all, this was home territory for the whole Scharnberg-Schümann clan, and the evenings there were also fascinating for us children.

But one topic was never touched on—politics. I do not remember a single occasion of someone bringing up a political subject or an event in contemporary history. Perhaps the grown-ups did discuss them after we children had been sent to bed, but I doubt it. I remember Prerow as a kind of oasis or an island existence or a long voyage when everyone is cut off from all events in ordinary life. My grandmother had no radio and did not want one, and she also had no telephone. She did subscribe to the small newspaper published in the neighboring town, but we were not interested in reading it and totally ignored it. Once a week, in the evening, a movie was shown in a local dance hall, but we were too young to go out on our own after dark. School, DJ service, and all other obligations of our regular lives were far away, and nobody seemed to miss them. We lived in a place beyond time. Prerow for us was the genuine and ideal vacation, in the best and most literal sense of the word.

There was another event during one of these golden summers prior to September 1939 for which I was envied by my friends and classmates: a trip to Sweden. Uncle Louis was captain of the *Nordwest*, a small freighter that regularly commuted every two weeks between Hamburg and the Swedish port of Göteborg. Uncle Louis had never married and had no children of his own, but he was very fond of us children. Therefore every summer he invited one or two of his nieces and nephews to go with him on the *Nordwest* to Sweden. My two brothers and my sister had already been, so now it was my turn.

My feeling of high expectation and enthusiasm was somewhat dampened when I embarked on his ship in our Brunsbüttel locks and discovered that my uncle had also invited my cousin Irmgard on the same trip. Since I was still prepubescent, girls, including cousins, were strange creatures. But actually she and I got along rather well. We spent unforgettable hours on deck passing through the Kiel Canal and then sailing on the Baltic Sea to Göteborg. The weather was warm and the sea calm. The cook, an especially kind man and an old friend of the whole family, always had something special and delicious for us to eat. There was also a gentle, funny, black-and-white ship's dog, *Seemann*, to play with. It was a fairy-tale voyage. In Göteborg, however, a small disappointment awaited us: the renowned Trollhättan waterfalls, one of the main tourist attractions of the city, about which my siblings had raved, were dammed up for construction and could not be visited. To compensate for this, my uncle invited us to a performance of a very large and grand circus where everything was action and spectacle and we did not have to understand the language. The waterfalls were soon forgotten.

On one of our strolls through the very modern and clean city, I had an experience that shocked me so much that I could not get it off my mind for months. In a showcase a Swedish newspaper was displayed, and on the front page I discovered a political cartoon about Adolf Hitler. There was the familiar mustache, the strand of hair over his forehead, and the NS uniform with the swastika armband. He had his mouth wide open and was facing a group of people symbolizing the European nations: the British John Bull, the French Marianne, the Dutch sailor with wide trousers and wooden shoes, and so on. They were huddling fearfully in one corner of the map of Europe and one of them said—my uncle translated the Swedish words for me—"Whom will he swallow up next?" It was a satirical, but not particularly biting, depiction of a worrisome situation for many Europeans. I, the eleven-year-old German boy, however, was profoundly shocked and horrified by this demonstration of anti-German sentiment, which was the way I interpreted it. Our beloved Führer, who already had done so much for us, was being ridiculed in an intolerable manner. I thought it was pure blasphemy, and I asked my uncle why they didn't forbid it. I remember a subtle smile on his face when he tried to explain to me that this was not Germany but *freies Ausland*, "free non-German territory," and among other phrases he used the word *Pressefreiheit*, "freedom of the press." But I found that a very unsatisfactory response and explanation. In thinking about it now, it occurs to me that until May 1945 this little cartoon was the only time in my life that I was exposed to any criticism of Hitler and of Germany, except for a few secretly picked-up news items from the BBC during the war that were not taken seriously anyway.

Our return voyage to Brunsbüttel was just as splendid as the trip out. When school began again around the middle of August, and we had to give oral reports in our German class about our vacation activities, my report was by far the most sensational and colorful of all because nobody else in our class had been abroad. The Hitler caricature, however, was not part of my report; probably my patriotic feelings were too deeply hurt, and I did not know how to deal with that.

In the summer of 1938, two weeks of my school holidays were quite different from those very civilian and individual vacations I spent on the Baltic coast and on the *Nordwest* during the Sweden trip. I participated for the first time in a DJ summer camp. Many years later in conversations with friends and acquaintances, I sometimes said jokingly that our generation spent more of its formative years from the age of ten to eighteen in camps, tents, and barracks than in the bourgeois surroundings of our parents' homes. In examining this statement now more closely and seriously, it becomes clear to me that it was not just a joke, that it comes fairly close to the truth. When I add up the months and years I spent in DJ summer camps, glider camp, KLV camp,[1] and premilitary training camps with time spent in the navy antiaircraft unit, the Reich labor service, the regular army barracks, and finally prison camp, I arrive at the astounding number of approximately thirty-six months of "camps" in less than eight years. During these months my life was regulated and regimented from morning to night, and there was always somebody telling me what to do. It is no wonder that even today I have a slightly neurotic aversion to any form of authority.

I have mixed memories of my first summer camp. I was very young, and it was the first time in my life that I had been away from my own family for more than a day or two. Two weeks can be a small eternity for an eleven-year-old boy, and I suffered from acute homesickness. If it had not been constantly impressed upon us that crying was unmanly—*ein deutscher Junge weint nicht*, "a German boy does not cry"—I would have wept often in the first few days. We slept in tents, on piles of straw. It was uncomfortable and noisy. The food was prepared by us and was miserable, sometimes actually inedible. The most hated activity was the *Frühsport*, "morning calisthenics."

Immediately after being awakened by bugle calls and shrill whistles at half-past six, we had to put on our gymnastics shorts, tops, and gym shoes, and then spend the next forty-five minutes before breakfast in long exhausting cross-country runs and endless, boring calisthenics.

At another place in these memoirs I have spoken about the normal DJ meetings, the premilitary and the ideological training. It is important that those remarks are not misunderstood that we felt it to be nothing but coerced service, stress, and pressure. Not at all. It was also a great deal of fun. That also applies to the summer camps. To be sure, in our camp there were some close-order drills, some lectures about the history of the party, and so on, but that part of camp life was not overemphasized. The NS Youth Ministry knew very well what appealed to children: team sports, swimming, excursions in the woods, singing, reading maps, determining one's position without maps and compass by the positions of the sun and the leaning of the trees (in our area, always from west to east because of the prevailing western wind). Even cooking our own meals and sleeping in tents had a certain romantic appeal after we became used to it. The most popular part of the day was the evening spent singing around the huge camp fire. We sang not just military marching songs, but also, more often than not, German folksongs, many of which were hundreds of years old. And at the end of the evening we told ghost stories.

The obvious parallels and comparisons to the Boy Scout camps are not surprising. After all, the origins of the Youth Movement and the *Wandervogel* tradition that influenced the Deutsches Jungvolk so strongly, as well as the founding of the Boy Scouts and Girl Guides before 1914, had one common denominator: the rebellion of the young against the philistine society of the Wilhelmian-Edwardian age.[2]

In the morning and at sunset there was the solemn color ceremony, the *Fahnenappell*. The whole camp stood at attention in an open square around the flagpole, and the two flags, the Hitler Youth flag, red and white with a black swastika, and the DJ flag, black with one white victory rune (⚡), were hoisted or lowered. Then we sang the two national anthems and the unofficial Hitler Youth hymn, "Vorwärts, vorwärts schmettern die hellen Fanfaren." One line of the latter read: *Ja, die Fahne ist mehr als der Tod*, "The flag rates higher than death." We took this line seriously and literally.

The NS Youth Ministry was quite successful in creating and cultivating a myth of the flag. Flags, ensigns, banners, and standards go back to the time of the Roman Empire. Today there are national flags, religious flags, military flags, and sports flags in every country of the world, and they all have a special symbolic function. For us young people at that time, the swastika and the victory rune were religious substitutes. That the DJ rune ranked in our estimation higher than the swastika may sound contradictory at first sight, but it is not difficult to understand. We boys and girls, ages ten to fourteen, felt

The victory runes on the special bugle flags distinguish these young musicians in this photograph of a typical "Fanfarenkorps" of the DJ. Courtesy of the Bundesarchiv Koblenz.

part of the new "people's community," and we were proud of it, even though this Volksgemeinschaft remained a rather vague and abstract concept for us. We were even prouder of having our own concrete DJ and JM world. That was the reason why our special uniforms (brown and black in the summer, navy blue in the winter for the DJ and dark skirts, white blouses, and white knee socks for the JM) meant so much to us. So did the various merit badges and our own musical bands with their special bugles and black-and-white *Landsknechtstrommeln*, "drums of the mercenaries," another tradition borrowed from the Youth Movement, and, above all, our own flag. That was our world, our organization, which we thought was clearly different from that of the older people, and we wanted it that way.

On one of the national holidays—it may have been November 9, because I remember that we wore winter uniforms—a big parade was held in our town. The marching column was very long. At least fourteen or fifteen NS units participated, each with their special uniforms and flags, as did several bands and drum-and-fife corps. The Deutsches Jungvolk was represented by two *Fähnleine*, DJ units, approximately two hundred boys, and since we were the youngest we marched at the end of the column. Traditionally the parade ended at a large square outside the Kiel Canal locks. A few minutes before the end of the ceremony, our leader, Lothar T., sixteen years old, had given us the order to listen only to his commands, not to the general parade leader. Quickly his instruction was whispered from file to file, and every Pimpf knew what to do. We squad leaders knew exactly what was to come and were looking forward to it. The Standartenführer placed himself on the sidewalk in the middle of the long column so that he could be heard by all marchers. Finally, he shouted at the top of his voice, red in the face from the strain, his last order of the day: *Formationen—HAALT!* All other units did stop marching more or less simultaneously, but not the DJ. Seemingly unfazed, we continued in step—Lothar T. had intentionally left a larger space between himself at the head of our column and the unit ahead of us—until about ten seconds later he shouted *Fähnlein 21 und 22—Abteilung—Haalt!* and all two hundred of us stood like a wall. For weeks and months afterward we told each other about the expression on the face of the Standartenführer, first astonished and then furious about this latest prank of the DJ. It was done just so that we could show our independence. Lothar T. was more popular among his peers than ever. Five years later, in 1943, he was killed in combat as a first lieutenant in the infantry on the eastern front.

4

As it actually happened

We enthusiastically celebrated every successful action of the NS government in foreign policy, especially in dismantling the Treaty of Versailles. The joining of Austria with the Reich in March 1938, the *Anschluss*, specifically prohibited by the treaty, created the new German province called *Ostmark*. We also cheered the cession of the Memelland by Lithuania in 1939. The NS propaganda ministry touted loudly and repeatedly the decision, a product of the Munich Agreement, to annex the Sudetenland to *Grossdeutschland* in October 1938. This new term for the Reich, Greater Germany, was officially introduced at this time probably in analogy to "Great Britain."[1] Other successes were the establishment of the "protectorate" of Bohemia and Moravia in March 1939 and the political liquidation of the sovereign state of Czechoslovakia, which had lasted less than twenty years since its creation in 1919. For all these accomplishments in foreign policy, we gave full and exclusive credit to the new NS government, only five or six years old, and primarily to the Führer.

A few years ago a book was published in the Federal Republic under the title *Did You Ever See Hitler?* The editor was an enterprising journalist who had interviewed a number of prominent and nonprominent Germans old enough to remember these times. These interviewees related the circumstances under which they had seen the Führer in person and what impression this encounter had made on them.

I saw Hitler twice. The first time was in 1935 when I was eight years old. Hitler and his retinue, in a long column of large black cars, were driving through our town returning from the dedication ceremony of a new polder at the mouth of the Elbe River.[2] After decades of skillful and laborious land reclamation work, the polder and its protective dike were finished. It had been named after the new chief of state Adolf-Hitler-Koog (today Dieksander

Koog). On his return trip to Berlin, the Führer was to pass through our town, and the news of this event had spread quickly. At the Kiel Canal the motorcade had to stop to wait for the ferry ramp to be lowered; besides, the ferry could not accommodate all cars at one crossing. More than a thousand people had gathered at this location, including my sister and me. She had been asked by my mother to look after me. For the first time in my life I experienced the phenomenon of a "mob" of people. It was a friendly, good-natured, and enthusiastic crowd, but a mob nevertheless. Individuals were no longer in control of their actions and movements. We were hundreds of meters from the raised ferry ramp, and when my sister lifted me up I could only see a thumb-size figure in a brown uniform standing on the ramp and saluting the crowd every now and then. He did not make a speech, there was no music, just hundreds of people who had come of their own free will to wave and cheer the Chancellor. I did not know the word "messiah" then, but here was clearly a situation of a savior, an anointed leader and his fanatical believers and followers who were expecting, or at least hoping for, salvation.

Now, in retrospect, it seems to me that the people were not just hoping for salvation from unemployment and material want, and they had come not only to forget the last war and the humiliating defeat. There was a profound longing for a new and higher meaning of life, for a splendid future—individually and collectively—which they saw incarnated in him. This gathering was no mass demonstration organized and choreographed by Albert Speer à la Nuremberg, with *Fahnenwald*, a "forest of flags," and *Lichtdom*, a "dome of searchlights," with stirring marches and impressive close-order drills executed by well-trained military and paramilitary units.[3] My sister and I were hemmed in among hundreds of ordinary citizens who had come spontaneously and who were swept away by emotions, ecstatic in the true sense of the word—beside themselves. Many had tears in their eyes.

The second time I was much closer to Hitler, perhaps just twenty meters away from him. He was on his way to Memelland, the area that in March 1939 had, under pressure, been ceded to Germany by Lithuania. The Führer and his public relations advisers had decided to go by ship to the regained territory, located in the farthest northeastern corner of the Reich, in order to receive the homage of the Memellanders. He embarked on the *Aviso Grille*, a destroyer-size ship, to sail from Hamburg through the Kiel Canal and along the German coast of the Baltic Sea to Swinemünde, a port at the mouth of the Oder River. There he was to change ships and travel the rest of his voyage on the *Panzerschiff Deutschland*, the much-discussed "pocket battleship," actually a heavy cruiser that at the time was the largest ship of the German navy and a more imposing vessel than the smaller *Aviso*.

The Führer's dislike and fear of the sea is often mentioned in Hitler literature and is explained by his Austrian, inlander background. On this occasion, however, he was willing to overcome his aversion to the sea, probably for representational reasons. Immediately after the voyage a number of fairly crude jokes about the "seasick landlubber Adolf," who had "fed the fish in the Baltic," made the rounds, a type of joke that because of its obvious lèse majesté did not particularly amuse us young people.

On this festive day in Brunsbüttel, however, nobody thought of inventing disparaging jokes. All members of the DJ had been ordered to be on the canal locks in uniform, as had the members of all other party organizations. The big locks and the entire area around them were packed with people, many wearing uniforms, many in civilian clothes, who cheered the approaching *Aviso*. When the ship tied up to the pier, I saw Hitler standing at the rail talking with members of his retinue. He wore his simple brown tunic and dark trousers. In contrast to one of his predecessors, the costume-loving Emperor Wilhelm II, on occasions like this Hitler did not appear in a fancy admiral's uniform. He looked at us with his blue eyes with a serious expression on his face. I, as did each of the spectators close to the ship, had the impression that I had made personal eye contact with him.

After the ship had secured all lines to the pier, an official with a megaphone asked the crowd to move back, not because he feared an assassination attempt or some similar act of terrorism—that was not considered an acute danger in those days—but because some members of the Führer's suite wanted to go ashore and some open space was needed. We slowly stepped backward. I walked over to the main lock gate to observe some of the escorting warships that were just then moving into the lock chamber. Suddenly I was confronted by a tall man in uniform and high riding boots who was rapidly striding toward me through the crowd. His dark bushy eyebrows and his square chin let me recognize him immediately as Rudolf Hess, the Führer's deputy. I probably would have considered it a unique honor to be knocked over by the second ranking man in the nation, but at the last moment I was pulled back by someone in the crowd and there was no collision.

These were the two occasions when I saw Hitler in person, my two "Hitler sightings." But the Führer was ever-present for all Germans. He was depicted innumerable times in the newspapers and the very popular *Illustrierten*, "illustrated magazines," in some kind of pose at some activity. When we went to the movies, which at our age at the time had become a ritual, every Sunday afternoon in one of our two local theaters, with the admission price of thirty *Pfennig*, there was always a short film preceding the main feature, sometimes a cartoon (we called all cartoons *Mickymaus-Filme*) and most certainly the *Deutsche Wochenschau*, the official newsreel of the week. In the latter there was always at least one segment showing the Führer "at work." But above all, Hitler's omnipresence was made possible by the young broadcast medium of radio. Hitler and especially Joseph Goebbels, later his Reichsminister for "people's enlightenment and propaganda," had very early in their struggle for political power recognized that through the invention and rapid development of radio a most effective propaganda tool was handed to them. It was tailored to their purposes, and they perfected and exploited its use. Soon after the seizure of power in January 1933, the mass production of a special radio set was ordered, the *Volksempfänger*, "people's receiver."

With this measure they demonstrated that the new regime did something tangible for the simple people, that even the ordinary household could now afford a luxury appliance which up to then had been reserved only for the rich. The heavily subsidized price for the receiver, a small, simple, black box, was set at a low, affordable thirty-five Reichsmark. The same motivation, a kind of populism, was later behind the construction and production of the Volkswagen (VW), at least that was the official propaganda line. Actually the mass production of the VW was part of the massive rearmament program, and the car was only available for the armed forces as an all-purpose vehicle.

Furthermore, the "people's receiver" was constructed in such a way that, except in border provinces, only the programs of German radio stations could be received. This informational isolation of the great majority of the population was important to the regime even before the war. Uncensored information and especially critical voices from abroad were undesirable and considered disruptive. Thus, the Chancellor and his government could firmly count on having a captive audience for all programs centrally created and distributed from Berlin. Many millions of listeners could be constantly exposed to the incessant series of mass rallies, parades, harvest festivals, opening ceremonies, memorial day celebrations, state funerals, and, above all, Hitler's speeches.

The Führer's talent as a political orator is generally recognized today by all Hitler experts. He did not discover this gift of his until after the World War, as he himself tells it in *Mein Kampf*. Nevertheless, in all the documentary films and records about the 1930s and 1940s that I have seen and heard, he is always portrayed as a kind of madman who, practically frothing at the mouth and with a shrill voice, screamed his almost incomprehensible messages at the audience. That is wrong. That is not the way it was, and that kind of caricatured portrayal is a disservice to the younger generations in the world who are interested in recent history, who, in the sense of Leopold von Ranke, want to know it *wie es eigentlich gewesen*, "as it actually happened."[4]

We know now that these speeches were carefully planned, prepared, and rehearsed. The arrival of the Chancellor at a rally was indicated by the playing of the "Badenweiler Marsch," the regimental march of his war unit, Regiment List. Thus this music served as a preparatory announcement that the head of state was present (comparable to the playing of "Hail to the Chief" in the United States). Hitler always began his speech in a low, sonorous voice, slow and almost halting in its delivery. He gradually raised pitch and tempo until he reached a crescendo, a climax that quite literally pulled the members of the audience out of their seats and impressed the millions of radio listeners just as deeply. He also was very conscious of not taxing the concentration span of his audiences too much. He rarely spoke for more than forty-five minutes and never more than an hour, in contrast to many other past, and present, totalitarian leaders who often harangued their audiences for three or four hours. Hitler wanted to avoid the inevitable soporific effect of long speeches, and he succeeded in this.

Three years after the Second World War ended, I had the opportunity to spend three months in Manchester, England. There I became acquainted with a young Englishman, Bill T., who was my age. He had spent some time in Heidelberg in 1938 as an exchange student. Bill told me of a mass rally in Heidelberg he had attended and at which Hitler spoke. He said that at that time his knowledge of the German language was still poor, and he understood little of the content of the Führer's speech. "And yet, Willy" he said, "I was sure the man was right."

I have never in my life seen or heard a speaker with more magnetic talent as a public orator than Hitler; his effect on a mass audience was nothing short of hypnotic. But there was a side effect of my early and repeated exposure to a master speaker in my formative years. When the Third Reich collapsed and we young people slowly and very gradually began to reorient ourselves, create new values for ourselves, and look for new role models, I made a noteworthy discovery about myself: I was physically unable to ever again listen to a political speech in which the speaker shouts down from his platform at his audience. This aversion to all noisy speech making has stayed with me to this day. I distrust those who raise their voices. I fully appreciate the German saying *Wer schreit, hat unrecht,* "He who screams is in the wrong." I also know that many Germans of my age-group know and share this feeling.

What impressed so many Germans in these three or four years before September 1939 was undoubtedly the fact that the NS government had achieved all their successes in domestic and, especially, foreign policy without war and renewed bloodshed. The people were deeply satisfied that the necessary and justified corrections of the Versailles treaty, as they saw it, could be made without force and violence. On the other hand, I know that there were alert and prudent observers—and my father was one of them—who realized that this kind of foreign policy, if it continued to be pursued unchecked, would inevitably result in a new war. For them this was a political gamble on a global scale for unacceptably high stakes.

Together with the rearmament plans—the introduction of universal military service, the organization and rapid buildup of an effective armament industry, the construction and extension of an efficient railroad and highway network for military purposes—there was also the preparation of the civilian population for a future air war. By government decree, the clearing of all attics of inflammable goods was ordered; several buckets filled with water or sand had to be standing ready; and manuals for the construction of *Feuerpatschen* were issued. Feuerpatschen was a new word for a primitive implement, a spade or rake handle, to which a wet rag was fastened; they were said to be useful for putting out smaller attic fires. On our street, the duty of carrying out these orders was given to my mother, of all people, a very private and nontechnical person. She was simply appointed, by mail, to be an air raid warden and even received a blue and white armband with the word *Luftschutzwart* on it. Today we know what the air war was really like, with carpet bombing, blockbuster bombs, phosphorus canisters (a forerunner of napalm), and firestorms, and these preparations seem pitifully inadequate and removed from reality. At that time, however, they were taken seriously, and my mother periodically had to climb up to the attics of her neighbors and friends and report on the progress of the preparations, a job she thoroughly despised.

As to the threat, the possibility, or even the probability of a future war, there was a deep split between the adult world and our young people's world. We differed profoundly in our attitude toward the phenomenon *Krieg*, "war." For most grown-ups war was a bitter and relatively fresh memory; the last one had ended less than twenty years before with high casualty rates. My mother had lost two of her brothers: Uncle Rudolf had not returned from a submarine mission in the Irish Sea; Uncle Richard, fourteen years old at the outbreak of the war, fell in the last days, late in October 1918, on the western front. Adults remembered the *Hungerwinter* of 1917–18, also called the "turnip winter," the influenza epidemic of the same year, the rationing, the long lines outside the grocery stores. And, above all, they remembered the humiliating defeat and ignominious end of the Imperial Reich, the dishonorable flight of the emperor, and the many immediate consequences of the war—the chaos in the cities and the catastrophic inflation.

For us children it was different. We believed that the German soldier was the best in the world. For us the *Dolchstosslegende*, the theory of the "stab in the back," was not legend but historical fact. The soldiers had not failed, but the *Heimatfront*, the "home front" did. The motto *Im Felde unbesiegt*, "Undefeated in combat," was carved into countless war memorials all over Germany, from small towns to large cities. In our children's games we rarely played cops-and-robbers or cowboys-and-Indians. We played war. Since nobody wanted to slip into the roles of *Franzmann* (French), *Tommy* (English), or *Iwan* (Russian), we always battled with our wooden rifles and tanks (wooden boxes on old baby carriages) against fictitious and invisible enemies. Since I had a fertile imagination and had read more than most of my playmates, I usually was given the role of combat messenger who, by his reports, could create a specific state of operations.

We got our "knowledge" of the World War from films and books officially promoted by the regime. Films like *Unternehmen Michael* or *Die Tankschlacht von Cambrai* and their glorifications of the German soldier filled us with deep admiration and enthusiasm. Books like Ernst Jünger's *In Stahlgewittern*, Werner Beumelburg's *Gruppe Bosemüller*, and Edwin Erich Dwinger's *Die letzten Reiter* conveyed similar messages, and they appeared on our Christmas and birthday gift wish lists. We devoured them furiously, loaned them to friends, and reread them many times. We were only vaguely aware of the existence of a pacifist literature, and we disliked all attempts to portray war as an unheroic and destructive experience. Copies of *All Quiet on the Western Front* and Arnold Zweig's *The Case of Sergeant Grischa* were thrown into the fire at the infamous book-burning ceremony on the Opera Square in Berlin in May 1933, and Remarque was denounced by name *wegen literarischen Verrats am Soldaten des Weltkrieges*, "because of literary treason against the soldier of the World War." Such works were placed on the index of forbidden books. Our role model was the *unbekannte Soldat*, the "unknown soldier," especially *der Grabenkämpfer an der Westfront*, the trench-war fighter on the western front. In drawings and paintings he was depicted with a tense and serious expression on his emaciated face alertly observing the enemy from under his steel helmet, ready at any time to defend the Fatherland, often against seemingly insurmountable odds. A real mythology was created here. War for us was not horror; despite the often graphic description in the war literature of the suffering and dying of individual soldiers, war was a human *Bewährungsprobe*, a test for man to prove himself of the highest order. Today, in the age of nuclear weapons, the peace movements in many countries, and the post-Vietnam frustration in the United States, all this may sound very alien and perhaps even repugnant, but that is the way it was.

In 1938 our playing with maps began in earnest, and we loved the "game." New maps were published on which, for example, the territory of the imperial Reich in 1914 was compared with the new borders of the Weimar Republic. The lost provinces and areas were marked in different colors: Alsace-Lorraine, the Saar area, Eupen-Malmedy (ceded to Belgium), Northern Schleswig, the Memel area, the Polish Corridor, eastern Upper Silesia. This state of affairs was then compared with a third set of maps showing the newly created Grossdeutschland. The numbers of square kilometers and inhabitants who had been joined to the Grossdeutsches Reich were added up: the Saar area, Austria, the Sudeten area, the Memelland. The Reich was expanding yearly and the official line was that we were beholden to the Führer, for it was his bold policy that had made all this possible. What was not openly stated but clearly implied was that not all lost territories had yet been liberated, but we were certain that it was only a question of time before the mission was complete.

45

The infamous book-burning ceremony in Berlin in 1933. The works of such "undesirable" authors as Erich Maria Remarque and Sigmund Freud were publicly condemned and thrown into the flames. Courtesy of the Bundesarchiv Koblenz.

We cultivated this popular game of map reading also on a global scale. On world maps we compared the huge expansion of the British Empire of Canada, South Africa, India, and Australia with the few German colonies in Africa, on the Chinese mainland, and in the South Seas before 1914, all of which had been taken away by the Versailles treaty.[5] Here, too, the message was clear: for two hundred years the British had swallowed up half the globe. The large French, Belgian, Dutch, and Portuguese overseas possessions also were not forgotten. For the late-coming Germans, only a few crumbs were left over with which to establish the modest colonial empire. That too ought to be corrected.

We continued to play these map games even more enthusiastically during the first years of the war, when we marked with little flags the advances of the Wehrmacht in the east, north, west, southeast, and in North Africa, following the regular and special news bulletins of the high command of the armed forces. The games came to an end in January 1943 with the military catastrophe at Stalingrad. After that there was no longer any expansion.

The summer of 1939 is remembered by many people on the European continent and in the United Kingdom as having been one of the most pleasant summers in a decade—warm and dry with blue skies, little wind, and daily sunshine for weeks on end. Many testimonies, letters, memoirs, and diaries from those days describe the almost palpable contrast between the beautiful natural climate conditions and the gathering political storm clouds in July and August of that year. (Similar observations can be found in the memoir literature about the summer of 1914.) Again and again it is pointed out that the people in Europe felt that something threatening and sinister was in the air, like a thunderstorm about to rage.

We twelve-year-olds felt little or nothing of this. We simply enjoyed the beautiful August weather. My family had returned at the beginning of the month from another unforgettable vacation stay in Prerow. To be sure, there were no sand beaches, no dunes, and no forests in or around Brunsbüttel, but our hometown had other things to offer, and it was easy to enjoy life there at the age of twelve. Whenever school and DJ service allowed us some free time, we spent it practicing swimming and diving in the Elbe River or the Kiel Canal. One of the most popular activities was to swim as close as possible to one of the passing ships until the pilot or the captain yelled a warning at us through his megaphone. This was a truly dangerous "sport," for we knew very well how powerful the suction of a sizable ship's propeller was. We pilots' sons made very sure that we always knew exactly which ships our fathers were taking through the canal, so that we could carefully stay ashore when one of them passed. It was unthinkable what would have happened to me if my father had discovered that his youngest son was among those "crazy swimmers" who complicated their demanding jobs.

The historical events of these last days of peace in August 1939 are well known. The nonaggression pact between Germany and the USSR was made then. We were totally dumbfounded by this treaty. For years we had been ordered in our instructional manuals and similar propaganda material to paint communism and all Communists in the darkest possible colors. Now came this abrupt, 180-degree turnabout. We tried to cope with the dilemma by saying that the Führer must have known what he was doing, but there remained a trace of skepticism even in the minds of us children. The true historical implications of the Ribbentrop-Molotov pact were unknown to us.

Events then followed each other in rapid succession, beginning with the back-and-forth maneuvers of German and Polish diplomacy. We young people were convinced that the Germans were in the right; that the Poles were just stubborn and uncooperative in helping to correct the wrongs of the

Versailles treaty by refusing to hand over the territory of the Polish Corridor; that Danzig, after all, was a German city and deserved to be reunited with the Reich; that the German minority in West Prussia was oppressed and mistreated; that the German radio station of Gleiwitz had been attacked by regular Polish troops.[6] That is what we heard over the radio, saw in the newsreels, and read in the newspapers, and that is what we believed. Expressions of skepticism about the veracity of these allegations by some adults, my father for example, were either ignored or swept aside with remarks like "What do these old fogeys know? They just want to gripe."

On September 1, 1939, the thundercloud burst. A few friends and I were sitting in an ice cream parlor in Brunsbüttel—there was no school on that day, and I do not remember why—when on the radio we heard parts of the famous (infamous) speech of Hitler's given in the Reichstag with the fateful words *Seit 4 Uhr 45 wird nun zurückgeschossen*, "As of 4:45 we are returning their fire." It was the beginning of World War II. To quote once again Lord Grey's saying about 1914, with a brief addendum, "The lamps went out all over Europe"—for the second time.

5

Many enemies, much honor

We know from countless contemporary reports and memoirs, and even from the first motion pictures and audio recordings, that in August 1914 people gathered spontaneously in the streets and public squares in many European cities upon receiving the news of mobilization and the declaration of war. They gathered in order to listen to the speeches of their respective leaders and to celebrate this course of events. What else is one to call this ardent enthusiasm of the masses, the devouring of the *Extras*, the special newspaper editions being issued almost hourly, the spontaneously formed parades of people, young and old, who marched through the streets singing patriotic songs? This astounding phenomenon is reported not only from Berlin, Munich, Hamburg, and Cologne, but also from Vienna, Paris, London, and St. Petersburg.

Even today historians have not been able to furnish a completely satisfactory explanation for this ecstasy of the masses in Europe. Granted, the people were tired of the seemingly perpetual series of crises in foreign policy, and they saw in a new war a kind of cleansing of the oppressive atmosphere. The English poet Rupert Brooke welcomed the outbreak of the Great War, rejoicing in it as an awakening from "a world grown old and cold and weary," as a cleansing, invigorating experience, "as swimmers into cleanness leaping." Thomas Mann calls the final chapter of his novel *The Magic Mountain* "Der Donnerschlag" ("The Thunderbolt") and in it he described how the outbreak of the war has precisely this cleansing effect on the decadent group of patients in the sanatorium in the Swiss Alps. They can be seen as a cross section of pre-1914 European society, and the "thunderbolt" scatters them all over Europe to their original homes. It is also plausible that a certain dissatisfaction and boredom of the people with the rigid Wilhelmian-Edwardian society played a role in their seeming ecstasy over the war's outbreak. They were

looking for something more exciting than the humdrum existence of their ordinary eight-to-six jobs, in the sense of Sigmund Freud's famous essay "Civilization and its Discontent." And yet, the wave of enthusiasm of seemingly
intoxicated masses in European cities in the early days of August 1914 remains a baffling, inexplicable, and uncanny phenomenon.

How different the situation was in Germany in the early days of September
1939! There were no mass rallies, no spontaneously formed parades, no
people singing in the streets. Most of the adults were sitting nervously and
anxiously by their radios waiting for further news. This was certainly the case
in our house. When I came home close to noon on September 1, my parents
and my Uncle Fäcks were sitting in our living room. Uncle Fäcks was a captain in the merchant marine and, after passing through the Kiel Canal, had
been told to tie up his ship in the Brunsbüttel harbor to wait for further orders. Thus he was our house guest for a few days. The radio was turned on,
and all stations played nothing but martial music. I remember my father saying, *Nu möten sei de Lüd mit Militärmusik opmuntern,* "Now they have to
cheer up the people with military music." The topic of their conversation was
whether England would remain neutral.

That was the mood of the grown-ups. For us young people it was completely different. For us war was the great adventure, the all-encompassing
event, the tremendous national cause towering now over all other matters,
the crucial test of the New Germany. We all had only one wish: to be a few
years older so that we could participate in and be present at the final triumphant victory, which we had no doubt about whatsoever. Which other nations, besides Poland, would be among our enemies did not concern us very
much, probably according to the adage *Viel Feind, viel Ehr,* "Many enemies,
much honor," one of the most fatuous of all sayings in the German language.

On September 3, England and France declared war on Germany. Immediately, the two largest vessels of the German navy, the new battleships
Scharnhorst and *Gneisenau* (more accurately, battle cruisers) were ordered
to anchor in Brunsbüttel to serve as floating antiaircraft batteries for protection of the locks—obviously a high priority target—against potential British
air attacks.

Because of family tradition, and because we lived in a maritime town, we
boys had a very special attachment to ships. We could estimate quite accurately their size and tonnage as they passed. At the age of five or six we already
knew every national flag on the stern of a vessel and often could identify her
by the company marking on her smokestack. Sometimes we overheard out-
of-towners (all "landlubbers" to us boys) on the canal ferry ask each other
whether, for example, the blue and yellow flag flying on a passing ship was
Swedish, Norwegian, Danish, or Finnish, and we, with the superiority of
youth, could only shake our heads over so much ignorance. Our expertise was

especially skilled concerning the German navy. Almost daily we saw destroyers, cruisers, battleships, submarines, and all other types of vessels passing through the canal. We knew every ship: the number of the crew, date of construction, speed, armament, and so on. We were truly in love with these ships, just like the boys in Günter Grass's *Katz und Maus*, who were also most knowledgeable about the navy.

There was another source for our expertise. All children have favorite toys, and in my case, after the usual teddy bear in my earliest childhood, the bright red fire truck, and sleek racing car, my favorites were ship models. I was about ten years old when this passion took hold. At first, my friends and I carved our own crude wooden models, but then there appeared in the display window of a variety store in town the first Viking models of ships of the German navy. We called them *Bleischiffe*, "leaden ships," although, of course, they were not made of the poisonous lead but were cast of a special heavy metal alloy. They were exact replicas of the existing German cruisers, destroyers, submarines, and, later, battleships. They were true to scale and were manufactured with careful attention to details of the superstructure—movable gun towers, for instance—and some of them were hand painted. But they were expensive. My first acquisition was the light cruiser *Leipzig* for 2.85 Reichsmark, an almost prohibitive price for a ten-year-old whose pocket money was fifty Pfennig per week. Our collectors' mania lasted for years. Every Pfennig and Mark was saved. At Christmas and birthdays all we wanted was "a new Bleischiff."

But our rapidly growing fleets were not just collectors' items. We spent many hours playing with them on the floors of our rooms. Soon harbor installations with piers, depots, buoys, cranes, and more could be purchased. We reenacted famous sea battles of the World War or, more often, created our own battles. At one point my friend Helmut's and my interests parted ways; I began also to collect foreign warships, especially famous vessels of the British navy, among them the renowned battle cruiser *Hood*, at that time the biggest warship in the world, while my friend limited himself strictly to models of the German navy and merchant marine.

Now, in the early September days of 1939, the largest and most powerful vessels, the showpieces of the new German navy, were anchored nearby to protect the town and the locks. That is how important Brunsbüttel was, and we lived there. Our enthusiasm and pride were boundless. In today's vernacular, we were in a state of a permanent patriotic "high." This condition of chronic intoxication was to continue through years to come.

The news from the front, which in these first weeks meant from Poland, was only positive. The report of the armed forces was transmitted by the official daily *Wehrmachtsbericht* on the radio and then printed the next day in all newspapers. The report always began with *Das Oberkommando der Wehrmacht gibt bekannt,* "The supreme command of the armed forces an-

Our favorite toys, the Viking ship models, in battle formation. They appear in this picture much as they did when we played with them.

nounces." The language of these bulletins was brief, concise, and seemingly objective, as though written by a general staff officer. The daily advances of the German troops were meticulously recorded, naturally without identifying the participating units, as were the names of the cities conquered and the rivers crossed, which Polish armies had been encircled, or how many enemy soldiers had been taken prisoner. The activities on the stationary western front, where at the *Westwall* and the Maginot line thousands of German and French soldiers were facing each other passively in a wait-and-see attitude, were briefly mentioned with one or two sentences, often reading *Am Westwall in der Nähe von X erhöhte Spähtrupptätigkeit*, "At the Westwall, in the vicinity of X, accelerated reconnaissance activity."[1]

A special role in the manipulation of public opinion and in raising the people's morale was assigned to the *Sondermeldung*, "special news bulletin." A standard formula was created: before the actual bulletin was read, the normal radio programs were interrupted several times to announce that a Sondermeldung was soon to be given. Next there followed a special fanfare with a classical, heroic musical motif by Liszt or Richard Strauss. Then came the reading of the text—for example, the conquest of Krakow and the number of prisoners taken. After that a military march was played. Later in the war the musical adornment was even more finely calibrated. There were many old and new military marches and soldiers' songs that we all knew. When a battle victory on the western front, in Africa, or the Balkans had been reported, it was followed by the playing of the "Panzer Song," the "Song of the Africa Corps" or the "Song of the Paratroopers." A few times the bulletins announced a success in submarine warfare—for example, that more than one hundred thousand tons of enemy ships had been sunk. Such bulletins were fairly rare at this early stage of the war, however, because the German navy did not yet have many combat-ready U-boats at sea. These navy bulletins were accompanied by the so-called "Engelland-Lied," a sentimental, patriotic drinking song from World War I with the refrain *Denn wir fahren gegen Engelland*, "For we are sailing against England." The great opponent on the ocean, after all, was England—that is to say, Great Britain.

For us young people, the war at this point in time took place on the radio, in the movie theater, the illustrated magazines, and the newspapers. All bulletins, reports, pictures, and films from the front were closely controlled and censored in Berlin by the propaganda ministry. For this purpose a unique instrument had been created, special units which we soldier-crazy boys did not take very seriously, but which were quite effective, the so-called propaganda companies. All reporters, combat correspondents, photographers, illustrators, and painters had been assembled in these units, and they had to portray the war in their media as was ordered by the ministry. The result was a total glorification of the war and of the magnificent roles that the German army, navy, and air force played in its conduct. These products then were offered daily and weekly to the population. A key word was always *Heldentum*, "heroism."

It stands to reason that on the Allied side similar efforts were made. I am thinking here, for instance, of the film series *Why We Fight* or *America at War*, which appeared after the United States had entered the war. But these productions were not so tightly controlled and manipulated as those in the Third Reich. I never saw, for example, during the long five and a half years of the Second World War any pictures of dead German soldiers. It would have been unthinkable in a totalitarian state to have private media companies send their war correspondents to the battlefront, as was done twenty-five years later during the Vietnam War, with interviews and combat scenes appearing every night in American living rooms. What we saw, heard, and read about were the unstoppable advancing German infantry soldiers and Panzer crews, the U-boat captain shouting *Torpedo-los* and the subsequent sinking of the enemy ship, the superior "ace" fighter pilot who had shot another enemy plane out of the sky and had an additional mark symbolizing another kill painted on the tail fin of his trusted Messerschmitt plane.

Military reverses were rare. When they did occur though, and the news could not be suppressed, they were played down. The *Panzerschiff Admiral Graf Spee*, one of our beloved ships, engaged in battle by three British cruisers off the mouth of the La Plata River in South America, had been damaged and had entered the neutral harbor of Montevideo, Uruguay. When the customary permission to remain there for twenty-four hours was not extended, the ship was scuttled. The skipper, Captain Langsdorff, committed suicide. The NS propaganda emphasized the heavy damage inflicted on the enemy ships and spoke of the "heroic suicide" of Captain Langsdorff (the euphemistic word *Freitod*, voluntary death, was used, not the usual term, *Selbstmord*), who could not bear to see his ship and crew being interned. Nevertheless we were confused and disturbed that a captain of a German warship had preferred to scuttle his ship rather than to go down heroically in battle. In our boastful conversations between classes at school, we finally came to the comforting conclusion that "they" would have to pay for the *Graf Spee* after the war. Naturally, we presupposed the "victoriously ended" war, and "they" were the uncooperative Uruguayans.

The German casualty rate in the war against Poland was relatively low. The force and speed of the attacking Wehrmacht surprised not only the Poles and the rest of the world but also the German people, and even the political and military leaders of the Reich. A new word, *Blitzkrieg*, "lightning war," was coined. It meant the tactically revolutionary concerted action of infantry, Panzers, and air force. The role of the *Stukas* in particular was triumphantly stressed in the newsreels. They were dive bombers that, with precision bombing and especially installed sirens, were to break not only the resistance but also the morale of the enemy forces. They were a kind of flying artillery, an absolute novelty in military history.

The conventional Polish army and air force were no match for the numerical, qualitative, and technical superiority of the Wehrmacht, and the war in Poland was over in a few weeks. It has been pointed out by historians and linguists that the word *Feldzug*, "campaign," rather than "Krieg," was preferred in the officially sanctioned phraseology, and the use of the term continued for years after the operation in Poland. Thus there was the Norway campaign, the western campaign, the Balkan campaign; after June 1941, even the invasion of the USSR was called the Russia campaign, a term which soon turned out to be pure irony. The word "Feldzug" clearly implies a military operation limited in time and with preparation, beginning, climax, and end. It even has a romantic, late medieval connotation of knights or sixteenth-century mercenaries setting out for a springtime Feldzug. The word "Krieg" on the other hand had, even for the most war-loving National

Socialists, a sinister, bloody, and endless connotation—one of the traumatic legacies of the First World War.

Since the total number of German casualties in the Poland campaign was so relatively low, only very few obituary notices appeared in our local newspaper, perhaps not more than one or two. That was to change drastically, especially after June 1941. From then on, during the next four years, literally hundreds of these notices appeared on the last page of our daily town paper. They were always adorned with the Iron Cross, and often the standard formula *Gefallen für Führer, Volk, und Vaterland* was used, "Fallen for the Führer, the people, and the fatherland." Sometimes one could even read the phrase *In stolzer Trauer,* "In proud bereavement," over the names of parents, wife, and children.

At the end of September 1939 the expected victory parade in Warsaw was arranged and films of it ran in every movie theater in the country. After that we had no more interest in that part of the war. The liquidation of the Polish state, sometimes referred to as the "fourth division of Poland,"[2] the annexation of the eastern part of Poland by the USSR, and the creation of the so-called *Generalgouvernement* of Poland we accepted as expected political and administrative measures according to the motto *vae victis,* "woe to the vanquished." We knew nothing of the suffering of the Polish people, especially the Jews, or of the establishment of the Warsaw ghetto and the disappearance of the *shtetl,* those unique East European enclaves of Jewish life and culture. It is worth noting that films of the miserable life in the Warsaw ghetto, produced later upon the initiative of Goebbels and planned for wide distribution, disappeared in the archives. They were never shown because the propaganda ministry was afraid that they would arouse sympathy and pity among the German people.

For us young people it was a special event when the first veterans of the Polish campaign came home on furlough and we saw them in the streets or at visits in our school. Some of them, very few, were decorated with the Iron Cross, which had been reissued on the first day of the new war. This medal goes back to the year 1813, the beginning of the wars of liberation from Napoleonic France. It was issued by the Prussian king for outstanding bravery in battle. Quite consciously the government had ceased awarding gold and silver medals customary at that time. The plain and unpretentious iron metal had been chosen for two reasons: to demonstrate symbolically the frugality and poverty of the Prussian state, and to indicate the militia character of the Prussian army during those wars. It was a kind of populist gesture of Friedrich Wilhelm III and his advisers Stein, Scharnhorst, and Gneisenau. In 1870, 1914, and now again in 1939, the order had been renewed. The medal that was not reissued was the *Pour le Mérite,* the highest combat award in World War I, in the American vernacular sometimes called "the Blue Max." It had been established in 1740, "the French Century," by Frederick the Great, but now it was felt that because of its French name it was no longer appropriate for the middle of the twentieth century. It was replaced by the new *Ritterkreuz*, the Knights Cross, a slightly larger replica of the Iron Cross but worn like the Pour le Mérite, on a ribbon around the neck.

These decorations were awarded very sparingly at the beginning of the war. For example, a lieutenant commander whose submarine had sunk the British carrier *Courageous* was only awarded the EK I, the Iron Cross First Class, and the members of his crew the EK II. Soon, however, a veritable flood of medals was awarded and the people began to comment mockingly about the medal inflation. It was rumored that Adolf Hitler himself had designed many of the new medals, badges, clasps, and armbands as an outlet for his frustrated artistic talent. Even the smaller branches of the armed forces had their own merit badges. There were close to one hundred of these decorations by the end of the war.

It is clear that the medals and badges were awarded, as they were and are in all armies, to strengthen and raise the morale of the troops, but the medal inflation of the Wehrmacht reached bizarre dimensions toward the end of the war. The simple Ritterkreuz, for example, had been upgraded again and again until there finally was the Knights Cross with gold oak-leaf clusters with diamonds and swords, which, I believe, was only awarded once or twice. These medals were worn on the uniform tunics during the first war years even in combat, a military absurdity since they could be a physical hindrance, especially for the infantry soldier moving through dense underbrush, and they could offer enemy sharpshooters a convenient target. But the psychological effect of the medals was considered so valuable that this practice was continued until camouflage uniforms were issued after the first year of the war on the eastern front. Finally the medals disappeared in combat situations.

We young people became experts in this area too. For us the most prestigious and admired decorations were the Knights Cross; the silver and the gold wounded badges for a soldier wounded six or more times; and the bronze, silver, or gold combat clasps issued during the later war years to soldiers who, in hand-to-hand combat, had "seen the whites in the eyes of the enemy" ten or more times (the official phrase for the prerequisite of this award). For us the wearers of any one of these medals were revered as demigods.

Our admiration and love for the military also expressed itself in a new collectors' craze. In addition to ship models, stamps, and coins, we began to collect postcards of war heroes. In my memory only we boys bought and swapped photographs of Günter Prien, submarine commander, for example, or Werner Mölders, fighter pilot ace, or Erwin Rommel, later named "the Desert Fox," whereas my sister and her friends concentrated only on collecting filmstars. The postcards were studio portraits of the soldiers in heroic poses, wearing dress uniforms with all their decorations.

The street scene in Brunsbüttel was changing rapidly; more and more people wore uniforms. Among the soldiers, the *Marine-Artilleristen*, the navy anti-aircraft gunners, clearly dominated, because two full battalions, called *MA-Abteilungen*, close to two thousand men, were stationed in and around our town. Their uniforms were the familiar gray-green color of the army, but their buttons, braids, and rank insignia were gold, in contrast to the regular infantry with their gray-green and silver. For us teenagers the Marine-Artilleristen were not much more than *Heimkrieger*, "home warriors," because they lacked the opportunity for and the experience of real combat. On the other hand, when we saw a "real soldier," an infantryman decorated perhaps with the Iron Cross and the Infantry Combat Badge, we talked about it for days. Naturally, the older girls much preferred dating such a hero over a common Marine-Artillerist, who at best could display the not very highly regarded *Flak-Kampfabzeichen*, the "antiaircraft gunnery badge." Nobody could imagine that three years later my classmates and I were to serve for fourteen months in the navy artillery.

Life in general in our town continued to take its normal course. The war in 1939 was not yet serious, especially in comparison with 1914–18. Air raids on the civilian population had not yet started. To be sure, rationing of food-stuffs, clothes, and shoes had been introduced immediately at the beginning of the war. Hermann Göring, the most popular NS leader, had been assigned, in addition to all his other functions, the administration of the war economy, thus the rationing plans. In a well-publicized speech he called himself a *guter Hausvater*, a "good head of house," and immediately drew the parallel to the First World War. That war, he said, had been lost because the home front had failed. Among the main reasons for this failure was the lack of consumer goods, and *Das wird sich nicht wiederholen*, "that will not repeat itself." Thus every person was given weekly food rationing stamps and monthly or quarterly stamps for textile and leather goods. But at this time rationing was considered more of a nuisance than a serious deprivation, and the rations and allowances were generous.

As of September 3, a complete blackout of all cities and towns was ordered. For every window in our house we had to install dark shades and wood slats on the edges so that not the slightest glimmer of light would shine through to the outside. That too was more of an aggravation than a serious reason for anxiety and fear, and soon a number of *Verdunkelungswitze*, "blackout jokes," made the rounds. We quickly acquired the habit of first pulling the shades and pressing the slats into place before turning on the lights when entering a room at night. If someone did forget to pull the shade, they were

57

quickly reminded by a shouted *Licht aus*, "lights out," from the outside. The blackout was strictly enforced by the police.

The propaganda machine was, of course, running in high gear, even though there was now much less fear and insecurity felt among the population than in the last days of August and the first days of September 1939. The main reason for this was the lightning success of the Wehrmacht in Poland. But the people did ask themselves, "How is the war going to continue?" After all, in the west there were the two formidable enemies of the First World War to be faced, France and Great Britain.

For us students at the Marne Gymnasium, a drastic change occurred at the very beginning of the war: we had to leave our school. Without warning the buildings were requisitioned by the navy and immediately converted into a naval auxiliary hospital. Teachers and students were dislodged and given provisional quarters in a much smaller school in town. This temporary arrangement continued for the duration of the war. For me it meant attending school in a different, quite unsatisfactory building for the next five years. In August 1944 I left school after having been awarded the *Notabitur* diploma (literally the "emergency" Abitur diploma) in order to serve the country first in the earth-brown uniform of the Reich labor service and then in the gray-green uniform of the *Panzergrenadiers*.[3] In the spring of 1946 our old school opened again after having been vacated by the navy and given back to the town and the education authorities. Thus I was able to spend my last year at the Gymnasium in our regular buildings and graduated in March 1947 after having passed the regular Abitur examination.

The move in September 1939 from our spacious school complex to a single, smaller building meant profound and painful changes in our daily student routine and in our curriculum. We had only one or two makeshift physical education classes per week since there was no gym and there were no playing fields. Neither were there our accustomed large auditorium and recess halls. Instead of our former well-equipped laboratories for physics, chemistry, and biology classes, we had to make do with a single poorly equipped lab installed in a neighboring social club. Several of our young male teachers were drafted. That too we felt to be a loss. Our two popular gym teachers disappeared, and their classes were then taught, in a fashion, by our art teacher, who was not trained for this and was no athlete at all. A popular joke among us teenagers was to imitate Mr. H. in gym class: he invariably introduced a new exercise on the high bar or the parallel bars by saying, "This is not the way to do it," because he himself could not do the exercise. In some academic subjects we were also shortchanged. Older teachers were called back from retirement to fill the gaps. Naturally, they did not have the energy, the enthusiasm, and the state-of-the-art knowledge in their respective fields previously evidenced by their younger colleagues who now were soldiers.

In a previous chapter I mentioned three teachers who made such a profound impression on me that they determined the course of my whole life. I was most fortunate that their subjects were the ones that interested me the most: German, history, and English. Miss J. and Mrs. U. were not eligible for the draft, and Mr. W. was not called up until later war years. Their teaching was excellent and their enthusiasm for their fields infectious. Years later, when I was a university student and later a teacher myself, I became close friends with all three of them. In many conversations we talked about the Hitler years and their work at that time. I often asked them about the difficulties of teaching in those years, such as how to convey knowledge and humanist values in such an inhuman and extremist milieu and time. Their reply was always the same, that almost every day they had to find acceptable compromises in their teaching between what was officially required and what they could justify in their own consciences as pedagogues and humanists. Mr. W., who was given to colorful and blunt language, phrased it like this: *Es war ein dauernder Eiertanz,* "It was a continual walk on eggshells."

Miss J., my German teacher for most of my years at the Gymnasium, tried to avoid this dilemma by concentrating on relatively neutral periods in German literature, the lyric poems and epics of the Middle Ages, baroque literature, and, above all, works of the periods of *Sturm und Drang,* classicism, and romanticism in the age of Goethe.[4] Even here she sometimes had to compromise. For example, in introducing us to the works of Heinrich von Kleist, she would have liked to select the drama *Prinz Friedrich von Homburg,* but instead we had to read *Die Hermannsschlacht,* a rather bloodthirsty and nationalistic play, because the authorities in Kiel and Berlin had so determined.[5] She was a Goethe specialist, and those of us interested in literature gained insights into the works and time of Goethe. The intelligence, depth, and comprehensiveness of her lectures and criticism were comparable to anything I heard later in various German and American universities.

The big drawback of this selectivity was, of course, that we remained almost completely ignorant of the great works of very contemporary German literature. I did not even know the name of Franz Kafka, for example, until the war was over; Bertolt Brecht was considered strictly a Communist author; Thomas and Heinrich Mann were "decadent"; Sigmund Freud was "Jewish/ destructive" *(Jüdisch-zersetzend).* Their works were not read, and not even their names could be mentioned in class. I am far from reproaching my teachers for these omissions. They did their best under the circumstances; they were professional pedagogues who took their tasks very seriously. There are only very few people who are destined for and capable of martyrdom.

It was at this time, as a twelve- or thirteen-year-old, that I was guided by these teachers to read serious works of literature. My parents' bookcases contained mostly books about ships and the sea, about the World War, and a few popular historical works, for example, *Von Potsdam nach Doorn*, a history of the Hohenzollern dynasty. I read much, just about everything in print in our house, including the adventure books of my older brothers and even the *Mädchenbücher*, "books for girls," of my sister, six years older than I. I read the whole *Goldköpfchen* series, of which she was very fond. I also read very fast, so much so that my father could not believe that I was able to finish a three-hundred-page book in two days. Once in a while he checked it because he thought that I had probably read very superficially or even just skimmed the pages. He was always surprised and, I am sure, pleased when I could provide all kinds of details about the just-finished book.

In the lower grades of the Gymnasium we became acquainted with the first examples of genuine literature, for instance, the realistic and historical novellas of Theodor Storm and Wilhelm Raabe. Especially popular among the literature enthusiasts in our class was the reading of classical plays out loud with assigned parts; thus we could demonstrate our incipient acting talents by declaiming the rolling, eminently quotable blank verse of high pathos in, for example, Friedrich Schiller's *Wilhelm Tell*. We also had to memorize and recite many poems, which were, in the fifth and sixth grade, the shorter and easier poems of the classical German authors Goethe and Schiller, the romantic and realistic poets, and even of Rainer Maria Rilke. We liked to read and discuss literary ballads by Schiller or Theodor Fontane.[6] But I cannot remember a single instance that one of us chose to recite one of the new NS poems, by Baldur von Schirach, for example, the Reich youth leader. Their literary quality was so poor and their pompousness and sycophantism so palpable that our teachers simply ignored them, although the printed versions began to appear in our new readers.

It was at this time that I became fascinated by the works of Karl May.[7] I do not remember which volume I read first, perhaps the first volume of the *Winnetou Trilogy*. My friends, classmates, and I were swept up by the Karl May reading frenzy, as were many generations of youngsters in Germany before and after us. We devoured volume after volume, following the hero, Old Shatterhand, through the American Wild West and Kara Ben Nemsi through Africa, the Near East, and the Balkans. The best and most popular books were told in the first person and were called *Reiseerzählungen*, "travel stories." There were sixty-five volumes of May's collected works. They contained everything that would appeal to a twelve-year-old—one hair-raising adventure after the other in exotic parts of the world with the hero always prevailing because of his superior physical and mental faculties and his equipment, his rifles, revolvers, and wonder horses. The hero was clearly portrayed as a superman, and, just like the comic strip character, Old Shatterhand/Kara Ben Nemsi always fought for noble and ethical causes against the forces of evil. The stories were told with much suspense and a flourishing imagination, and there was a great deal of humor in them. That the hero was a German, and emphasized this fact often, naturally pleased us. We also accepted that he was, in spite of the dozens of eliminated opponents, basically a peace-loving and mild-mannered man who often stressed his being a Christian. There circulated many rumors about the real Karl May: that he had been a failure as a writer in his lifetime; that he had never actually been to any of the places in the world that he described so vividly and graphically and thus was a fraud; that he had spent time in jail for petty theft. Who cared! We followed our hero on his adventures covering half the globe; and in our children's games, and certainly in our dreams, we identified with him.

In school our intoxication with Karl May was barely tolerated, and my parents also looked askance at my new reading mania. All too often the light in my room stayed on until long after midnight. I knew almost nobody, among my friends at the time, who did not pass through a similar Karl May phase. Some years ago an internationally known literary scholar told me how he had discovered the works of a hitherto little-known German writer in the 1950s. Klaus F. said, "I was reading the first volume of his works, and I was seized by a reading mania *(Lesewut)* which I have experienced only once before, as a boy with Karl May."

But this must be said too. Karl May has to be read at a very young age. I have friends, especially in the United States, who out of curiosity or professional interest have picked up a Karl May volume and begun to read. Without exception they gave up after fifty or a hundred pages, shaking their heads about my childhood love affair with the Karl May books. The weaknesses and flaws were all too apparent to these trained literary historians and scholars: the endless repetitions, the crass sentimentality, the palpable kitsch, the often egomaniacal boastfulness—all that we did not see at the ages of twelve or thirteen, and if we did we suppressed all criticism. Even today I have more than twenty Karl May volumes in my private library, and once in a while I like to leaf through one.

In a previous chapter of these memoirs I have reported some subtle and some blatant examples of NS propaganda in German textbooks. Another example, and by far the most pernicious and downright immoral one, came up in religion class. The subject was usually taught at eight o'clock in the morning. We students often were still rather sleepy and just went through the motions of the lesson, despite the efforts of our teacher Miss B., a competent pedagogue and a devout Christian whose brother was a Lutheran bishop and head of the dioceses of Schleswig-Holstein. Although the main emphasis in religion classes was on Bible studies, on Christian doctrine, history of the Christian church, and Martin Luther's works, broader topics of ethics were also included. It was on the latter that, on one particular morning, class discussion was livelier than usual. The subject was euthanasia. We really woke up when one of my classmates, Jürgen K., one of the most zealous and enthusiastic DJ leaders, quoted an example from our arithmetic book. I cannot reproduce it verbatim, but the problem was phrased in approximately this manner:

> In the province of X in the Greater German Reich, there live about forty-five thousand incurably ill mental patients. For their housing, food, medical, and nursing care the state has to provide ninety thousand Reichsmark per patient per year. It costs three hundred thousand Reichsmark to set up a new farm with land, house, barn, cattle, seed corn, and so on.
>
> Question 1: How many Reichsmark does the province X have to spend per year for the care of these patients? Question 2: How many new farms could be established for the same sum total of expenditures?

The message was quite clear: if these patients were not there anymore, many new farms with healthy families could be created. It was an unsubtle invitation to mercy killing for the benefit of the new Volksgemeinschaft—phrased more plainly, it was an invitation to officially sanctioned murder.

The dispute between Miss B. and Jürgen K. became heated. At first I participated and supported my classmate's position, but I soon held my tongue. Jürgen K.'s arguments became more and more brutal and his voice grew shriller. Miss B.'s position was the Christian and humane one: "A society must be judged morally by its willingness to care for its weakest and most vulnerable members." At the end of the hour Jürgen K. was considered a kind of minihero in class because he had "let a teacher have it." I did not participate in this ritual of patting the new class hero on the back, rather, I stood aside in a pensive mood. Naturally, this was noticed immediately by the others and I was called a teacher's pet, a spoilsport, and worse. But even at the age of twelve or thirteen, I felt that there was something fundamentally wrong with the arithmetic problem and Jürgen K.'s argument for killing helpless individuals for a "higher cause."

A few days later my beliefs and scruples were reinforced. Miss B. had been so upset about the course of her class and our arguments that she had brought it up in the teachers' room. At the next suitable occasion Miss J., my German teacher, took me aside, which she sometimes did because she was interested in my progress in reading and writing. Her earnest admonition culminated with, "No, Willy, under no circumstances can you and your classmates argue about life and death in such a manner. That is amoral." I have never forgotten those words.

Jürgen K. and I were also the main participants in another episode that throws a special and disturbing light on the student morale in German schools and, to be sure, in the Third Reich. Every four or five weeks we were assigned a *Hausaufsatz,* "home essay." It had to be fairly long and substantial, and it was important for our final grade of the term. When Miss J. returned the papers, Jürgen K. and I were asked to read our essays aloud to the class. We each had received a Grade 1, which was very rarely awarded, perhaps once or twice during the whole school year. The topic of the essay was *Ein Lagererlebnis,* "a camp experience." I had written about my impressions as a DJ camp guard standing alone for two hours at night in a rainy forest, and I evidently had captured the details of the dark and slightly scary nature scene. I had attempted to create an effective *Stimmungsbild,* a "mood picture," of that night, and my teacher was impressed. She also had high praise for Jürgen K.'s essay. He had written a small drama about two DJ units from different parts of the town who were living in a kind of permanent feud. It had an impressive climax and a subsequent reconciliation in camp. He too received the highest mark. But the catch was that he had copied the story verbatim from one of the many boys' books with which Miss J. was not familiar. I knew it, but it did not even occur to me to announce this fraud publicly. Denunciation of, or "ratting on," a fellow student was unthinkable. The whole class felt Jürgen K.'s cheating and his good grade to be unjust, but at the same time he was admired to some extent because he had been clever enough to get away with it.

All this is not atypical of the attitude of students in German schools concerning the topic of cheating. I know from school novels and novellas of the nineteenth and early twentieth centuries that this was true in the more distant past. I know from personal experience that this was the case during my own school years, and from many recent conversations with teachers and students in Germany I have learned that little has changed even today. I have no illusions about the situation in American colleges, where the honor code does not always work perfectly. Or, to use another example, the often-quoted high moral standards at English public schools and their emphasis on honesty and fairness are not always and under all circumstances adhered to. But, generally speaking, the code in both those systems works. What makes the situation at German schools so alarming and troublesome is the fact that attempted or accomplished cheating is a cult among German students. They who cheat the most and are the most inventive are the most admired members of the class. Innumerable examples from literature and from my own experience could be listed here: formulas in mathematics and chemistry written in the palms of one's hands; vocabulary lists pinned on the inside of skirts or dresses; translations of difficult Latin texts like Tacitus or Livy ordered by mail; tables of historical dates and names deposited in the lavatory, and a hundred other tricks.

I know of no satisfactory explanation for this unflattering phenomenon in the German education system. Obviously one could interpret it, and this has been done, as a youthful protest against the adult world, against any authority.

The stress of competition for good marks and similar reasons have also been mentioned. While that is true for other countries as well, however, there is in their schools no generally accepted cult of cheating, no overt acceptance of a moral defect by all students. It is a kind of moral anarchism in the system that is a perplexing phenomenon and a disturbing issue.

Our parents, of course, were kept in ignorance about all this. It would have been contrary to their most basic concept of morality, although in their youth they probably had performed similar tricks. One comforting note, however, needs to be recorded: the ugly cheating practice ceased suddenly and completely as soon as we entered the university. For us young students in Göttingen and Bonn, plagiarism, for example, was considered unacceptable and reprehensible, as is any violation of the academic honor code for my students now.

In the spring of 1940 there was a joyful reunion in our family. Since late August 1939 my oldest brother, Hans, had been interned at Las Palmas in the Canary Islands. He was a sailor on the SS *Madrid*, a smaller passenger ship of a Hamburg shipping line which regularly commuted between Hamburg and Buenos Aires. It was part of his prescribed service of several years, a basic requirement for admission to the merchant marine school. At the beginning of September 1939 the ship had been surprised by the outbreak of the war and had sought refuge in the Spanish Canary Islands, where Germans could count on a friendly reception from the benign neutrality of Franco's Spain. Other German captains acted similarly, and thus there were hundreds of young German merchant sailors sitting in what today is a holiday resort, and they were "bored stiff," as my brother told us later. Most of them wanted to go home for the chance to participate in the great war adventure. Hans had volunteered several times for service on support vessels for German raiders operating in the Atlantic, but so far had been rejected since the list of volunteers was very long. He then was "lucky" in a different way. He developed a fairly serious hernia and was flown back to Germany for the operation.

Our family knew nothing about this, and thus one day our oldest brother arrived suddenly and totally unexpectedly at my parents' house. Everybody was overjoyed, and the event was appropriately celebrated. My father, however, the farseeing realist, had mixed feelings about this happy event. Many years later my brother quoted to me my father's first words upon seeing his oldest son: *Jung, nu büst du wedder to Huus un nu must du doch noch in'n Krieg,* "Boy, now you are back home and now you have to go to war after all." It had been quite agreeable for the war veteran of 1914–18 that his oldest son should sit out this new World War in a relatively safe place in a neutral country, far away from any combat action, but of course he was not able to express this sentiment out loud.

Hans's return had another slightly comical, but also annoying, consequence for my parents. Upon his arrival, my brother had dropped his baggage in our kitchen. After the first happy greetings, my father caught sight of his duffel bag and immediately ordered: *Rut mit dat Ding,* "Out with that thing." But it was already too late. A few cockroaches had found their way out of the bag into our kitchen. Thus, for the next few years, we had to cope with this pest that was acceptable on an older ship in those days but was most inappropriate in the kitchen of a German *Hausfrau.* My parents tried every known insecticide and fumigation device, but it took years before we could get rid of the ugly nuisances. My mother was especially mortified by it, and every time we had visitors she thought she had to explain in detail how it happened that cockroaches had invaded the apartment of a very middle-class German family.

My father's anxiety over my brother's future was only too justified. At first Hans was allowed to attend the merchant marine school for eighteen months, but as soon as he had acquired his A5 diploma, the mate's license, the real war began for him. As a third, second, and finally, first mate, he served on various ships in the North Sea, the Baltic, the Atlantic, and the Mediterranean. He lost seven ships in three years, was torpedoed, mined, and bombed, but he survived all disasters. In May 1945 he arrived healthy and unscathed at my parents' house in Brunsbüttel.

6
Something
exciting
was going on
again

The nonevents on the western front in the war winter of 1939–40 were later called the *drôle de guerre*, the "phony war." In the German vernacular *Sitzkrieg* was used in analogy and contrast to the furious *Blitzkrieg*. Basically, these expressions are just grim oxymorons, since a war is never phony. Although the French and German soldiers were sitting in relative safety in their bunkers and casemates of the Maginot line and the Westwall, they did suffer casualties, dead and wounded, there also.

Four weeks before this "phony war" came to an end, in April 1940, the public was surprised and shocked by the operation *Weserübung*. It was the attack on and occupation of the Scandinavian countries of Denmark and Norway. My father and his colleagues had, of course, noticed both the increased eastbound traffic through the canal in the early days of April and also the presence of army units on board many of the troop transports. But even for these veteran maritime experts the direction and the objectives of the assault were unknown. The preparation for the operation was a triumph of secrecy. We young people were once again full of enthusiasm because "something exciting was going on again," *weil jetzt wieder etwas los war*. We were also thrilled because in an amphibian operation like Weserübung the navy, our beloved ships, had to play a decisive role.

I do remember, however, that even in the conversations, comments, and observations of us thirteen-year-olds sometimes somebody expressed reservations: "But Norway and Denmark are neutral countries, and they were neutral in the 1914–18 World War. They had nothing to do with Versailles." But such skeptical voices were quickly silenced by the NS propaganda, which repeatedly emphasized that Norwegian waters had been mined by the Allies as early as April 5 and that, at the time of the embarkation of German troops, British convoys were already on their way to Norway. In other words, Great Britain was ready to commit the same act of breaching Norwegian neutrality as had Germany. British troops did indeed land on the Norwegian coast almost simultaneously with German forces. Thus the preventive nature of the invasion was stressed, as was, of course, the strategic importance of securing the North European flank.

As in September 1939, we followed the progress of the operation intensely, and the military successes soon quieted critical voices among the people in Germany. Certain losses were admitted: the new heavy cruiser *Blücher* was sunk by Norwegian shore torpedo batteries in the Oslo Fjord. It capsized with heavy losses in army and navy personnel. The sinking of all ten destroyers— which were almost all the modern destroyers the German navy had at that time—while attempting to capture the all-important iron ore port of Narvik in northern Norway was never really admitted at the time. There were only reports about the heroic fighting of the flotilla Kommodore Bonte and his crews. Other serious losses were not mentioned at all, such as the sinking of the light cruisers *Königsberg*, at Bergen, and *Karlsruhe*, near Kristiansand. The reports of the supreme command of the armed forces also kept silent about the participation of German submarines during the entire operation, because there was none. That part of Weserübung was a complete failure.

What did appear more and more frequently in the propaganda media were reports about Norwegians willing to collaborate with the German authorities, among them most prominently Vidkun Quisling, who soon became the second most powerful man in the occupational government. Only after the war did I learn that on the Allied side "Quisling" became synonymous with "dishonorable collaborator" and "traitor."

We played our customary game with maps and little flags, and the expansion of the Greater German power sphere was indeed impressive. The strategic advantage resulting from the occupation of the northern neighbors was twofold: the all-important supply of Swedish iron ore via the port of Narvik was secured (50 percent of the German steel production at that time relied on Swedish iron ore); and the German submarines and surface units had an incomparably more advantageous operational basis against Great Britain as compared to the situation in the First World War. This was, of course, very clear to my father, the veteran submariner, whose U-boat, on every mission in 1914–18, had to find its way with great difficulties out of the "wet triangle" of the German Bay into the open Atlantic. I do not remember how he, the born pessimist, reacted to the triumph of the Norway campaign, but I do know that he and many other Germans were still looking anxiously to the west where the opponents and victors of the last war were waiting, their armed forces unscathed and fully intact. The nervous question "What will happen in the west?" had not been answered by the operation Weserübung. It had only been postponed.

The answer was given on May 10, 1940. Once again it began with a special bulletin and a formulation that was to be repeated over and over during the following years: *In den frühen Morgenstunden des 10. Mai sind starke deutsche Verbände auf breiter Front zum Angriff auf————angetreten,* "in the early morning hours of May 10 strong German units launched a large-scale offensive against————." Most people were taken aback that this large-scale offensive included the neutral Low Countries of Belgium, Holland, and Luxembourg. The inclusion of Holland in particular was unforeseen. After all, this country had been able to retain its neutral status all through World War I; it had granted asylum to the last German emperor, Wilhelm II; and commercial and cultural ties between the two countries had always been close. The relatively Germanophile attitude of the Dutch people turned overnight into a grim and lasting Germanophobia. It was caused by the unexpected and unprovoked attack, by the bombardment of Rotterdam, which was seen as a symbolic act of brutality against civilians, and by the beginning of the persecution of Dutch Jews, later immortalized by the fate of a young Dutch girl, Anne Frank.

Today, fifty years later, there exists a veritable library of historical presentations and analyses of the military and political events in Europe in May and June 1940. A brief enumeration may suffice here: the surrender of the armed forces of the Netherlands after five days, of the Belgian troops two weeks later; the surprise breakthrough of the German army in the Ardennes Forest, thus outflanking the Maginot line; the escape of the British Expeditionary Forces at Dunkerque (even today it has not been fully clarified why the German Panzers were stopped, giving the BEF the chance to cross the Channel); the collapse of the French armed forces; the fall of Paris on June 14; Italy's late entrance into the war; the armistice with the new French government headed by World War I hero Marshall Pétain on June 22. The whole West-Feldzug had lasted six weeks.

The excitement among us young people was boundless, and the German people in general registered the achievements of the Wehrmacht with, at first, incredulous pride. Again and again the comparison with the stationary trench warfare of 1914–18 was made and was, of course, supported and cultivated by the NS propaganda apparatus. The daily bulletins from the supreme command of the armed forces had carefully and consciously given the names of Belgian and French towns, rivers, and areas which still had a sinister and bloody connotation for the German population: Flanders, Arras, Verdun, Cambrai, the Somme, the Marne. The overwhelming victory had been achieved at a relatively low price. Twenty-seven thousand German soldiers had been killed in the western campaign (this figure was not given at the time)—a fraction of the casualties in a single World War I battle. The war seemed won. We were sure that the elimination of Great Britain was only a matter of time. The trauma of 1914–18 had disappeared. Versailles was now a closed chapter of history.

That was the tenor of the meticulous reporting by the *Propaganda-Kompanien* of the campaign and the armistice signing ceremony. The newsreels and documentary films were utilized to the fullest, paying careful attention to the symbolism of it all. For example, the signing of the French-German armistice agreement was arranged to take place in the same railroad car and at the same place, Compiègne, a hundred kilometers north of Paris, as it had in November 1918. This historic car had been carefully preserved and exhibited by the French in the army museum in Paris. The German authorities had it moved to the same place near Compiègne, which the French had turned into a memorial park celebrating the French triumph in 1918. It was complete with a monument and commemorative plaques placing blame for the war on "the criminal pride of the German Empire." The arrival of the French and German delegation was filmed and soon shown in all German movie theaters. The German delegation was headed by Hitler himself. He was shown reviewing the honor guard to the tune of the traditional Prussian *"Präsentiermarsch,"* "honor guard march," and then leading the seating of the delegations, the signing itself, and then the dynamiting of the *Schandmonument*, "monument of disgrace."

What was deleted in this documentary film was what was later called the "Führer's jig," a very short scene in which Hitler, after leaving the railroad carriage, could not quite suppress his feeling of satisfaction and joy and slapped his thigh. The reason for this omission? It would have shown the demigod in an all-too-human, gloating reaction that would not mesh with the public image of the serious and self-controlled Chancellor, and now also *Feldherr*, "master strategist," an image that had been carefully constructed and fostered by the propaganda ministry. I saw this scene for the first time many years later in an Allied documentary film.

Among us young people there was no feeling of hatred against the French similar to that which can be seen in certain works of German literature, especially during the Napoleonic wars and the French-German war of 1870–71. We simply felt superior, as members of a nation whose soldiers had just achieved a stupendous success. This had nothing to do with the "master race" theory because its theses impressed us as so abstruse and farfetched that we never took them seriously, as I have pointed out previously. It was just that the "stab-in-the-back" legend, that the German soldiers were never defeated in World War I, seemed to have been confirmed by the historical events of the last six weeks. Again and again we were exposed to films in which the triumphantly advancing Wehrmacht units were often juxtaposed with sequences of long columns of Belgian, French, and British prisoners of war who were moving slowly and with dragging feet to the rear, many of them wounded, their

uniforms in disarray, their exhausted and sad faces often shown in close-up—
embodiments of totally demoralized armies.

Especially sensational for us were reports that some of the strongest border
fortifications—for example, the Belgian Fort Eben Emael, considered im-
pregnable by military experts—had been conquered by applying *neuartige
Kampfmittel*, "new weapons systems." It was the first engagement of paratroopers and airborne units, who had landed their glider planes on top of these
fortifications. The first pictures showed these elite soldiers in their jumpsuits
and differently shaped helmets, and we simply stood in awe of these new heroes who with their coups de main had made military history.

The term "new weapons" was used later in the course of the war quite
often, especially when military reverses began to affect the morale of the population, and it had to be boosted. In the final phase of the war, the "new" or
"secret" weapons played an important and effective role in strengthening the
people's endurance and will to hold out, thus actually prolonging the war. It
goes without saying that there was extensive footage in the newsreels of a victory parade of German infantry soldiers who marched down the Champs
Elysées past one of their commanding generals. They even tried to perform
the traditional *Parademarsch*, the goose stepping. If it lacked the usual precision and uniformity, that only increased the effectiveness of the scenes
on the viewers. We told ourselves that these were combat troops who in the
previous weeks had other things to do than practice goose stepping on a parade ground.

These days of triumph made the task of Goebbels and his people in the
propaganda ministry an easy one. Nevertheless, they did not refrain from pure
falsification of facts and excessive hyperbole. I remember two examples. In
one broadcast about the Dunkerque evacuation, a BBC interview with members of the British Expeditionary Forces was quoted. The German commen-
tator closed with these words: "It is a complete mystery to us with whom the
British Broadcasting Corporation conducted these interviews. After all, for
days now the German air force has not allowed a mouse to cross the Channel," *lässt seit Tagen keine Maus mehr über den Kanal*. In reality, the British
succeeded in evacuating a total force of almost three hundred forty thousand
British and Allied soldiers. The other example concerns the air raids of the
Luftwaffe first on the RAF fighter installations and then on London, the
Blitz. In one news bulletin it was stated that the London dock area had been
hit so heavily by incendiary bombs that "these blazes could in all probability
not be extinguished in this war." That was sheer hyperbole, and nonsense
from a military and technical point of view, but many people believed it.

The summer of 1940 was the zenith of Hitler's political and personal career. For more than four years in the First World War he and his comrades had

suffered in the trenches with always the unattainable objective, Paris, staring them in the face. Now, twenty-two years later, Hitler himself stood in the French capital as the German head of state after a lightning victory over the renowned French army. The comparison between the young corporal Hitler and the Feldherr Hitler, was, of course, heavily exploited and embellished in the media. Strangely enough he denied himself a triumphant entry into Paris and visited the city only once at dawn, when streets and plazas were deserted. On the other hand a gigantic victory parade in Berlin was organized and choreographed like a Wagnerian opera. In a speech to the Reichstag, publicized as his great *Friedensrede*, "speech of peace," he reported about the recent events to the assembly and announced promotions and awards of high medals. This was the first indication of the medal and promotion inflation. A number of generals were promoted to the rank of General Fieldmarshal; in the entire First World War only three of these titles were bestowed. Göring was given a completely new title, *Reichsmarschall*, and was awarded the *Grosskreuz zum Eisernen Kreuz*, "Grand Cross of the Iron Cross," a medal that probably weighed half a pound. The most important aspect for Hitler was his peace offer to Great Britain on the basis of "dividing the world." He was ready to guarantee the status quo of the British Empire; and except for the return of its former colonies, Germany, he proclaimed, had no further territorial demands in the world.

For us young people and for many other Germans, this seemed to be a very generous and fair offer, and we could not understand its refusal by the British government. We were not aware of the total distrust of the British concerning any of Hitler's promises. We did not know that the Führer, by his frequent breaches of international agreements during the previous two years, had forfeited all credibility, and, above all, we did not know the phenomenon of Winston Churchill.

Many historians and Hitler experts attribute the Führer's self-aggrandizement, which later became more apparent, to this time, to these days of triumph. Some even use the clinical term "megalomania." At this time the title *Gröfaz* was bestowed upon him by one of his most ardent admirers, General Keitel. It was an acronym for *Grösster Feldherr aller Zeiten*, "greatest strategist of all time." It was quickly picked up, probably first by the acid-tongued Berliners, and used to ridicule Hitler in his new pose as the superior general because of the exaggeration implicit in the term and its closeness in sound and spelling to the existing derogatory slang word *Fatzke*, "fop, dandy." The word "Gröfaz" gained real currency in the later years of the war, although its use, of course, was strictly forbidden and could get an incautious speaker into serious trouble. Hitler's conceit about his own talents was to have dire consequences for the German people and the course of the war, as

71

evidenced in his continuous and apparently apodictic meddling in strategic decisions beginning with the German defeat at Stalingrad in January and February 1943 and ending with the fighting in Berlin in April 1945.

After the categorical rejection of Hitler's peace offer by the British, the NS government ordered the Wehrmacht to prepare for Operation *Seelöwe*, "sea lion," the invasion of the British Isles. The first step had to be the gaining of absolute air superiority over the Channel and southern England. In his customary overbearing manner, the new Reichsmarschall Göring took charge of this task and offered guaranteed success in a few weeks, or, at most, months. Thus in the late summer of 1940, the air war over England began, which the British today still call the Battle of Britain. The Luftwaffe and the RAF suffered heavy casualties, but the Germans blinked first. The Spitfire and Hurricane pilots, soon to be celebrated in Churchillean rhetoric, attacked the bomber squadrons of the Luftwaffe with a passion and fury that the German pilots, accustomed to easy victory until then, had never experienced. The outcome was uncertain and could have gone either way. At this point the NS leadership made an error that some historians today see as *kriegsentscheidend*, "decisive for the outcome of the war." Instead of pursuing the original plan to put the airfields and radar installations of the RAF fighter command out of action, a new target was chosen in order to break the morale of the British population—London. Neither objective was achieved, although the propaganda assured us again and again that a breakthrough was imminent.

As always we observed the course of events with the greatest interest and admiration for our pilots. In the newsreels the enemy planes fell out of the sky in droves; our own planes never did. We also had already calculated how long the invasion of England would take to complete. According to our estimate, it would only take about six to eight weeks *weil wir mit Holland, Belgien, und Frankreich in sechs Wochen fertig geworden sind,* "because we took care of Holland, Belgium, and France in six weeks." Once again it was my father who kept a cool head. He knew nothing about planes and air war, but a great deal about ships. He knew the British navy and British sailors, and he warned against underestimating them. He did not particularly like the British, but he respected them highly. *De Engelsman is noch lang nich kaputt,* "The English are far from being down and out," is how he often phrased it. This "defeatism" was a matter of considerable irritation to my brother Rudi, four years older than I, and me. My father was no student of history, and I do not think that he knew much about Napoleon's unsuccessful preparations to cross the Channel in 1807, and I am certain that he was not aware of the fact that the last invasion of the British Isles had occurred in 1066. But as a naval expert he could only shake his head about the halfhearted invasion preparations of the German navy, for example, the assembling of hundreds of river barges in the jump-off ports on the French Channel coast. He knew that these vessels were totally unsuitable for crossing the treacherous Channel waters with hundreds of thousands of army soldiers on board and landing them on the southern English beaches.

During the air raids on London, the Houses of Parliament, among many other buildings, were hit and damaged. Guided of course by the propaganda ministry, we saw in this a symbolic act: the weakness and imminent demise of the decadent democratic form of government, which was far inferior to the one based on the *Führerprinzip*, the "leadership principle," as in Germany, Italy, and Spain. We knew that since May 10 the commanding figure in the British government was Winston Churchill. Even some of his most famous rhetorical phrases were quoted, such as "I have nothing to offer but blood, toil, tears, and sweat." How seriously the NS regime took the new prime minister was shown by the fact that he now became the main target of the propaganda campaign. He was always referred to with epithets like *Lügenlord*, *Trunkenbold*, *Gallipoli-Verlierer*, (Lord of Lies, Drunkard, Gallipoli Loser.)[1] Sometimes the verbal abuse took on bizarre forms. I remember a short newspaper column that analyzed Churchill's name; it was hyphenated as "Church-ill" and then translated as *kranke Kirche*, "sick church."

Here is a personal example of the effectiveness of the propaganda from our everyday student life. We had to write an essay in our German class on the subject *Krieg und Propaganda*. In my puerile imagination I invented a satire about the sinking of the British passenger liner *Athenia*, one of the first ships torpedoed by a German submarine. Churchill, first lord of the admiralty at the time, had tried to portray the sinking as a brutal act of the German navy. The attempt was modeled after the successful exploitation of the *Lusitania* sinking in 1915. The NS propaganda, of course, vehemently denied any breaking of international law. In my satire I wrote about the "Lord of Lies" who had accused the German U-boat commander of having fired ropes by rockets over the superstructure of the ship and having then pulled the *Athenia* to the bottom of the sea, a version that Churchill had dreamed up in a drunken stupor. I was quite proud of this original treatment of the subject, and I was very surprised when I received an unusually low grade. Besides showing the propaganda effect on young minds, it is another example of the deep concern my German teacher, Miss J., had about the constant brainwashing to which her students were exposed.

In general we had a severely distorted view of Great Britain, its people and history. The darker aspects of empire building were emphasized, for example, in the widely distributed picture album, *Robber Nation England*. On July 3, 1940, a British contingent of the Mediterranean fleet attacked and destroyed the French fleet in Oran in order to prevent these powerful units from falling into German hands. Churchill later called this attack on the former ally one of the most difficult decisions of his life. The NS propaganda immediately drew the parallel to the unprovoked assault of a British squadron on the Danish fleet in Copenhagen in 1807, pointed out that to "Copenhagen" another country had become a verb in the English language, and called all of this immoral. Anti-British movies were produced and shown in all German film theaters. An example, slightly later than 1940, was *Ohm Krüger,* a film about the Boer War (1899–1902) in which the English soldiers were the villains and the Boers the heroes. I remember one exceptionally blatant propaganda scene to expose the hypocrisy of the alleged "Christian" nation of England: at the end of the service in a South African church, an English clergyman slowly and solemnly walked down the center aisle, and while the black congregation sang a final hymn the reverend distributed alternately Bibles and rifles, a Bible left, a rifle right, Bible, rifle, rifle, Bible. The intended message was clear: on the one side the Anglican Church was spreading Christ's words, "Love thine enemies"; on the other side, it was distributing weapons to the "primitive" blacks for killing Boers.

At school we learned about the tradition of the English public schools and their role in training the political, social, and military ruling class. In our textbooks we read about, and our English teacher lectured on, these institutions whose history in some cases went back four or five centuries to pre-Elizabethan times. On the other hand the exclusivity of these schools was denounced in our textbooks because they were there only for the privileged ruling classes, not for the people. As proof of this, photographs of the school uniforms were shown and ridiculed: tails for the boys at Eton; blazers, ties, and straw hats for Harrow, and so on. We, with our brown-and-black and navy blue DJ uniforms, looked condescendingly upon such "antideluvian" school uniforms, and we even felt a little sorry for our Etonian and Harrovian contemporaries in their "straightjackets." The positive aspects of the public schools, about which our teacher spoke, for instance, their codes of behavior and language usage, went completely past us at the time, made no impression on us, and were not absorbed at all.

Ridiculing the enemy was a popular tactic of the propaganda. Thus a member of the propaganda companies composed a journalistic piece about a bomber squadron of the Luftwaffe preparing for another raid on British targets, briefing of the crews, filling the fuel tanks, testing machine guns, arming the planes with new bomb loads, and so on. One particular crew member, more probably the reporter, had thought of a special practical joke. They had collected a number of men's used umbrellas and had attached clever messages to each of them. They took them along on their mission and after having released their bomb load on their target, they also dropped the umbrellas on the English countryside. The reporters then speculated about the confusion and embarrassment of the people in England who found one of the umbrellas. In this manner the airmen allegedly made fun of the civilian character of the

British government. Prime Minister Neville Chamberlain on his peace missions in 1938 had always been shown carrying an umbrella, and it had become a symbol for the old-fashioned, out-of-date nature of British society. We laughed about the customary garb of Englishmen in the city of London and in Parliament, dark three-piece suits, bowler hats, and umbrellas. We compared them with our smoothly uniformed military and political leaders in Germany. Again, this appeared to us as further proof of the decadence and superannuation of the whole democratic system. A German soldier or member of the NS leadership carrying an umbrella in public was unthinkable. We could not even imagine that the younger members of the English "umbrella brigade" could overnight, if necessary, change from their drab attire into uniforms and turn into first-rate soldiers. We also did not realize the deeper symbolism of all this—that is to say, the absolute dominance of the civilian over the military in British society. For us only the soldiers counted, the military, the war. Anything civilian was less important and had to take a back seat.

Of these years I remember several episodes that throw a certain light on a phenomenon which, both during and more especially after the war, was much discussed and was even treated in literature: the fear by adults, mostly parents and teachers, of children as potential informers. Bertolt Brecht deals with this topic in one scene of his play *Furcht und Elend des Dritten Reiches* (1935–38), *Fear and Misery of the Third Reich*, written while he was in exile in Denmark. He called the scene, one of twenty-four, *Der Spitzel*, "The Informer." It is mostly a quarrel of a married couple in which the wife reproaches her husband for not having been cautious enough while expressing political opinions in the presence of their young son, a DJ-Pimpf. It is supposed to portray the poisoned atmosphere in a totalitarian state when fear even drives a wedge between parents and children. I saw this play in the 1960s in East Berlin and was not impressed. Everything sounded much too contrived.

I first remember a short scene from our daily family life. My brother and I had been on DJ and HJ duty in the evening and were returning home together. Naturally, both of us were in uniform, my brother in the air-force blue of the *Flieger*-HJ,[2] I in the navy blue of the DJ, both of us wearing the insignia of our respective ranks and various merit badges. As we entered our living room, only my father was there. He was leafing through *Mein Kampf* and was listening not very attentively to a Hitler speech that was just then being broadcast. He looked up and said: "Look, you always tell me that I am not a good National Socialist. But here I am sitting reading Hitler's book and listening to the Führer's speech, and two of my sons are leaders in the Hitler Youth. There is no better National Socialist than I anywhere." The open sarcasm of his remarks was, of course, not lost on us, and we did not particularly like it. But we had far too much respect for our father than to start a family quarrel about politics. The idea of denouncing him in public or bringing charges against him because of these and many other critical remarks he made about the party and the regime never occurred to us. Such an idea was so alien that it was totally beyond our imagination.

The second scene I remember was at about the same time and concerns an odd incident that upset the people in our town, especially the pilots' community, considerably. It was discussed with much intensity and passion, and we teenagers did not hold back with our opinions. Fortunately, it had no serious consequences for my father and his friends. One of our neighbors, Pilot G., was involved in a collision inside one of the canal locks. As he was taking a ship into a lock chamber at slow speed, his order to reverse the engine had not been executed promptly enough, and the ship had hit one of the huge lock gates. The vessel's bow and the gate were damaged and the lock chamber was out of commission for a few days. It was the type of accident that sometimes happens, and all professional sailors know this and live with it. Under normal circumstances, all cases of collision are brought before the *Seeamt*, "maritime board," where a group of experts conducts hearings to determine the cause(s) of the accident—technical failures, weather conditions, communication problems, and so forth. Occasions where the captain or the pilot was held responsible were rare. This case, however, turned out to be different. The Gestapo interfered.[3] They sensed sabotage and accused Pilot G. of having deliberately attempted to put the lock installation out of action. Our neighbor was found guilty and given a jail sentence of several months. My father and his friends were furious, and in their private conversations gave vent to their anger. One of their most reliable and competent colleagues had been judged and sentenced by ignorant and meddling laymen, and his career had been destroyed.

We children sometimes overheard our parents' rather vehement discussions, and we later, among ourselves, repeated the arguments and opinions that sounded so convincing to us. I remember very well one morning, as we were taking the bus to school, we expressed our opinions about the G. case loudly and bluntly: *Die dämlichen Gestapoheinis haben doch keine Ahnung von Schiffen und Seefahrt*, "the stupid Gestapo jerks know absolutely nothing about ships and the sea." By chance, my aunt, Tante Emma, and her friend were riding in the same bus that morning. They were seated up front and were listening to our loud talk. At one point Tante Emma said to her friend, as she later told my mother, "Listen to them in the back. They are the real experts." Fortunately, we boys and my aunt and her friend were the only bus riders that morning. No one else heard us and therefore no report of our secondhand, but dangerous, criticism of a government agency could be made. My aunt, however, told my parents about the incident, and that was the end of the discussion about Pilot G. in our house, at least in the presence of us children.

The third episode having to do with denunciatory fear happened in our school. It caused quite a stir, but it was never discussed in our classes and even in our recess conversations only hesitantly and furtively. During our trips to and from school in the commuter bus, Mr L. was mentioned more and more often. He was one of our English teachers. We, in the lower grades knew him only by sight, since he only taught in the upper grades. His nickname was "Ovambo." Mr. L. was an Anglophile. According to our older schoolmates, he constantly expressed his admiration for the British Empire in his classes, emphasized the century-old victorious tradition of the British navy, and spoke of the special character of the English people—tough, stubborn, and proud. He also warned against belittling them and writing them off as a military opponent. His most severe critics among his students were Werner D. and Ludwig M., both of them pilots' sons from Brunsbüttel and our neighbors, and both of them relatively high-ranking DJ leaders who were much admired by us younger students. One day Mr. L.'s "tirades praising England" became too much for these two. They brought formal charges against him. Mr. L. was arrested, and his trial was held in a neighboring town. Werner D. and Ludwig M. were called as main witnesses for the prosecution, and Mr. L. was sentenced to six months in jail for "spreading defeatism and undermining people's morale." He disappeared from our school and never returned. Much later I heard that he had survived the war, but I do not know any more details about his life and career.

It was the only example of denunciation of which I am aware that took place in our school, neighborhood, and town. The reaction of the adults, his colleagues and our parents, is quite revealing. Herr L.'s colleagues were stunned, but I do not think that they were actually afraid of us. They were quite cautious in the classroom and often stayed away from risky subjects in their teaching, as I have mentioned in a previous chapter. In our neighborhood, the family of Werner D. consciously hushed up the event. I had strict instructions from my parents never to even talk about it. I am certain it indicated their embarrassment and shame over the fact that, due to the initiative of the son of their friends, a person had been put in jail and his career ruined. That was so unusual for them and their concept of morality and decent behavior that they refused ever to talk about it. It was for them, as my father told me many years later, a further sign that *die Zeit aus den Fugen war*, "the times were out of joint." Even we younger people shied away from discussing the "Ovambo affair," and it damaged our image of the two witnesses who in all other respects were our role models.

A last memory about Werner D. is in order here. Like all young men in his class, he had volunteered for service in the armed forces as soon as he had reached the age of seventeen. He was an outstanding soldier and had rapidly advanced in the Wehrmacht, so that after only a year and a half he was promoted to second lieutenant in the army elite division Grossdeutschland. During his last furlough, he, his younger brother Helmut, and I had staged an improvised snowball fight in our street. Werner was not wearing his uniform tunic, only breeches and a sweater. A passing neighbor, whom we called a *Kanarienvogel*, "canary bird," because of the bright yellow uniform of some kind of NS functionary, said patronizingly, *Na, Werner, ein bisschen mit den Kindern spielen?* "Well, Werner, playing a little with children?" Werner was furious and said to us later; "I wish I had had my jacket on. Then that idiot would have had to salute me," and Helmut and I could only wholeheartedly agree. It is another small example of our lack of respect for many of the local NS people, especially in comparison with real soldiers. When Werner's furlough was nearly over, he paid a farewell visit to my parents. My father accompanied him to the door and said to him: *Jung, koom gesund no Huus,* "Boy, come home in one piece." Our friend waved for the last time as he was going down the steps and shouted: *Mook wi, Herr Schümann,* "Will do, Herr Schümann." He was killed in combat a few months later near Charkov in the Russian Ukraine.

My second brother, Rudi, was exactly Werner's age, to the day. Thus the traditional birthday parties were held alternately year after year in our house and in the house of his family. Rudi had volunteered for service in the air force, which was a matter of course for him because he was an enthusiastic adherent of the glider sport. For years he had pedaled his bicycle every weekend to the glider slope, Hoopen, near our town, where the topographical structure of the landscape and the almost permanent west wind was especially favorable for this sport. There and in several glider camps he had fulfilled the prerequisites for the A-test (beginners), B-test (intermediate), and finally for the C-test. The latter was not easy to attain. One of the tasks was to stay in the air in a motorless plane for a considerable length of time and perform a number of difficult maneuvers. It required considerable flying skill and study and knowledge of wind, weather, cloud formation, and so on. He proudly wore the blue badge with the three white wings of the C-pilot. All of this was, of course, preparation for military flying in the Luftwaffe. Rudi was all the more disappointed when, after his basic training, it was discovered that he had faulty vision and could not pass the vision test. It was the end of his dream of becoming a fighter pilot, a goal he had cherished for years. I remember well the deep disappointment he expressed in his letters home. I am sure he had already seen himself as one of the "glamor boys" of the air force. My parents, however, were quite pleased about this turn of events, although they tried not to show it. By 1941 everyone knew of the high-risk existence of fighter pilots, although German casualties in the air operations were never admitted by the NS propaganda.

Since Rudi was a trained electrician, he attended an air force school for airplane mechanics and then spent the next three years as a member of the ground crew on a military airstrip in the vicinity of Leningrad. When the general retreat of the Wehrmacht on the eastern front began, he was transferred to a *Luftwaffenfelddivsion*, "air force field division," newly formed infantry units composed of surplus air force personnel. He was wounded in combat near Danzig (Gdansk) and managed to obtain a berth on one of the last German hospital ships out of Danzig. He reached a Danish port, and from there he made his way hitchhiking and on foot to Brunsbüttel, arriving there in April 1945. My parents were overjoyed at having one of their sons back home—damaged and emaciated, but alive. In many later conversations, my brother and I agreed that his physical defect of faulty vision had very probably saved his life. The casualty rate among German fighter pilots in the last years of the war was horrendous, and the chances of survival for them for three years were very small indeed.

7
My Lord,
doesn't this
ever stop!

In the spring of 1941 I was fourteen years old and thus, according to long family tradition, my confirmation was imminent. My parents and their parents and all our ancestors, as far as we could trace them back, had been members of the Lutheran Church, which in our part of Germany was considered to be an approximation of a state church. All of us children had been baptized as infants, and it was a matter of course that we would be confirmed. In former years it was customary that the confirmands attend the confirmation classes held by the pastor once or twice a week. Now, in the not-very-church-friendly climate of the NS state, our attendance was sporadic to say the least. We always found some excuse or pretext to cut classes despite my mother's gentle admonitions.

Our family, like the majority of people in northern Germany at that time, were not regular churchgoers. We attended church services on special occasions: baptisms, confirmations, weddings, funerals. Some of us went to church on Christmas Eve for sentimental reasons. On a normal Sunday, only a few pews were occupied in our Lutheran church, which was not very spacious anyway. It was the only real church in our town. There was also a small Catholic chapel, but it did not even have a permanent priest. As a small child I had attended *Kindergottesdienst*, Sunday school, fairly regularly, not because of my parents' insistence, but to keep my playmate Helmut company; his mother was a devout Christian. There and in religion classes in elementary school and Gymnasium—where religion was an established part of our school curriculum—I acquired my religious education, and it was sparse and fragmentary. Only after the war did I really become acquainted with the Bible, learned more about the history of the Christian church, and studied the theological writings of the church fathers, of Martin Luther, and of the theologians of our century. That was done through self-study or in connection with my scholarly pursuits in the fields of history and literature. We grew up *wie kleine Heiden,* "like small heathens," as one of my teachers rather sadly told my parents at one point. It was a formulation that we at that time did not mind hearing.

But there had to be a confirmation. That was an unshakable tradition in our town and in our family, and with the elaborate celebration came presents, flowers, and cards. The spiritual aspect of the ceremony, our first partaking of Holy Communion, meant nothing to us, nor did the announcement of the pastor from the pulpit that we were now fully recognized members of the congregation. We were far too young and immature to register the full implication of all this. Our lethargy and indifference were encouraged by the ambivalent and, at times, clearly antichurch position of the NSDAP and its organizations, including the HJ and DJ. Some of my fellow confirmands appeared for the ceremony in their DJ uniforms. That was out of the question for my parents. They had purchased my first real suit with long trousers for the occasion—but at least they did not force me to wear a tie, which according to our dress code at the time would have been hopelessly out-of-date and far too civilian. Each of us received a *Konfirmandenbrief,* a handsome document adorned with a colored reproduction of Caspar David Friedrich's painting, "Cross in the Mountains,"[1] and a special biblical quotation selected by the pastor, the *Konfirmandenspruch.* My mother was quite elated by all this, but for my friends and for myself, the ceremony, the document, and the whole tradition of "coming of age" meant absolutely nothing. It was not until 1945, after the war and after the NS regime had ended, that I voluntarily went to church for the first time and participated in a church service.

In late winter and in spring of the year 1941, the Blitzkrieg started rolling again with the seemingly unstoppable advances and conquests of the Wehrmacht. The theater of war was now expanded from Europe to another continent, North Africa. The very designation of the newly formed units of the armed forces, *Afrikakorps,* inspired us. We admired the new lightweight uniforms and the *Tropenhelme,* "pith helmets." World War I memories were awakened; for example, we remembered General Lettow-Vorbeck, who held out and continued to fight the entire four and a half years in *Deutsch-Ostafrika,* today Tanzania, against overwhelming South African and British forces and did not capitulate until November 1918. His autobiography and other glorifying accounts of his heroics were among our favorite books, and the very singable marching song "Heia Safari," about the former German colony, now became very popular. It paid special tribute to the *Askaris,* the native black soldiers who remained steadfastly loyal to their general and the emperor to the very end of German rule and beyond.

Now a new legend was born, that of Erwin Rommel, "the Desert Fox," commander in chief of the Afrikakorps. We knew his name as that of a gifted and bold divisional commander and tactician during the western campaign, but now his name became a household word for everyone. As always, we followed with passionate interest the mobile warfare and the back-and-forth maneuvers of the German Afrikakorps and the British Eighth Army along the North African coastline of the Mediterranean. It soon became known that here, despite the savagery of battle, a special chivalrous kind of fighting was adhered to on both sides, which impressed us greatly, especially when compared to the later events on the eastern front. I know of one authentic example of this, a personal experience that an English friend told me a few years after the war. Dennis E. was a lieutenant in the infantry and had been captured by the Germans in one of the battles around Tobruk.[2] He and his fellow prisoners of war were moving in a long column toward the German-occupied hinterland. He was exhausted and very thirsty, and he stepped up to one of the Panzers temporarily parked on the side of the road and asked for a drink of water. The German tank commander handed him a twenty-five liter container that was fastened to the turret. Dennis eagerly put the unwieldy container to his lips and started to swallow. But it was not water; it was gasoline. It was a terrible although understandable error made by the German officer. In every army in the world there are annoying and potentially dangerous defects, malfunctions, and poorly designed equipment. Here it was the fact that the containers for water and gasoline had the same color, the same shape, and the same size. It was a first-rate SNAFU, as the American soldiers in World War II coined the phrase. This particular SNAFU could have been fatal for my friend, but the tank commander was so horrified about his mistake that he jumped off his vehicle, quickly helped the injured Dennis into a staff car, and rushed him to the nearest field hospital where he was treated immediately. Fortunately, the burn wounds in his mouth and palate were only superficial and he suffered no serious and lasting damage. Dennis E. closed his narrative with these words: "That's the kind of war it was in 1941, tough but humane."

Less than two months after Rommel's landing in Tripoli, in April 1941, the next campaign began, this time in southeastern Europe against Yugoslavia and Greece. Once again it lasted only a few weeks and ended with the capitulation of the two nations. I remember that in the special bulletins certain famous place names from ancient history were singled out, for example, the Thermopylae. In school we had learned about the heroic battle there of the Spartan King Leonidas against the Persians and had memorized the poet Simonides's epigram: "Go tell the Spartans, thou who passeth by / That here, obedient to their laws, we lie." But it appeared a matter of course to us that such heroic actions against German Panzers were impossible, and thus no new legends could be created. Nothing seemed impossible for the Wehrmacht to achieve. After we had seen pictures of the German flag being hoisted on the Eiffel Tower, we casually accepted the fact that the flag was also flying over the Acropolis.

The last part of the Balkan campaign was the conquest of the island of Crete by paratroopers and airborne units. There soon were rumors that this operation had been very bloody and the casualty rates among the elite troops unusually high, but of course this was never officially admitted. It is a fact, however, that the Crete conquest was the last large-scale action of German paratrooper units from the air. The propaganda emphasized the heavy British losses of ships and personnel during the final evacuation of the island.

We found it absolutely in order that practically all the countries of the European continent from the North Cape to Crete were part of the Greater German power sphere or, as in the case of Spain, were headed by a Germanophile government. The three exceptions, neutral Portugal, Switzerland, and Sweden, were small countries and appeared to be of little strategic and geopolitical importance. All of this was constantly brought to our attention by the NS propaganda ministry and hammered into our consciousness every day with pictures, films, maps, verbal and written presentations, and analyses.

All the more shattering was the news of an event in the Atlantic at the end of May 1941: the initial triumph and then the sinking of the battleship *Bismarck*. It was the first serious setback in the war for the German armed forces. Elsewhere I have spoken about our love of ships and our knowledge of the vessels of the German navy. We had known for several years that a new battleship was being built in a Hamburg shipyard, and we had followed with great interest the construction of the dreadnought which was supposed to be superior to any existing warship in the world. In the days before the launching of the new giant on February 14, 1939—Hitler himself was to be present—we had played a game of guessing and betting about the name of the ship. The final unveiling of *Bismarck*, done not until the actual launching ceremony, definitely met with full approval of us boys. From our point of view Otto von Bismarck had been the most prominent figure of German history since Frederick the Great. He was considered the statesman to whom Germany owed its long-overdue unification. We saw "the Iron Chancellor" as the founder of the Second Reich. Therefore it was most appropriate that the new battleship should carry his name, a ship that was said to be the crowning achievement of the German shipbuilding industry, superior in size, armament, speed, armor, and range.

Now the construction was completed. We had also heard that the most competent and best-trained specialists and experts of the whole German navy had been selected for service on the *Bismarck*, the best sailors, machinists, navigators, gunners, communication people, and radar specialists. The "best and most powerful battleship in the world," as it was loudly and boastfully proclaimed in the newspapers, was also manned by an elite crew. For its shakedown cruises in the Baltic, it had to pass by our hometown. A large group of us boys had gathered on the Elbe dikes and waited excitedly for the arrival of the ship. It passed us at slow speed, huge and powerful, yet slender and elegant, and it made an unforgettable impression on us. The *Bismarck* was the sensation of those days, and we immediately adopted it as our *Lieblingsschiff*, our favorite ship of the entire navy.

Some weeks later its passing through the Kiel Canal locks became a source of great amusement for our whole town. The vessel was so large that it could sail through the locks and the canal only with the assistance of several tugboats, each guided by a pilot. The naval authorities had insisted on having as the pilot in command on the bridge of the *Bismarck* the man who had last taken one of the smaller battleships *Gneisenau* or *Scharnhorst* through. The logic of the admirals was that this man would be the most suitable and experienced person to pilot the new giant during the delicate and difficult maneuvers in the relatively narrow locks and the *Graben*, "ditch," as the canal was often called by my father and his colleagues with calculated understatement. Unfortunately, the last *Gneisenau* pilot had been Herr Benno C. He was regarded as a buffoon among his colleagues. He talked too much, drank too much, and was not taken very seriously. He most certainly was not the best man for the job, instead he was the worst. The whole town laughed about the imbecility of the admirals, but the passage of the ship was accomplished without incident. We children of pilots' families were especially amused; for us the real sailors were the professional merchant mariners—our fathers.

At the end of May 1941, the *Bismarck* was engaged in its first battle action. It and the new heavy cruiser *Prinz Eugen* met two British capital ships in the Denmark Strait, the battle cruiser *Hood* and the battleship *Prince of Wales*. The encounter was very brief. The *Hood* was hit by a full broadside of the heavy guns of the *Bismarck* and blew up. There were only three survivors. We saw the battle as proof of outstanding German technology and seamanship, especially the superior fire control of our Lieblingsschiff. Our excitement was boundless and we acted as though we ourselves had been present.

It was all the more difficult for us to cope with the following events. The *Bismarck* had gained access to the open Atlantic and presented a serious threat for the vital British convoy traffic from and to Canada and the United States. This fact and probably revenge for the destruction of the *Hood* led to the famous Churchill order: "Sink the *Bismarck*." A large British task force including carrier-based torpedo planes was assembled to chase the "scourge of the sea." The outcome is well known. The ship's steering mechanism was put out of action by a torpedo hit. It was unable to maneuver purposefully and was finally sunk by the concentrated action of the superior British forces. There is a theory that it was scuttled by its crew. There were few

The battleship *Bismarck,* our *Lieblingsschiff,* is seen on its last voyage north from the deck of the heavy cruiser *Prinz Eugen.*

survivors of the crew of more than two thousand officers and men. British ships left the scene in the middle of the rescue operation because of fear of U-boat attacks.

We were dumbfounded and numb with pain. The NS government declared a special national day of mourning for the *Bismarck* and its crew. For weeks afterward, we young people in our discussions tried to find answers to the question of how this catastrophe could have happened. We asked many questions, but of course only among ourselves, not publicly. We could not understand why the ship had been sent out into the open sea without a single protective escort (the *Prinz Eugen* had been ordered to separate from the *Bismarck* after the engagement in the Denmark Strait and arrived at the French Atlantic port of Brest for repairs five days later). Where were the renowned German submarines when the ship needed help so badly? And what had happened to Göring's highly praised Luftwaffe? After the war a number of books and treatises about the events appeared, some of them written by serious historians and naval experts, and a feature film about the final destiny of the

Bismarck was produced by a British company. But none of these examinations really gave a totally satisfactory answer to the questions that we fourteen-year-old boys asked at the time. Even before the loss of the ship, my father frequently expressed skepticism about the naval construction plans: "What do we need these big ships for? Now that we have them, the naval command has to look for a big shelter for each of them." As a realist and naval expert he knew that the Battle of the Atlantic could only be won by U-boats, not by capital ships and surface raiders. The subsequent years proved him right once again. The battleships *Gneisenau, Scharnhorst,* and *Tirpitz,* sister ship of the *Bismarck,* played no significant role in the German naval operations anymore. They were eliminated by submarine commandos *(Tirpitz),* surface battle *(Scharnhorst),* and air attack *(Gneisenau).*

In my personal life at this time, I had to make a decision as far as my membership in the Hitler Youth was concerned. I was fourteen years old and thus could no longer remain in the DJ, except as a leader with a higher rank than I had. Therefore I had the choice of joining either the general HJ or one of the special branches of the organization. The former was not popular among us Gymnasium students. It had the reputation of being flabby and lax and having no spirit, and most of its members (aged fifteen to eighteen) were developing other interests—jobs, girls, entertainment. Moreover, its meetings were held in the evening. For these reasons two friends of mine and I chose to join the Flieger-HJ, which had much smaller units and was considered an elite branch. In my case there was the additional incentive of following in my brother the C-pilot's footsteps. To show our new interest in flying and airplanes, we applied in the early summer for participation in glider camp, which was held not far from our hometown. The purpose of the camp was to accumulate thirty "starts" in a glider, brief takeoffs and landings, and then pass the A-test. The most important requirement was to stay in the air for thirty seconds and execute a few simple maneuvers to prove that we had complete control over the plane. Our gliders were very different from the popular hang gliders of today. They were real airplanes constructed of extremely light wood and plastic fabric with a seat for the pilot, a joystick, and pedals for the flaps. After passing the A-test we would be allowed to wear a new badge on our uniforms, a blue medal with one white wing in the middle.

All this came to naught. A German writer of the romantic period, Jean Paul, characterized the German summer as a *grün angestrichener Winter,* "winter painted green." The summer of 1941 was just that: cold, rain every day, and, for us especially annoying, wind from the east, the wrong direction. Thus we rarely had *Flugwetter,* "flying weather." When conditions were favorable for a few hours, we had to work hard to propel a glider into the air. Two strong rubber ropes were fastened to the nose of the plane. Eight of us boys were assigned to each rope, and we had to run down the slope pulling as hard as possible. Four other boys held the tail of the plane. When there was enough tension, the order *Los!* was given, and they let go. The glider was catapulted upward and sailed down the slope, with some luck catching a bit of current which enabled the pilot to stay aloft a few seconds longer. He then landed in the field below. The start crew had to run down and drag the glider up to the original starting point for the next camper to take his turn. It was strenuous work, but we did not mind it because each of us wanted to have his thirty starts recorded. Because of the miserable weather conditions, nobody achieved that goal.

On some days there was no flying at all, for gliding in rainy weather can be quite hazardous. On those days there was nothing to do. Nobody was in charge. Our two instructors cared only about the actual flying. It did not help that our lodgings were quite primitive: no lockers and no beds. We slept in hammocks in the hangar and ate off a few rickety wooden tables, and there were not even enough of them. There were no showers and just four sinks for washing up. Boredom and lethargy were pervasive, and morale was low. All this was aggravated by the fact that we were poorly and insufficiently fed. An innkeeper in the village below had been commissioned to cook for the whole camp, about fifty hungry boys. Three times a day some of us had to take a hand-pulled cart to the inn to pick up our food, which was almost always watery and tasteless soup and some loaves of bread and sliced sausage or cheese. There was never enough food, and we were always hungry. There was no good reason for this since the rations for the German population at that time were still quite sufficient. Months later we found out the real reason for this deplorable situation in our glider camp. The innkeeper and his wife were crooks and black marketeers. They had simply diverted large portions of our food into their illegal black market trading. They were arrested, tried, and jailed. But that did not help us glider campers during that summer. We came home without the A-test and half-starved. My memory of this camp even after almost fifty years is still an unpleasant one.

On June 22, 1941, the German people and the world were once again surprised and shocked by another special bulletin. The Wehrmacht had begun its large-scale attack on the Soviet Union, Operation *Barbarossa*, the Russia campaign—which soon turned out to be anything but a campaign. I happened to be home that morning running an errand for the glider camp, and I clearly remember my very unpolitical mother's reaction to the news broadcast on the radio: *Mein Gott, hört denn das niemals auf?* "My Lord, doesn't this ever stop?" It is quite possible, even probable, that her reaction represented that of the majority of the German population.

In our glider camp we had no newspapers and no newsreels, just one small radio which provided us with the most essential information about the events on the new eastern front. Operation Barbarossa appeared to proceed according to plan. One overwhelming victory after the other was announced. The names of the conquered cities and areas were farther and farther away from the German border: Smolensk, Kiev, Novgorod, the Crimean peninsula. The number of prisoners taken soon ran into hundreds of thousands. The advance of the German army seemed once again irresistible. For us the fall of the two capital cities of the USSR, Leningrad and Moscow, was just a matter of time, and that would be the successful end of the eastern campaign.

In a previous chapter I have spoken of contemporary historians who have isolated a few "war-decisive" mistakes of the German political and military leadership. According to these experts, the attack on the USSR belongs in this category of fundamental errors. The main reasons for this sensational turn of events discussed in the propaganda of the time were economic, strategic, and ideological. The latter was perhaps the most decisive motivation. It was a mixture of anti-Communist ideology, which had only briefly been suppressed by the Ribbentrop pact less than two years before; of racist theories that proclaimed the superiority of the Germanic peoples over the Slavs; and of vague dreams of a *Germanisches Weltreich*, a Germanic empire from the Atlantic Ocean to the Ural Mountains. The often-quoted *Drang nach Osten* played an important role here, the desire for expansion eastward, to secure new *Lebensraum*, a sphere of existence for the "overpopulated" Greater German Reich.

This ideological component of the strategic thinking of Hitler and his government led to the abusive treatment of the civilian population of Soviet Russia. It enabled the Soviet government, which had already evacuated Moscow, to unite the Russian people and inspire them to take up the fight against the aggressors from the west. Stalin's regime, which up to then was by no means consolidated, could now proclaim the "Great Patriotic War." Stalin himself for the first time became a genuinely popular leader of his people. The horrendous treatment of Soviet prisoners of war (mass starvation), the systematic recruitment of forced labor among large parts of the population, the raging of the SS special units and their aim of genocide, the elimination of whole segments of the Russian population, especially Jews, make up undoubtedly the worst and most shameful chapter in the entire history of Germany. The consequences for the course of events of the war and, even worse, for the reputation of Germany and of the Germans in the world were catastrophic.

Adolf Hitler in his book and in innumerable speeches had proudly called himself a "student of history." How often did we hear the phrase *Wir lernen aus der Geschichte,* "we learn from history." As we know now, he had learned nothing. The Gröfaz made exactly the same mistakes as Napoleon Bonaparte. He had the same misconception of the vastness of Russia, of Eastern European climate conditions, and of the stubbornness and the tough will and resistance of the Russian people. The latter in particular testifies to an abysmal underestimation of the new enemy.

The immediate sufferers on the German side were the millions of army and air force soldiers, many of whom had to pay with their lives or their health for the fundamental errors of the NS government. Very soon the news from the eastern front spread furtively—that this was a new, brutally hard kind of war, that the number of German casualties was much higher than in any previous campaign, that the spirit of sacrifice of the "Iwan" (the name for the Russian soldiers since World War I) was outstanding and difficult to break.

Today there stands a monument in a Moscow suburb which indicates how far the Panzer spearheads in November 1941 had advanced during their assault on the Soviet capital. It is said that the tank crews could actually see the spires of the Kremlin. But that is as far as the Wehrmacht ever got. The rapid deterioration of essential roads during the *Schlammperiode,* the "mud period," the early advent of the Russian winter, and the ferocious counterattacks of the Red Army put a stop to any further advances. Now it became obvious how poorly the Wehrmacht was prepared for winter warfare in the east. The infantry soldiers in their ordinary uniforms, their thin overcoats, and leather boots were helplessly exposed to Siberian temperatures. Massive and severe frostbite, often leading to a loss of limbs, was the consequence. The motorized units became immobilized because the tanks and other vehicles simply did not function at forty or fifty degrees centigrade below zero. Even the simplest and most robust weapons, like the rifle 98 and the machine gun 34, became inoperable because the lubrication oil froze. The whole military machine was designed to function in Central European conditions. Here, close to Siberia, men and materiel failed.

In the daily *Report of the Armed Forces,* the phrase "heavy fighting in the central segment of the front" appeared for the first time, and then more and more often. At first we were taken aback and very astonished, and we asked ourselves naively, "Heavy fighting against whom?" After all, the Red Army as a fighting force had, for all practical purposes, ceased to exist, as we had been given to understand for some time by the propaganda media. Now Goebbels and his people went to great lengths to conceal the true nature of the military situation, where a catastrophe was barely avoided. But German losses were never admitted, nor was the yielding of territory publicly recognized. The names of cities were given only when they were conquered and occupied, the names of rivers only when they were crossed in an eastward direction, never the reverse.

A new terminology was invented at this time which in later years, when military reverses became the norm rather than the exception, was extensively used and perfected. Thus, when a German unit was encircled by enemy forces, the phrase *sich einigeln* was used, "to establish a hedgehoglike defense." If our own troops were pushed back, the word *Rückzug*, "retreat," never appeared in the reports, but it was called *Frontverkürzung*, "shortening of the front line." The idea behind those and many other euphemisms was never to admit that the Wehrmacht had lost the initiative. It was done linguistically by consistently avoiding the passive voice and only using active verbs, not "our troops were forced to retreat," but "our troops shortened the front line." The photographs in the newspapers and the film clips in the newsreels only showed scenes where the inventive and imaginative talents and the spirit of the soldiers enabled them to cope with all adverse conditions, the mud, the cold, the ice, and the snow of the Russian winter.

We young people had an inkling of the existence and the scope of the crisis when the government decided on a measure they would have never undertaken except in a true emergency situation. In a large-scale propaganda initiative, the entire population was asked to participate in the *Winter-und Wollsachen-Sammlung*, to collect winter and woolen clothes and equipment. In every city, town, and village, collection points manned by NS functionaries were set up. People were to donate warm clothing, felt and ski boots, even snowshoes and skis from their private possessions for the suffering soldiers on the eastern front. My mother, for example, took some long woolen stockings and a knitted vest and received as a receipt a rather fancy document beginning with the words: *In dankbarer Anerkennung der Spendenbereitshaft von Frau Schümann*, "Gratefully recognizing Mrs. Schümann's willingness to donate————." Very soon we saw in the newsreels long trains and columns of trucks filled with the people's gifts rolling east, where they were enthusiastically welcomed by the troops. The soldiers were now equipped with heavy sweaters, a woolen cap under their helmets, and practical ski boots. They went into the next battle with grateful smiles on their faces *für die Heimat*, "for the people at home." There was even the often-repeated story of a soldier going on guard duty in a mink coat. Poor planning and lack of preparation were, of course, never mentioned.

Later a new medal was created for the participants in the winter war. Like the ribbon of the EK II, it was worn in a buttonhole of the uniform tunic, and the cynical *Landser* immediately named it their *Gefrierfleischorden*, "frozen meat medal."[3] Nevertheless, for us, the wearers of the medal soon became the real heroes and combat veterans, because the immense suffering and the sacrifices of the German troops around Moscow in the winter of 1941–42 had become a reality even for us young people. In later war years we saw fewer and fewer soldiers with the "frozen meat medal" ribbon in their buttonholes. The rapidly increasing casualty rates depleted the ranks of the infantry soldiers most of all. Toward the end of the war, hardly any of the veterans of 1941 were left in the combat units that had started out in Operation Barbarossa full of confidence and sure of victory.

8

Amerikabild

hile the winter war in the central sector of the eastern
front, especially near Moscow, was raging, the world was totally confounded
by the surprise attack of a Japanese carrier fleet on the main operational base
of the U.S. Pacific fleet in Pearl Harbor on December 7, 1941, the "day that
will live in infamy," as President Roosevelt with skilful rhetoric branded it immediately. In conversations in later years with many American friends of the
generation old enough to remember, I have heard again and again how well
they remembered that day and even the hour of the breaking of the news about
Pearl Harbor, where they were and what exactly they were doing at that very
moment. It is a common phenomenon at times of national catastrophes.

For more than thirty years now the United States has been my second
home country. I have been asked by my family here, friends and acquaintances, and my students what our reaction in Germany was to this sensational
event that expanded the war, hitherto a largely European affair, into a truly
global conflict. Strangely enough, my memory of this day and the subsequent
declaration of war against the United States by Germany and Italy three days
later is astonishingly imprecise and vague. It is difficult to explain why all this
made no deep and lasting impression on us Germans, but especially not on
the young people. In later years I have often tried to reconstruct what we knew
about the United States of America then, what our perception was at that
time of the New World.

We did not know much about American history. In our history lessons at
school, the Revolutionary War had been treated in connection with British
history. About the Civil War we had learned not much more than that it had
been one of the bloodiest conflicts in the nineteenth century. Of the U.S.
presidents we knew the names of George Washington, one of the founding
fathers of the new republic, and Abraham Lincoln, the liberator of the black

slaves. We were much better informed about the lives and deeds of Hannibal, Julius Caesar, and Alexander the Great. American history from the sixteenth to the end of the nineteenth century lay at the periphery of our historical knowledge and consciousness. In our history classes about the twentieth century we had learned a little about the role of the United States during the age of imperialism and colonialism, although we had only a vague idea about the geographic location and the political situation of the Philippines, for example. I do not think that the name Theodore Roosevelt meant anything to us. The construction of the Panama Canal had been touched upon in our geography class as a vast improvement for global maritime traffic. In short, our history and geography lessons were completely Eurocentric.

We were, however, aware of the emergence of the United States and Japan as two new world powers following the Great War, one of the key results of that conflict. We learned that the appearance of the American Expeditionary Force in France in 1917–18 had profound consequences, not so much because of the relatively limited participation of the Pershing forces but because of the psychological lift for the exhausted, bled-white French and British troops, and, in reverse, the demoralizing effect upon the equally tired and depleted German army. In the NS propaganda and in many Hitler speeches the "betrayal" of President Woodrow Wilson's Fourteen Points of the Allied war aims was repeatedly mentioned and maligned. From September 1939 on, the tone of the war propaganda against Franklin D. Roosevelt had become increasingly aggressive and accusatory. Every measure of the American government in support of the British war effort—the Lend-Lease Act, the shooting order, the Atlantic Charter, the phrase "arsenal of democracy"—was sharply and vehemently criticized as a flagrant breach of neutrality. After Churchill, Roosevelt was next in line as the main target of the hate campaigns of the NS propaganda machine. He was portrayed as a man totally in the hands of "Wall Street Jewry." In our naive and youthful minds we probably thought at the time that, since the United States was in a quasi state of war with the Axis powers anyway, why not make a clean sweep of it and replace a disingenuous state of affairs with a real war?

The United States of America had been in the nineteenth and also in the twentieth century the main emigration country for Germany. Among the many millions of Europeans who left their home countries and went *nach drüben*, "over there," the German contingent was numerically among the largest. In certain parts of the country the German element was especially felt. Some cities like Milwaukee, Cincinnati, and St. Louis had large German quarters. In our English and history textbooks there were photographs of highway signs in towns and cities like Bremen, Hanover, Leipsig, and Holstein and pictures of stores and restaurants with German names. The histories of towns like King of Prussia and Germantown were told. The Amish

German Settlements in the U.S.A

1. Holstein (Nebraska) — 2. Bremen (Ohio) — 3. Frankford (Missouri) — 4. Leipsic (Ohio) —
5. Westphalia (Missouri) — 6. Münster (Ohio) — 7. Hanover (Kansas) — 8. Emden (Missouri)

This page from our seventh-grade reader, printed in 1939, pictures authentic signs from German settlements in the United States.

settlements in Pennsylvania and Ohio with their archaic language, virtually unchanged since the eighteenth century, were not forgotten, nor was the existence of many German newspapers, especially in the Midwest. The contributions of General Steuben to the Revolutionary War and the achievement of Carl Schurz, a senator and secretary of the interior at the time of Abraham Lincoln, were glorified. In one of our history textbooks we even read an often-told but historically incorrect legend. At the time of the war of independence the motion to declare German the official language of the new republic had allegedly been defeated in favor of English by only one vote. The authors of this textbook could not refrain from speculating about the possible course of world history if that motion in Philadelphia had passed.

As to the individual and private world of the German people, there was hardly a family in Germany in which not one or more members had emigrated to America in the second half of the nineteenth and the early twentieth century, to "the land of unlimited opportunities" where "the streets were paved with gold," phrases which for many people were only slightly exaggerated. In the popular theater plays, and later in films, "the rich uncle from America" was a common stereotype. In my own family there are two relevant examples. My paternal grandfather went across the Atlantic in the early 1890s to try his luck, planning to have his family, including my father, an infant at the time, join him. He was never heard from again. Family lore has it that he participated in the Alaska gold rush and perished somewhere in one of the rough mining camps. The other example was the brother of my future sister-in-law who, having emigrated around 1930, became a professional soldier and was killed as a sergeant in the army air corps on December 7, 1941, at Pearl Harbor. But in the NS propaganda and NS ideology training, the phenomenon of emigration was sharply opposed and criticized as a loss of "valuable German blood."

What did we know about American literature? In a phrase—almost nothing. The literature of the English language was British literature. The names Emerson, Hawthorne, Melville, Whitman, Dickinson were unknown to us. I began to read their works only after the war. Mark Twain was considered a children's author, and *The Adventures of Tom Sawyer* and *The Adventures of Huckleberry Finn*, in translation, of course, were popular Christmas or birthday gifts for twelve- and thirteen-year-olds. Harriet Beecher Stowe's international best-seller *Uncle Tom's Cabin (Onkel Toms Hütte)* I read privately, also in translation, and devoured it because of the clear presentation of good and evil. Prominent writers of the twentieth century like Hemingway, Faulkner, Fitzgerald, O'Neill, and Wolfe were ignored in our English classes, just like their forefathers of the eighteenth and nineteenth centuries.

One curious exception deserves to be mentioned here because it illustrates the thinking and the manipulation of the NS propaganda ministry. During the last years of the war, there arose a severe scarcity of paper. It meant, among other inconveniences, that people who usually gave books as presents at Christmas, confirmation, and birthdays were now deprived of doing so. The bookstores and their windows were empty. Then suddenly during the pre-Christmas season of either 1943 or 1944 many copies of John Steinbeck's novel *The Grapes of Wrath*, translated as *Früchte des Zorns*, appeared in the display windows. Even in this shortage situation the government deemed it expedient and well advised to provide enough pulp to print thousands of copies of this book. The reasons for this generosity are easy to see: by widely distributing this critical and accusatory novel, the "brutal character of the exploitative capitalistic system" in the United States was to be exposed. The implied message was that a country that treats its farmers so callously and drives them into poverty and misery must be rotten, decadent, and immoral and deserves to fall. One result of this sudden flurry of Steinbeck popularity was that many a book lover found five or six copies of *Früchte des Zorns* under his or her Christmas tree in 1943 or 1944.

Those were the components that formed our *Amerikabild*, our perception of the new enemy country. If any of us worried at all about the gigantic human and industrial potential of the United States—there were the memories and lessons of World War I—we found plausible comfort in convincing ourselves that America was far away; that it was much too late for this potential enemy to be of significant help to Great Britain and Soviet Russia; that it would take months and probably years to organize the armament industry in such a vast country; and that there was, after all, the German submarine fleet to prevent the delivery of massive aid to British and northern Russian ports. The Battle of the Atlantic was just then raging in all its fury and seemed to be tilting our way. We were sure that the war would be ended with a German victory by the next summer at the latest. The *Schwarzseher*, the pessimist in our family, my father, who knew the United States well from his sailing days and who, as a veteran submariner, remembered the decisive role of the United States navy and merchant marine in the fierce convoy battles of 1917 and 1918, warned us emphatically not to underestimate the new enemy. We young people ignored his warnings as we had done so many times before. We were still in an optimistic and confident mood.

The question regarding the real reasons for the German and Italian initiative to declare war on the United States has never been answered and explained in a totally satisfactory manner. For some historians it is the third "war-decisive" error of the German government. (The shifting of the German bombing raids from the British fighter plane installations, the airfields, and radar stations, to London in 1940 was the first mistake; the unprovoked invasion of the USSR in 1941 the second.) At first, however, this event of global significance had little effect on the military situation at the eastern front or in

North Africa. In our own little private world it also did not bring about any changes for the moment. Naturally, we registered later with satisfaction the initial overwhelming victories of our new ally Japan in the South Pacific: the fall of Singapore; the conquest of Indonesia and the Philippines; the seemingly unstoppable Japanese thrust toward Australia. But these events lay months ahead in the future. In December 1941 we were concerned with other things much closer at hand.

In our private lives, New Year's Eve 1941–42, the third winter of the war, was the last celebration of an unforgettable tradition of our neighborhood; after that most participants scattered during war-related service. Even before the war it had become customary that my mother, father, and we children gather in our neighbor's house, at the family D's, to greet the new year. A pattern had developed over the years. We children were allowed to stay out until nine-thirty or ten o'clock thoroughly enjoying ourselves making mischief on this one night of the year. It was a tradition very similar to Cabbage Night—the night before Halloween—in many parts of the United States. Most popular were two kinds of mild and nondestructive vandalism: one was unhinging the garden gates of our neighbors and depositing them in the front yards of another neighbor down the street; and even more popular was setting off firecrackers close to a neighbor's house or, if possible, in their staircase if they had forgotten to lock the front door of the apartment house. Most of the time our neighbors were good-natured about those New Year's Eve pranks. They simply picked up their gates the next morning without making much of a fuss about the inconvenience. They also were tolerant of the firecracker noise. After all, it was New Year's Eve.

At about ten o'clock we went inside to join our parents who were gathered in the living room of the D's. Sometimes one or two other families with their children were there also. The gentlemen drank rum grog,[1] the ladies red wine grog, and we youth were served a hot punch with a few drops of wine. New Year's Eve was the only day of the year on which we had a late supper; sausages and potato salad or some very special open-faced sandwiches were eaten just before midnight. The best part of the evening was listening to the conversation of our parents—though "conversation" is not the right word. They told stories: my mother about her home in Pomerania and growing up in a large family; Frau D. about her experiences as a young elementary school teacher in the Ruhr valley; Herr D. about ships and his four years as an internee in Australia during the First World War. The star of the evening was my father. After the third glass of grog he began. He was a master storyteller, had seen a great deal of the world, had unusual experiences in many countries, and always selected the most interesting episodes. They were without exception fascinating to all of us and almost always funny; thus he never spoke about his war experiences, many of which must have been hair-raising. When he did mention "the War," World War I, it was only to relate an exotic and humorous episode with an effective point and climax. We children, after a few years, knew what was going to happen and looked forward to this special evening and my father's stories, some of which we soon knew almost by heart but never became tired of hearing. My father's favorite yarns were about Wilhelm II, the last Hohenzollern sovereign of the Reich, *Willem Kaiser*, as my father called him. He had an ambivalent attitude about his former commander in chief. He knew the glaring personal weaknesses of the Kaiser very well—his vanity, his predilection for fancy uniforms, his desire always to be center stage. Yet on the other hand, Wilhelm II represented for my father the *gute alte Zeit*, "the good old days."

In 1908, during his year of compulsory navy service,[2] my father took part in one of the emperor's big annual parades in Danzig, the *Kaiserparaden*. Kaiser Wilhelm, as was well known, was an ardent navy fan. The participating naval contingent had practiced goose stepping for weeks, although naturally they could not hold a candle to a parading Prussian Guard unit and their precision marching. Nevertheless, this public performance of the Imperial Navy would probably have turned out satisfactorily except for an all-too-human organizational error. As my father told it:

> I was standing in one of the last rows, twelve abreast, all of us in parade whites. We were waiting for the order to start marching, but there was a slight delay. Unfortunately, right behind us was the next formation also waiting impatiently. They were heavy cavalry, cuirassiers, also twelve abreast, with their big neighing horses, the riders with shining breastplates and lances. Sailors and horses have little in common and they do not trust each other. Suddenly the cuirassiers started moving, and when the big beasts came closer and closer, we became frightened and started running because we did not want to be stampeded. We pushed forward the rows ahead of us and they also started running, so that finally, instead of an impressive naval marching unit, a horde of fleeing sailors ran past His Majesty on the reviewing stand. It was not a pretty sight.
>
> Shortly thereafter the customary parade review was to be held. Four thousand sailors stood at attention in a square formation, everybody with a guilty conscience and expecting a blazing dressing down by our unit commander, a captain. But it never came. As Captain B. was about to begin, a personal adjutant of the Emperor galloped into the open square, pulled up his horse in front of him and proclaimed in a loud voice: "*Beim Vorbeimarsch der Marine haben Majestät dreimal 'vorzüglich' und viermal 'sehr jut' jesagt*. During the Navy's march in review His Majesty exclaimed three times 'excellent' and four times 'very good.' " Thus we were the heroes of the day.

In Low German my father added, *Willem Kaiser sei ümmer bloos dat, wat hei sein wult*. "William Kaiser saw only what he wanted to see."

All this was told with dramatic effect, descriptive power, and a great deal of humor. We children especially laughed and shouted with joy about the punch line, the emperor's verdict. My father enjoyed the effect of his story, chuckled a little, and laughed with his eyes. Many years later, when a few of those who had been present at these New Year's Eve parties got together and reminisced about them, there was always somebody who said sooner or later, "And then Herr Schümann began to tell his stories."

In the same winter the various DJ and HJ units of our town were planning the customary annual *Elternabend*, "parents' night." They were named and modeled after similar meetings organized by the schools in order to promote closer relations between the members of the youth organizations and their parents. A typical program of these meetings consisted of gymnastics demonstrations, musical presentations, sing-alongs, and sometimes the performance of a short play, often but not always with a political message.

I remember one of the latter, although we did not participate ourselves and were only spectators, because it was performed by a unit of a neighboring town. The climax of the one-act play was the final scene, which took place in the living room of a bourgeois family. A visitor, waiting for the man of the house, stood in front of the bookcase and read out loud the titles of the books in the front row: Adolf Hitler, *Mein Kampf*; Joseph Goebbels, *Vom Kaiserhof zur Reichskanzlei*; Alfred Rosenberg, *Der Mythos des 20. Jahrhunderts*; Felix Dahn, *Ein Kampf um Rom*; and a dozen other "clean" titles, books by NS authors or writers acceptable to the regime. Then, since the owner of the house still had not arrived, the visitor pushed aside some of the volumes of the first row and read the titles of the second: Karl Marx, *Das Kapital*; Lenin, *Gesammelte Werke*; Thomas Mann, *Buddenbrooks*; Heinrich Mann, *Der Untertan*; and others, all of them "Communist" or "decadent" authors and therefore on the NS index. After naming each title, the actor who played the role of the visitor waited for the audience's reaction, which did come as expected, but the laughter was always restrained. None of us young spectators had read any of the works and we knew only a few authors' names from hearsay. The play ended with the appearance of the book owner, a pathetic and obnoxious figure who was horrified about the discovery of his real political convictions. He stuttered some silly explanation for the existence of the forbidden books, that he had "forgotten" to burn them.

The play was supposed to be a political satire to expose the "beefsteak National Socialists," those brown on the outside, red on the inside. Our sympathies were, of course, on the side of the visitor who had unmasked another miserable political hypocrite. But I also remember that we did not like the simplistic plot and the rather primitive treatment of such an important subject, and we were sharply critical about it on our way home. Even as young teenagers we resented being enlightened with a club.

99

In general not too many parents attended these meetings, but for us participation was mandatory, and we also had fun doing them. For this particular event in 1942 we had selected a nonpolitical play, *King Thrushbeard*, based on the Grimm Brothers' fairy tale. We had rehearsed for weeks in January and February of that winter. I had been cast in a major part in the play; it was the first time for me to perform on stage in front of an audience, and I suffered abysmal stage fright. But nothing went wrong and we thought we had well earned the respectable applause of the spectators. I was personally complimented by several people who said that I had shown real acting talent, which was new to me, but naturally I was proud of this discovery. A few days later we received orders from "upstairs," the NS party leadership of our town, to repeat our whole program for a much larger and very special audience. What had happened?

For several days the heavy cruiser *Prinz Eugen* had been anchored in Brunsbüttel under the protection of the massive navy antiaircraft artillery units in and around our town. After its participation in the battle of the Denmark Strait, the ship had been berthed for months together with the battleships *Scharnhorst* and *Gneisenau* in the French Atlantic port of Brest and had been exposed to heavy air raids by the RAF. Therefore the German naval command decided to have the three capital ships break through the English Channel to reach safer German ports in the North Sea or the Baltic. After careful preparation, and with massive protection by naval escorts and fighter planes, the bold operation was successfully carried out. The propaganda praised it as a splendid accomplishment, as a coup de main in the best tradition of the German navy. Churchill was said to be furious about the failure of the Royal Navy and the Royal Air Force to prevent the operation. It was interpreted as a fiasco for John Bull. I remember though that our reaction was somewhat mixed. Of course we were proud of our ships and their crews, but it was difficult not to see that the celebrated breakthrough was, basically, an escape from the effectiveness of the enemy's air force. That was also the way my father saw it.

Now we could lay our eyes on one of the participants in the operation, and, despite our doubts about a German naval "triumph," we were happy to have the cruiser back. It turned out that we were to do something concrete for her crew, because that was the order from "upstairs," to repeat the full program of our Elternabend to entertain part of the *Prinz Eugen* crew. The captain planned to grant liberty to as many of his sailors as was possible without jeopardizing the safety of the ship. He knew, of course, that, in a small town in the third year of the war there was not much excitement to be found for sailors going ashore for the first time in weeks or months. Therefore he had turned to the local NS functionaries for help, and they again had turned to the HJ organizations. Thus it came about that one evening we played, sang, and danced in the largest hall of our town in front of three or four hundred young sailors. We did our best, but our audience at first showed only moderate enthusiasm for our program, and the applause after each number was restrained. Actually, we understood full well that these veterans, after months of extreme stress and combat exposure, showed only limited interest in a fairy-tale play performed by thirteen- and fourteen-year-old boys and girls.

But the evening was not a failure, and we owed that to one of our dance groups. The oldest BDM girls, ages seventeen and eighteen, were members of a branch in their organization called *Glaube und Schönheit*, "Faith and Beauty."[3] A group of them performed in our program. When the curtain rose, eight young, attractive women were standing on the stage dressed in tight-fitting white gymnastics shorts and shirts, ready to do their number, Swedish gymnastics with ball and hoop accompanied by music. The Lords, the nickname for all sailors in the German navy, literally jumped out of their seats with enthusiasm, and the whistling, hooting, and footstamping never let up during the whole fairly long exercise. The final applause for everybody, including us younger members of the cast, was gigantic, and we were proud to have been part of such a successful event. When I came home and told my parents about the course of the evening, my father was highly amused and laughed about the very human reaction of his young navy comrades.

The *Prinz Eugen*, nicknamed the "lucky ship," did survive the war, but its end came in a very inglorious manner after the war. At one of the American nuclear bomb experiments at the Bikini Islands, it was among the ships anchored in the atoll in order to study the effect of an atomic explosion on war and merchant ships. Like all other guinea-pig ships, the *Prinz Eugen* was heavily damaged and later scuttled.

At the end of May 1942, the Royal Air Force deployed for the first time one thousand heavy bombers in a night air raid on the German city of Cologne. It resulted in heavy damage and severe losses among the civilian population. The NS propaganda branded the raid immediately as a *Terrorangriff*, "terror attack," and this term was used consistently in the news from then until the end of the war. It was the beginning of the systematic and at least partial destruction of practically all large and middle-sized German cities. From then on, many people in Germany began to lead a double existence: work and relaxation in the daytime, cave dwelling at night—that is to say, many either slept in air-raid shelters or at least hurried into them as soon as the sirens began to wail. There were enough shelters. Even in our small town, for example, all state-owned apartment houses had been provided with bunkers in their backyards. They were ugly monsters with walls and ceilings of reinforced concrete up to fifty centimeters thick. Construction had begun immediately after September 1939, and now we children spent many nights not in our own beds, but in bunk beds that one of our neighbors had built for his children and for us in the bunker. We quickly got used to it and, at least in the beginning, found this change of everyday life quite adventurous.

Another change of attitude in our family and among friends and neighbors was evident in how people adjusted to new and different circumstances. In our part of the country late summer and fall often brought severe thunderstorms which usually arrived and departed with the ocean tides. It was quite customary that our very cautious parents awakened us at night and made us get dressed and wait in the living room for nature's explosions to abate. My father had a metal box with all important documents, bankbooks, and other valuable papers next to him so as to be able to leave the house quickly if lightning should strike. To this day this box is called the *Gewitterkasten*, "thunderstorm box," in our family. From 1942 on, however, the danger from human actions, bombing and strafing, became infinitely greater than potential destruction by natural causes. When there was a rumbling noise in the distance that upon coming closer was recognized as thunder, most people turned over in their beds thinking, "Good. It is *only* a thunderstorm."

We sometimes asked ourselves what had happened to our renowned Luftwaffe and all its celebrities, the highly decorated fighter plane aces, who had not only not prevented air raids like the one on Cologne but had not even been able to inflict serious damage on the attacking bomber squadrons. Nevertheless, we were still unshaken in our conviction that the Wehrmacht was superior to the armed forces of any other country in the world. The real extent of the devastation was, of course, never reported, although rumors about it were beginning to spread. Doubts in and skepticism about the political and military leadership were, at most, expressed in *Flüsterwitze*, "whispering jokes." For example, people furtively called Reichsmarschall Hermann Göring "Hermann Meyer." He was supposed to have said at the outbreak of the war that if any enemy planes ever reached Berlin *will ich Meyer heissen*, "you can call me Meyer," a common expression in German approximately equivalent to the English saying "I'll eat my hat."

In June 1942, relatively late in the year, the long-awaited new German attack on the eastern front, which we confidently thought would deliver the coup de grace to the Red Army and end the war in the east, began. It was the offensive on the southern part of the front in the direction of the Caucasus and the oil fields around Baku. We know now that the new plans represented a radical change in the strategic thinking of the military high command in the Führer's headquarters—ultimately of Hitler's own thinking. No longer did military considerations have the highest priority; economic ones did. The main goal of the offensive was to secure the almost unlimited supply of raw material, especially oil, metal ores, and food provisions. There were again the initial stupendous victories. The special bulletins announced triumphantly that the Crimean peninsula was finally completely in German hands; that the

German flag was now flying on the Elbrus, the highest mountain in the Caucasus and in all of Europe. The Red Army suffered enormous losses again, but it did not collapse. On the contrary, the German offensive came to a halt in the late fall on the banks of the Volga River and ended with the military catastrophe at Stalingrad.

Few Germans, and certainly not we young people, knew anything in the summer of 1942 about the change in the strategic thinking of the high command of the armed forces and of the Führer. For us the new conquests in southern Russia were definite proof that the Russia campaign would be over by the end of the year, that the end of the Communist regime was imminent. What was not clear to us, and I remember that it was a frequent subject of discussion among us, was what was to come after the final defeat of the Red Army, and what were the concrete German war aims in Eastern Europe?

It may have been at this time that I read a magazine article that pretended to offer a brief glimpse into the future. It was a short, sentimental, utopian "mood picture" of a German *Wehrbauernfamilie*, a family of farmer-soldiers who had settled somewhere in the vastness of the Russian plains not far from the Ural Mountains. The farmer, a veteran and army reservist, has just returned from a day of strenuous plowing of the fertile black soil on his new homestead. His blond wife greets him in the door, surrounded by a host of fair-haired children, and she carries on her arm an infant who, of course, is also blond. She has just fed and milked the healthy cows in the barn and now is waiting to feed her husband a nourishing homegrown supper. After the meal, the farmer and his wife stand outside the front door slowly letting their eyes roam over the land, the many acres that make up their property now. They talk about their neighbors, German settlers like themselves, about the beautiful future ahead of them, about the children who have found a new home here. They are very much aware of their mission to secure this land as part of the Greater German Reich and to make it flourish through their diligent and conscientious labor. They also are ready to defend the land by force of arms if necessary, just like the medieval farmer-soldiers in the borderlands of the Holy Roman Empire.

Not a word was said in the article about the former inhabitants and owners of the land. Had they been dispossessed, driven out, or worse? Where were they now? The legitimacy of the settlers also was not questioned. What right did this fictitious family have to be here? What was a German family doing here in the Ural Mountains two thousand miles east of their homeland? I do not remember whether we seriously believed in such utopian visions of the future, but this one must have made a certain impression on us. Why else would I remember in detail such a poorly written and basically outrageous piece of journalism?

9

What must
not be,
does not
exist

n the summer of 1942, at the beginning of the long school vacation, I was to participate in another camp. This time it was a *Wehrertüchtigungslager*, abbreviated WE-*Lager*, which had just been established by order of the Reich Youth Ministry in Berlin and was quite different from any other camp I had attended so far. "Wehrertüchtigung" is an untranslatable word and means, approximately, the training of body and mind in preparation for military service. Participation in a WE-Lager was compulsory. The aim was to prepare fifteen- and sixteen-year-old boys for our future—inevitable—service as soldiers. The duration was six weeks, longer than any of the other camps in which I had participated. The most attractive feature was that the instructors were real soldiers.

We young people had our own very definite positions and feelings, vis-à-vis the military and the party. Our positive attitude toward everything military was absolute. We were ardent worshipers of all *Soldatentum*, "soldiership," especially the German one, and within that the Prussian variation. Many of the books I read as a child and as an adolescent were works in which the soldierly virtues of courage, loyalty, duty, service, endurance were glorified, especially in the First World War, but also in the Franco-German War of 1870–71, in the Napoleonic wars, which we knew only as the *Befreiungskriege*, "wars of liberation," and the many armed conflicts in the centuries before. Of the Middle Ages, we were especially interested in the descriptions of battles and fighting, such as the knightly duels in the *Nibelungenlied* and the *Gudrunsage*.[1] In earlier historic times of Northern and Central Europe, we were most impressed by the reports of wars by the Germanic tribes against the Imperium Romanum. Even in reading Norse, Germanic, and Greek mythology we were most inspired by the fighting heroes and gods: the Norse

god of thunder, might, and war, Thor; the almost invincible Siegfried; and
the virtually invulnerable Achilles.

Wars and battles for us were not just inevitable modes of existence in the
history of humankind; they were the culmination of all human life in which
man (never woman) could prove himself and display his most laudable qualities. Cowardice in battle, flight from combat, and disloyalty were under all
circumstances negative and dishonorable. Defeat in battle or a lost war was
always explained by the numerical superiority of the opponents (the defeat of
the individual Burgundian heroes in the *Nibelungenlied* by the antlike masses
of the huns; Germany "against the world" in World War I); by the failure of
political leadership despite the heroic deeds of the soldiers (defeat of the Prussian army in 1806); or by the treachery and perfidy of the enemy (Siegfried's
slaying by the insidious Hagen in the *Nibelungenlied*). All this was a roman-
ticization and glorification of war, which now, in retrospect, appears to be particularly dangerous for the maturation of young minds. Our view of the world
and of life in this respect was closed and unshakable. Objection to and devi-
ation from it, as in all the pacifistic literature after World War I, was considered perverse and decadent and was forbidden anyway. The incarnation of
heroism for us was the unknown German soldier in the trenches of the western front, courageously holding his position, often against overwhelming
odds, doing his duty, and often paying with his life for the greater cause of the
Fatherland. The steel helmet, the field-gray uniform, and the Iron Cross became symbols of the highest fulfillment of duty and unquestioning willingness of sacrifice.

Our attitude toward the NSDAP and its struggle for power was much more
ambiguous. To be sure, in the NS literature, the fighting aspect of the party's
rise to power was emphasized. Hitler's book, after all, appeared under the title
My Struggle, and early members of the party were called *alte Kämpfer,* "old
warriors." Hitler's war service as a courageous and decorated combat soldier
was constantly referred to. Even party members who had lost their lives in
street fighting and beer hall brawls in the Weimar years were revered as mar-
tyrs. For example, two Doric temples containing the coffins of the sixteen victims of the ill-fated march on the *Feldherrnhalle* were erected in Munich.[2] At
the annual memorial service in remembrance of the putsch on November 9,
1923, a national holiday, their names were read out loud in countless rallies
all over Germany and the audiences responded with *Hier,* "present," after the
reading of each name. The surviving members of the putsch were awarded a
special medal, the *Blutorden,* "blood medal." The flag carried during the
march was called the *Blutfahne,* "blood flag," and was later used to conse-
crate new party flags, banners, and standards. The student, Horst Wessel,
who had written the text of "Die Fahne hoch" and who was killed during

civil-war–like riots in Berlin, was elevated to a mythical figure, and his song became part of the official national anthem of the Third Reich. Hitler Youth member Herbert Norkus, also a victim of street fighting, became a martyr and role model for the HJ, and his life and death were immortalized in books and films.

Despite these and many similar attempts of NS ideologists to equate the struggle of their party with soldiers' achievements in military history, to place their victims in the ranks of the fallen comrades of former wars, such efforts never really took hold among German youth. There are several reasons for this, some of which are relevant here: the weight of tradition; the world historical dimension of battles and wars; and the human quality of the living representatives of the two worlds.

On the one hand, there was more than a thousand-year-old history in which the exemplary and decisive role of the Germanic warrior, the medieval knight, the mercenary of the sixteenth century, the Prussian grenadier, the militia man of the Napoleonic wars, and, finally, the trench war veteran of the Great War were made to stand out. On the other hand, the thirteen years of fighting by the NSDAP, which was not more than a bloody and violent partisan political struggle despite the efforts by the NS propagandists to create and promote a new tradition, seemed artificial and failed.

Moreover, the genuine soldiers of the past fought for emperor and Reich, for king and state, for the protection and defense of the Fatherland against foreign enemies who were often portrayed as a threat to the existence of the *Heimat*, "homeland." The brownshirts of the 1920s and early 1930s battled political opponents, especially the "Reds"—the Communists and Social Democrats who were persistently denigrated, but nevertheless they were Germans. There was a mythical aura around names like Barbarossa, Prinz Eugen, Seydlitz, Blücher, Moltke,[3] and also around famous historical battlefields: Belgrade, Leuthen, Waterloo, Königgrätz, Sedan, the Somme.[4] In comparison with the famous emperors and generals, figures like Horst Wessel and Herbert Norkus appeared to us like pygmies, and their battlefields were anonymous beer halls, back alleys, and tenement corridors.

The living representatives and heroes were the many former soldiers, veterans of World War I who were now our fathers, teachers, friends, and neighbors, men we respected and admired, despite occasional youthful rebelliousness. We had no respect for the local functionaries of the NSDAP who had not achieved very much in their bourgeois careers, who often had a rather dubious past, and who now occupied positions of power in our town because of their low party membership number. We did not believe their pretentious idealism and often made fun of them. Our attitude was not affected by the fact that a few of the highest members of the NS hierarchy, Hitler, Göring, and some others, were genuine combat veterans.

The NSDAP was painfully aware of this dichotomy, the enormous difference between their own public image and that of the military. That is the generally accepted explanation for a special event in March 1933, a show produced after careful preparation and with much pomp, the *Tag von Potsdam*, the Day of Potsdam. It was the attempt to overcome the polarizing opposites of *Preussentum*, "Prussianism," and National Socialism and everything they stood for. The new government, less than two months old, had chosen the *Potsdamer Garnisonskirche*, "Potsdam garrison church," for the celebration, as it was one of the symbolic centers of Prussian tradition. In its vault stood the coffins of Frederick the Great and his father. The decorations in the nave were the flags of all the Prussian Guard regiments. This was the place where the Reichspräsident and former Imperial Generalfeldmarschall Paul von Hindenburg was to meet *den einfachen Soldaten des Weltkrieges*, "the common soldier of the World War," the new Reichskanzler, Adolf Hitler. The encounter was staged with cinematographic precision and attention to details. The military symbols were placed in the foreground, in the most visible places. The field-gray uniforms dominated over the brownshirts; the steel helmets over the SA caps; the traditional regimental flags over the swastika flags; the Prussian military marches over the NS songs. The climax was the deep bow of the Chancellor before the President and their handshake. Hindenburg appeared in parade dress uniform with all his medals, wearing the old-fashioned spiked leather helmet and carrying his marshal's baton; Hitler, in calculated contrast, dressed in formal bourgeois attire in a Prince Albert coat.

Many historians see the Day of Potsdam as a psychological success for the new regime. Even if total synonymity between Preussentum and National Socialism had not been achieved, at least an impressive attempt had been made by the new leaders to bridge the gap. They were well on their way to exploiting the prestige and nimbus of Prussia and its army tradition for their own purposes. The documentation of the event, especially the picture of the Hindenburg-Hitler handshake, was distributed to all media and eventually found its way into our textbooks in school.

I was not even six years old at the time and have no specific memories of the celebrated day, but, I am, of course, familiar with the many pictures and films about the Day of Potsdam. But despite these and many other efforts of the propaganda ministry to enhance the image of the typical National Socialist, there remained in our consciousness a colossal difference between the representatives of the Wehrmacht and the NSDAP, between the soldier and the party comrade, between *Soldat* and *Parteigenosse*. All this is not to say that we children and adolescents were not enthusiastic young adherents of the new ideology. We were convinced of the legitimacy of the German mission; we very rarely had any doubts about National Socialism as a political philosophy;

The Reichspräsident von Hindenburg and the new Reichskanzler Hitler shaking hands on the Day of Potsdam, March 1933, which was supposed to symbolize the definitive coalition of the Armed Forces and the NSDAP. Courtesy of the Bundesarchiv Koblenz.

and we believed in the new order that was bound to take the place of the antiquated and decadent forms of society. The war that was forced upon us, as we saw it, was a stepping-stone toward creating an entirely new *Weltordnung*, "global order." But the Wehrmacht was the force guaranteeing that it would come about in the near future.

So in the summer of 1942, we were thrilled at the prospect of having genuine members of the armed forces, all of them combat veterans, as our camp instructors in the WE-Lager in Gudendorf, a small village not far from Brunsbüttel. Gudendorf is located on the *Geest*, an elevated land ridge in the center of Schleswig-Holstein with an attractive landscape of small hills, woods, and many *Knicks*, hedgerows enclosing and separating fields. It is topographically very different from the flat, almost treeless, windswept marsh around Brunsbüttel and was ideally suited for infantry training. We had to wear the black-white-red HJ armband with a swastika on our upper left arm, though our camp uniforms were not our own regular HJ uniforms but special army fatigues, including peaked caps and army boots.

The camp routine was in many ways similar to what we were used to from other camp experiences: early rising (6 A.M.); color ceremony; close-order drills; daily room inspections; ideology training. What was different and exhilarating for us was the military air of all activities: new uniforms, heavy emphasis on marksmanship and field exercises, map reading, the art of camouflage, setting up defensive and offensive positions for infantry units, many night exercises. This specific camp was set up for the training of air force communication personnel. Evidently there was at that time a lack of trained specialists in this specific branch of the armed forces. Consequently, in addition to all other activities, we learned *funken* every day for two hours, the operation of a wireless telegraph in Morse code. Many of us achieved the goal of transmitting and receiving thirty letters per minute, which was considered a very respectable speed and was due to our enthusiasm and strong motivation.

Our instructors had been selected according to merit, pedagogical talent, and ideological reliability. Most of them were former DJ and HJ leaders. All of them had seen real combat and wore their various combat decorations. For them this assignment certainly was a respite from the hell of the eastern front, although, naturally, they never admitted it. It was most exciting for us when they talked about their combat experiences. But once again I noticed that, just like my father concerning World War I, these veterans never mentioned the bloody, gory, and violent incidents of which, undoubtedly, they had seen plenty. Most certainly they never spoke of acts of heroism, their own or their comrades'. What they did regale us with were funny stories, and we were the most appreciative and attentive audience imaginable.

One of our sergeants, a native of Schleswig-Holstein, like most of us, for some reason had served in a Swabian division from near Stuttgart. We had learned that a field switchboard operator had to cut in, in certain intervals, on telephone conversations especially on vitally important lines. The standard formula was: *Sprechen Sie noch?* Pause. *Sprechen Sie noch?* If there was no response, then a brief pause was followed by, *Ich trenne* ("Are you on the line? Are you on the line? I disconnect"). One day our sergeant was conveying an important telephone message to somewhere on the eastern front. Suddenly he heard the excited voice of the operator who shouted breathlessly in the broadest Swabian dialect: *Schwätzn Se noch? Schwätzn Se noch? Ich zerruppe.* ("You're still yakking? You're still yakking? I'll rip"). Gone was the vital connection before our sergeant even had the time to translate the Swabian idiom into High German.

For unknown reasons, probably because of a clerical error, I was ordered in the summer of 1943 to participate in a second WE-Lager, this time a pure infantry training camp. It did not even occur to me to trace the error and protest against this unheard-of repetition. Thus I spent that summer also in Gudendorf and was considered the most experienced camper. We all felt very much like young soldiers, hoping to apply soon the skills we had been acquiring since the age of ten and prove ourselves.

After returning from the WE camp in August 1942, our regular school days began again. Two months later, however, they were interrupted for me by a new order to stand by for service in the *Kinderlandverschickung* (KLV). The KLV was an operation initiated by the central government to move children from cities threatened by potential air raids to "safe" areas, more rural and centrally located places beyond the range of enemy bombers at the time. (The British government had taken similar steps during the heavy raids on London and other English cities in the fall and winter of 1940–41.) Accompanied by one or two experienced teachers, entire school classes were transported to central and southeast Germany, where they were lodged in youth hostels, rural inns, and similar accommodations. In our province of Schleswig-Holstein, the cities of Kiel and Lübeck were considered high-risk locations, and many children from there were being evacuated to Austria, now officially called *Ostmark* instead of *Österreich*. Though this distance put considerable psychological stress on parents and children, no exceptions were allowed. Orders were orders, and they had to be carried out.

Room and board were provided for the children, as were their educational and medical needs, though in a rather provisionary and sometimes primitive manner. Then it was decided in Berlin to do something for their *ideologische Betreuung*, "ideological care." That at least was the official line, and the Hitler Youth was commissioned with this task. Today I am convinced that we *Lagermannschaftsführer* and *Lagerunterführer*, we who had been selected for this service, were not much more than babysitters who were to take some of the burdens and responsibilities off the shoulders of the accompanying teachers. Basically, we were supposed to keep up the spirits of young children and combat homesickness and other stress symptoms with daily, planned activities. Unfortunately, none of us Hitler Youth personnel were suited for such a sensitive task. We were neither mature enough nor did we have any special training.

In the fall of 1942, I was on my way, dressed in my navy-blue DJ winter uniform, carrying a very heavy suitcase. In my contract it was explicitly stated, to assure my parents, that I would not suffer any negative consequences in my education since, after all, I would be absent from regular Gymnasium classes for a period of five to six months, close to half a school year. Promotion to the next grade was practically guaranteed. My teachers had been instructed to hold special tutorials for me after my return in order to cover the material I would miss during my absence.

It was my first long trip alone, but the spirit of adventure and the prospect of the unusual—no school routine for months—clearly outweighed any secret anxieties and worries about the long journey and about the new assignment. I traveled by train via Hamburg, Berlin, and Leipzig to Vienna, where I had to report to a central KLV office. From there a group of us was ordered to go to the Semmering, a famous spa in the foothills of the Alps. We were housed in a luxury hotel while participating in a special five-day workshop. The program of this workshop was a strange mixture of totally irrelevant and useless lectures ("Germany's Geopolitical Situation in the World" and "History of the NSDAP") and some helpful instructions and suggestions as to what to do with ten- and eleven-year-olds on long winter afternoons and evenings, especially in stressful situations so far from home. What I remember most of these days is the incomparable Alpine landscape at the Semmering Pass. For the first time in my life I saw high mountains covered with everlasting snow.

At the end of the course we got our assignments. A friend of mine and I were sent to Amstetten in lower Austria, he, being sixteen years old, as Lagermannschaftsführer and I as Lagerunterführer. We arrived late in the evening. Our "camp" was a pleasant and cozy—*gemütlich*—looking rural inn in which thirty boys from a school in Kiel and their teacher were housed. The next day, right after school, we were supposed to begin our duties. But for me it never happened. In the middle of the night I stumbled out of bed to inform my friend that I felt miserable, and I collapsed in the hallway. I was running a fever of over forty degrees centigrade (103°F) and was immediately taken by ambulance to the nearest hospital, where I was diagnosed as having diphtheria. Right away the ambulance took me to a larger hospital with a diphtheria isolation ward in the town of Waidhofen an der Ybbs. In this ward, a large hall with twelve beds, not all of which were occupied, I spent the next eight or nine weeks.

As soon as my fever had been lowered and I could swallow again, I felt fine. The majority of my fellow patients were small children whose parents could only communicate with them from behind closed windows during visiting hours. A few weeks later a soldier who had served on the eastern front and had suffered severe frostbite on both feet was admitted. Gangrene had set in and then he also contracted diphtheria. He was a Berliner and always in a good mood despite his ghastly wounds. The dressings on his feet had to be changed three times a day, and we had to endure the sight of his black footstumps and the infernal stench of rotting flesh. The reason for his perpetual good mood was at that time incomprehensible to me, but I thought a great deal about it. He told us again and again that because of his feet wounds he would never have to go back to the hell of the eastern front. I found that quite unheroic, but considering his severe mutilation I could not help wondering whether perhaps there was some justification for his attitude.

The medical care for us was first rate. For the first and only time in my life I was attended by Catholic nurses, nuns with their old-fashioned, wide-brimmed headdresses. They were without exception competent, friendly, and always ready to help. They brought as many books and magazines as they could find for me (the hospital did not have a library). I never read as much and as voraciously as I did in those hospital months, up to ten or twelve hours a day. The food was, of course, Austrian cuisine, and I quickly got used to it, with the exception of the caraway seeds that seemed to be the favorite spice of the hospital kitchen staff. Sometimes even the bread and the fried potatoes were covered with caraway seeds.

Finally the day of my discharge arrived. My new travel orders read "Breitenstein am Semmering, convalescent home for diphtheria patients." I finally arrived there, but only after considerable detour. After I had dragged my monster suitcase to the railroad station and had found the right train, I stepped into a train compartment. The only other occupant was a very impressive-looking man wearing a brown-yellow party uniform with silver bars, braids, stars, and other insignia of his rank with which I was not familiar. I threw him a smart salute, sat down, and he immediately drew me into an animated conversation. He was a friendly, somewhat garrulous type who seemed to be very self-assured. When I told him of my destination he said immediately, "That is wrong. Breitenstein is only a convalescent home for scarlet fever patients. You have to go to X" (I do not remember the name of the town). I was so impressed by his self-assurance, his knowledge of the KLV—he said that he had daily contact with the program—and his uniform, that he easily convinced me that somebody had indeed made a mistake. I changed trains at the next station and traveled to X. Of course, there had not been a clerical error. I spent a miserable night in the railroad station of X and arrived at Breitenstein a day late. But nobody really cared about punctuality, and they just laughed about my explanation, that on the train I had been persuaded by a high party functionary to change my travel plans. About a month later I again saw my acquaintance from the train compartment. He was in the middle of giving the eighty boys of the neighboring convalescent home their monthly haircut. He was the official KLV barber. I was so ashamed of my gullibility and my unquestioning acceptance because of his fancy dress uniform that I pretended not to recognize him, and he too acted as though he had never seen me before.

That whole affair was a miniature version of the *Köpenickiade*, a famous incident from the Wilhelmian era. In 1906 a shoemaker in an army captain's uniform had turned *Köpenick*, a town not far from Berlin, upside down, including occupation of the town hall and confiscation of the cash strongbox.

All of Europe laughed at the time about this excessive respect paid to a Prussian uniform. I, too, had been dazzled by a fancy uniform, but in 1942 I did not know the name Köpenick nor the literary version of the episode, *Der Hauptmann von Köpenick*, nor the name of the writer, Carl Zuckmayer, because he was one of the forbidden authors.

I stayed in Breitenstein for about eight weeks, and they are among my most cherished times as an adolescent. The village, located not too far from the Semmering Pass, was a spa with a magnificent view of the Alps. We lived in a small villa, in which most of the time there were not more than eight or nine convalescents. Each of us had our own room, and the food was unusually good and varied. After all, we were here to recuperate from a serious illness. A relatively young nurse, Schwester Maria, in her late twenties, was in charge. She was a friendly, outgoing person and determined our daily routine with much Austrian charm. We slept a great deal, sat in the wintry sun, and made small nonstrenuous excursions. Politics and the war seemed far away. It was an insular, almost idyllic existence. But not quite.

After a while we noticed that Schwester Maria, despite her usually happy mood, at times became very quiet and withdrawn, and once or twice had tears in her eyes. Finally, she revealed to us older patients the reason for her worry. She had a brother whose unit was fighting in the encirclement battle of Stalingrad. Despite sharp censorship, the news from there became progressively more gloomy. I do not know what became of her brother because I left the home at the beginning of February 1943, but her concern was all too justified. Of the ninety thousand German soldiers of the Sixth Army who surrendered in Stalingrad, only five thousand came home years after the war had ended. All others had perished in Soviet prison camps, among them probably Schwester Maria's brother.

One day my travel orders arrived. My KLV service was over. I was allowed to go home. I broke up my long train ride by stopping over in Vienna for a few days, where I became an eager tourist visiting the palaces of Schönbrunn and Belvedere, the Hofburg, St. Stephen's Cathedral, and many other sites. All of them were still intact. The air raids on Vienna had not yet begun. Everything was larger, more splendid, more metropolitan than in any other city I had ever been in. The traces and the aura of the former capital of a European empire were easily seen and felt, even for me, a very young student of history. After that there was the long journey home by train. I felt very much like a widely traveled person, a kind of globe-trotter. After all, I had been away from home for five months, longer and farther away than any of my friends and classmates. This feeling of superiority was enhanced by a little episode that occurred shortly before my arrival in Brunsbüttel.

For the last leg of my trip, about fifteen kilometers, I had to use a little commuter train, which we fondly called "Rosa." It was mostly used by students and workers whose school and jobs were in Itzehoe, one of our larger neighboring towns. I shared a compartment with a few workers who were talking in the gemütlich Low German language of north Germany. At one point one of them turned to me and asked in somewhat labored High German, *Sie können uns wohl gar nich vers-tehn, was?* "I guess you cannot understand us at all?" He had noticed a badge on the sleeve of my uniform jacket, *Südost. Niederdonau*, "Southeast. Lower Danube," which all of us KLV veterans had sewn on, although it was against regulations. Evidently my friendly neighbor considered me an Austrian, and his use of the polite *Sie* in addressing me made me feel even more grown-up and proud. I replied nonchalantly, and with a slightly superior air, in my best dialect-free High German, *Keineswegs. Ich verstehe auch Plattdeutsch,* "Not at all. I understand Low German too."

That was my first excursion into the big world. My parents were happy to have me back home. At school I had to tell my classmates about my various experiences. All of my teachers were most understanding and helpful, so that around Easter 1943 I was promoted to the tenth grade.

Many modern historians consider the German defeat at Stalingrad, the annihilation of an entire German army, the turning point of the war in Europe. There had been serious military reverses in 1941 and 1942 also, which I have mentioned and commented on in these memoirs: the loss of the battleship *Bismarck*; the failure of the army to take Moscow in the winter war of 1941–42; the first large-scale attack of the RAF on Cologne. Another major setback was in the late fall of 1942 at the Battle of El-Alamein, where the advance of the Afrikakorps driving to conquer Alexandria had come to a halt. Then there was the catastrophe of Stalingrad. It could not be suppressed in the reports from the high command of the armed forces, and it also could not be glossed over, as had been the case with other minor reverses. It served, however, to shift the NS propaganda machine into high gear. The whole dimension of the defeat was never admitted, the enormous casualty rates, the unheard-of number of prisoners taken by the Red Army. Exact numbers were consistently reported only in German victories. Goebbels and his people now chose a new tack in their efforts to boost the morale of the German people: grim determination and perseverance against all odds.

The most conspicuous illustration of this is the well-known declaration of total war. A conventional plebiscite was out of the question and none had been held since the 1930s. Instead, a great public spectacle was staged in the Berlin *Sportpalast*. Goebbels, who as a speaker and mass demagogue was almost as gifted as Hitler himself, delivered his famous "Speech of the Ten Points." I remember it well, some of the phrases even verbatim, because it was broadcast at prime time on all radio stations. I reacted with similar excitement as the mass audience did in the Sportpalast. Goebbels announced a program of total mobilization consisting of ten points. After each new measure, he shouted a question at his carefully selected audience: *Ich frage Euch: wollt Ihr den totalen Krieg?* "I ask you: do you want total war?" With every answer the spectators were pulled out of their seats and roared their approval. That was the NS version of a plebiscite, a masterpiece of political and rhetorical demagoguery. Even my sober and skeptical father could not entirely escape the effect of the grandiose show. He said: *Nu ward dat ernst,* "Things are getting serious now."

A veritable media offensive was then launched to lift the spirit of the population. I remember a short story in a newspaper about a village blacksmith who from morning to night worked hard at his strenuous job. One of his sons had fought at Stalingrad and was now reported as missing in action. But the father did not give up; he channeled all his worry and grief into his work for the war effort. The final scene showed the grieving blacksmith standing at his anvil forging iron. With every stroke of the hammer he said to himself *Für eine neue Sechste Armee!* "For a new Sixth Army!"

In all areas and activities the new *Durchhalte-Mentalität,* "hold-out mentality," was stressed and promoted. In our history classes at school the nearly fatal crisis of Prussia in 1762 at the end of the Seven Years' War was emphasized. Frederick the Great's state was faced with total annihilation, but then was saved by holding out until the "miracle of the Brandenburg dynasty" came about, the sudden death of the Czarina Elizabeth and the consequent peace treaty of Hubertusburg that was favorable for Prussia. The end of the First World War was interpreted even more one-sidedly in that a German victory had been virtually within reach, but the lack of staying power of the home front, especially the political Left, had led directly to defeat and humiliation, the infamous Dolchstosslegende. In the NS ideology training course, the near obliteration of the NSDAP after the failed Munich putsch in November 1923 was treated in detail. The party's survival and final victory, its seizure of power in 1933, was attributed in our training manuals to the "unshakable faith" in final victory, in the "hold-out mentality" of the Führer and his people.

Film production was affected also. No longer was the main emphasis placed on films that glorified the victories and triumphs of heroic fighter-plane aces and submarine commanders decorated with the Knights Cross, but on films that illustrated the Durchhalte-Mentalität. The best-known example is the color film *Kolberg,* although it was not completed until 1945. It was produced at high cost with a glittering cast of some of the most popular film actors and actresses and literally thousands of extras. It was based on an event in 1806 in which the small fortress of Kolberg in Pomerania held out for months against the overwhelming numerical superiority of the French forces despite the total collapse of the Prussian nation in general. Even in the area of popular music, special hit tunes were commissioned and promoted with texts like *Es geht alles vorüber*, "Everything will pass," or *Davon geht die Welt nicht unter*, "The world won't come to an end because of that" sung by the best-known and most beloved movie stars, including Zarah Leander and Marika Röck.

All this was made possible by the total and absolute control of the nation by the government. People's lives, all of their activities at work and at home, including very personal spheres, were centrally guided from Berlin. Another example of the complete domination and regimentation of people's minds by means of the media was evident one morning in all German cities, towns, and villages, where there appeared large posters on walls and in store windows. They showed a big black figure in a threatening pose, but no explanatory text. Everybody asked about the meaning of this and a large-scale guessing game began. The answer was given a few days later by millions of new posters on which the figure was identified as *Kohlenklau*, "coal snatcher." It was a newly invented symbol for waste of fuel, especially valuable coal.

By this gigantic operation—today it would be called a media blitz—people's attention was to be directed to the unconscionable waste of fuel in factories and households, to the idea that this wastefulness was a serious threat to the nation's energy supply, and to the plan that all citizens should contribute their share in stopping this depletion of resources. Whether the aim of the campaign was achieved is difficult to ascertain, but people did become more conscious of and careful about their fuel consumption. The word "Kohlenklau" was immediately integrated into the German language and was even varied in the vernacular. Toward the end of the war the shortage of able-bodied soldiers became critical. Certain military and party officials were ordered to comb through all units, factories, and offices searching for available men capable of frontline duty. These officials immediately and with black humor were dubbed *Heldenklaus*, "hero snatchers."

The year 1943 had begun with a serious military defeat at the Volga River. The days of lightning victories, of proud special bulletins, and military triumphs were over. In the spring of that year the Battle of the Atlantic tilted in favor of the Allies. As of May 1943, Allied convoys were no longer attacked by U-boat wolf packs.[5] The defensive systems, escort vessels, and planes flying air cover equipped with radar or sonar had become so effective that the losses of submarines could no longer be sustained. We were not told any details of this new situation, but we did notice, of course, that the special bulletins about submarine warfare were no longer coming. In the same month North Africa was lost, and the Afrikakorps, now called *Panzerarmee Afrika*, surrendered at Tunis. The proud achievements of the Desert Fox were now only memories. More than a quarter of a million German and Italian soldiers became prisoners of war. Once again, we never learned the exact number of losses. The Allied conquest of Sicily was followed by Mussolini's resignation and the collapse of Italy's Fascist regime. In July 1943 the German army on the eastern front initiated one of the last German offensives in that theater of war. It culminated in the tank battle at Kursk, which, despite heavy losses on both sides, ended in a stalemate. This biggest tank battle in history was played down by propaganda, obviously because no great victories were achieved. I did not learn details about the battle at Kursk until after the war.

Among the series of failures and defeats, there was one event in the summer of 1943 that brought home to us the true meaning of "total war" and profoundly horrified the people, especially in our part of the country: the air raids on Hamburg at the end of July and beginning of August. There had been bombing raids on German cities by the RAF for more than two years, but in most cases they had been attacks on military and industrial targets: weapons and ammunition factories, shipyards and U-boat pens, railroad junctions, and similar strategic targets. In Hamburg the civilian population in their living quarters was attacked mostly with incendiary bombs that caused the horrendous *Feuersturm*, "fire storm," about which even today the people of Hamburg speak only hesitantly and with horror.

The loss of life was heavy. Many of the victims suffocated in the large area fires because the fire storm consumed the oxygen in the air and at the same time created artificial hurricane-like gusts of wind causing the fires to spread even more rapidly. It was a tactic employed again by the Allies against Dresden in February 1945 and against Tokyo beginning in May 1945. The daily bulletins of the armed forces spoke only of the heavy damage in the Hanseatic city, but news of the real dimension of the devastation spread quickly. After all, it was our neighboring city. Many people, including my family, had relatives and friends there. My aunt and uncle lived in Barmbek, not far from the center of Hamburg. They survived but lost all their possessions when their apartment house was flattened. An endless stream of evacuees poured into the surrounding towns and villages. Many of them were taken by special trains into areas further inland and housed there in very provisionary quarters. They brought with them the horror stories of desperate people who leaped into the water of rivers and canals in order to extinguish the burning phosphorus on their clothes and their skin. Many of them drowned or suffocated there. They described families who were trying to escape the inferno and were glued to the boiling street asphalt, where they burned like living torches. They also spoke about the helplessness of the firefighting forces. It was a litany of pure hell, and it was the first time in my life I experienced the real feeling of *Grauen*, "horror."

Even from a distance of sixty miles we could see a gigantic cloud of dark smoke which hovered for days over the city. This feeling of terror and helplessness was intensified by the complete failure of the air defense. Even in the military bulletins the customary phrase "heavy losses were inflicted on the attacking 'terror' squadrons" was omitted. The surprise attack was achieved by a simple technical innovation by the British. Their planes had dropped millions of small strips of aluminum foil, which made the *Würzburg-Geräte*, the German version of radar, inoperable, so that the night fighter pilots had no guidance and the antiaircraft gunners were firing blind. These aluminum strips covered the streets of our town and the surrounding fields after the raids. Before their real function was recognized, the local authorities warned us not to touch them with bare hands, since they might be a diabolical device by the enemy to poison civilians.

Eighteen months later the real dimension of the damage, the totality of the destruction, was brought home to me personally. I was by then a regular army recruit in a regiment stationed in Hamburg. One day our training schedule read "Street fighting." It was and still is the type of combat most dangerous and therefore most hated by all infantry soldiers. Where did we practice? Not on our regular training grounds outside the city but in the dead parts of Hamburg, in Hamm and Hammerbrook. We took a subway train to these completely deserted districts. We recruits and our instructors were the only living humans there plying our grim trade for days among the thousands of rats and piles of rubble: attack on and defense of a destroyed town. All this happened inside the limits of a once pulsating and vibrant city. Churchill's euphemism of "dehousing" was a stark reality here.

As to the actual effect of the aerial bombardment of German cities there still exists a difference of opinion. It seems that the majority of military historians believe that the bombing had, at best, mixed results. The German people's resolve and morale tended to be strengthened rather than undermined, and the industrial capacity was rebuilt rather quickly after each raid.

Despite these serious reverses on all fronts—on land, at sea, and in the air—one idea that never entered the minds of us young people was that the war was lost. In my innumerable discussions, conversations, and lectures abroad after the war, it is *the* subject where I encountered the least understanding and the strongest reaction of incredulity. The constantly repeated question, especially in England and in the United States, was how we could continue to believe in final victory in view of the rapidly deteriorating military situation from 1943 on, and also considering the assassination attempt on Hitler in July 1944, and even in the last months of the war, when superior numbers of Allied forces from the west and east had set foot on German soil. I will discuss this seemingly blind and absurd attitude in detail in a later chapter covering the last year of the war. At this point I can only simply state that I know of no one in our school, in our neighborhood, or among my friends, to say nothing about the Hitler Youth, who ever mentioned the possibility of losing the war. There is no way of knowing the feelings of the adults at that

Hammerbrook, one of the most heavily damaged parts of Hamburg in the firestorm of July 1943, was the area where we infantry recruits practiced street fighting.

time—my parents, for example—but I suspect that many, perhaps the majority of them, rejected the idea emphatically, perhaps according to the motto *Was nicht sein darf, ist nicht,* "What must not be, does not exist."

10
Tough times—
tough people
(and soft heads)

Jn July 1943 my close daily contact with my family came to an end. Until then my friends and classmates and I had grown up as "normal" children in normal middle-class homes despite the various interruptions. We had our own rooms or shared them with our siblings. We had been provided with three meals every day prepared by our mothers. On six days of the week there had been the daily routine of school from eight o'clock in the morning to one or two in the afternoon, a great deal of homework in the afternoon and at night, and DJ or HJ duties every Wednesday and Saturday afternoon. There was not much free time except during school holidays. When we were not occupied, we went to the movies, engaged in sports (soccer, gymnastics, field handball), and we pursued all activities typical of children and adolescents. All that came to an abrupt end. We became soldiers. I was sixteen years old.

The number of casualties, especially on the eastern front and in North Africa, rose rapidly, and the Wehrmacht command had greater difficulties in compensating for the heavy losses of combat personnel by new recruitment. Conscription age was already set as low as seventeen, and at this time the authorities did not want to lower it further, probably to avoid the onus of conducting a *Kinderkrieg*, "children's war." Therefore various measures were taken to provide the essential replacements for the combat units: ethnic Germans who were not German citizens were drafted; volunteers were recruited in occupied non-German countries—for example, in the Low Countries and in Scandinavia; many men who had been exempt from military service for reasons of health or had enjoyed occupational deferment were now reclassified.

One of the most ingenious and effective acts was the mobilization of the upper Gymnasium classes. These students were not to be deployed in actual ground combat but instead in the defense of the home front, in the air defense system. The high command of the *Ersatzheer,* "replacement forces," had been convinced that the duties of thousands of adult antiaircraft gunners could just as well be performed by sixteen-year-olds. By issuing this order the armed forces gained at once seventy to eighty thousand mature and trained soldiers for combat duty. That was the beginning of the service as *Luftwaffenhelfer* or *Marinehelfer* for practically all male Gymnasium students in Germany, and it continued to the last days of the war.[1] We of the Jahrgänge 1926 and 1927 were the first contingent. The two highest grades of a Gymnasium were moved to an antiaircraft battery emplacement. Special uniforms were created for the *Flakhelfer,* blue-gray for the Luftwaffenhelfer and navy blue for the Marinehelfer. After a period of about six weeks' basic training and specialized instructions on guns and fire guidance equipment, we were slowly moved into the battery units and took over the duties of the grown-up soldiers.

When this new scheme was announced to the public, it was emphasized that our education would not be seriously impaired. In most cases the teachers came to the batteries and conducted their classes there. For our school a special arrangement had been made. Our class had been assigned to two *Leuchtgruppen,* "searchlight emplacements," that were part of a fourteen-unit searchlight battery. Since there was something for us to do as gunners only at night, we were able to attend regular classes in our old school. The two Leuchtgruppen had been selected because they were located only two or three miles distant from Marne; thus our school could easily be reached by bicycle. Emplacement four, *Diekhusen,* became our home for the next fourteen months. We led a double existence: regular school in the morning; homework and further special training on equipment in the afternoon; duty at night when there were one or more alerts, which became more and more frequent as the RAF increased its activities. My duties were either to operate part of the *Leitrichtgerät,* a kind of direction finder, or act as *Befehlsübermittler* (BÜ), "telephone operator." Thus for over a year, almost every night I turned a wheel or accepted or conveyed telephone messages.

At our school there was a short farewell ceremony to which our parents had been invited. Our principal, whom we formally had to address as *Herr Direktor,* although informally everybody called him *Chef,* "boss," gave a farewell speech full of pompous phrases like *Pflichterfüllung,* "doing one's duty," *Dienst am Vaterland,* "service to the Fatherland," *Harte Zeiten—harte Menschen,* "tough times—tough people," and similar highfalutin words. His use of the last phrase was especially unfortunate because it nearly ruined the whole solemn ceremony. All of us boys were familiar with the story of how a witty Berliner had added to a *Harte Zeiten—harte Menschen* poster the disrespectful phrase *und weiche Birnen,* "and soft heads." Not all of us managed to keep a straight face at this point in the ceremony. *Oberstudiendirektor* M.

was a party member but not a particularly rabid National Socialist. He probably thought that for an officially arranged ceremony he had to use officially sanctioned jargon.

After the farewell ritual my father and I went to the bus station. He was very quiet on the way and looked quite depressed. Finally he broke the silence: "I had hoped that you would be able to finish your Gymnasium studies without further interruptions. And now this." It was difficult for him to get used to the thought that, in addition to his older sons who were absolving their war service at rather exposed posts, now his youngest son also was to wear the uniform of the armed forces at the age of sixteen. I am sure that he was also afraid that under the circumstances I would never be able to finish the Gymnasium, acquire the Abitur diploma, and thus some day, after the war, whenever that would be, matriculate at a university. That had been his dream for me for years. After all, I would be the first *Akademiker* in my family, and he had done everything in his power to make this dream come true. But at this moment, on this day in late July 1943, the future did not look very promising for any of us.

For us boys this radical change in our lives was one big adventure, and we applied all our enthusiasm and energy to the new tasks. At first, however, there were some disappointments and setbacks. It began with our uniforms. Some of my classmates and I were not fully grown. At that time I was about five feet four inches tall and weighed 125 pounds. The supply depot simply did not carry uniforms for such short lightweight soldiers. Thus we had to accept uniforms that were three sizes too big, and in which we looked like scarecrows. It was a trivial concern, but for sixteen-year-olds appearances matter greatly. Fortunately, my mother was a fairly competent seamstress and was able to correct the worst flaws, and a few weeks later all of us received fitting uniforms.

Another disappointment had to do with close-order drills, marching in various formations, saluting, and so on. For disciplinary reasons much emphasis was placed on this part of basic training even in the navy artillery, although all of us, since the age of ten, had not only learned and executed all orders but many of us had taught and supervised basic training routines for more than four years. Nevertheless, once again for six weeks, two hours every day, we drilled hard. But that did not bother us particularly; we simply accepted that as a soldier's lot. The big difference, however, was that now we had to drill with rifles and bayonets. Unfortunately for us they were not the standard hand weapons of the German infantry, rifle 98 or 98K (for *kurz*, "short"). Instead we were trained with captured rifles, in our case French *Chassepot* rifles from World War I. At the daily manual-of-arms drills, this rifle came up to my ears, and with attached bayonet it was a good foot taller than I. We short Marine-

Close-order drill as navy artillery recruits. I am the last on the right. The rifle plus bayonet would be a foot over my head.

helfer presented a strange, slightly comical picture at our drills, and we were painfully conscious of this impression.

A further cause of discontent was the order that Marinehelfer had to wear the black-white-red HJ arm band at all times in public with our dress uniforms. We emphatically and unanimously rejected this, not because we had overnight become young anti-Nazis, but because we considered ourselves soldiers now. We knew that we were doing men's jobs and we wanted to be seen as men. We looked at the whole Hitler Youth "business," *den ganzen Hitler Jugend-Kram*, as being part of our past, when we were children and civilians. Consequently, when our basic training period was over and we had to appear in public on our daily bicycle trips to school, we took off our arm bands as soon as we left our emplacements. Thus, we could hardly be distinguished in our appearance from real soldiers. Later we did not even wear the arm bands in our emplacement at inspection and similar occasions because our CO, a

MA-Obermaat, "navy artillery boatswain," was a good-natured and easy-going man who cared little about HJ arm bands and similar extraneous matters, which were not directly related to running an efficient Leuchtgruppe.

There was a last issue that caused frustration among us sixteen-year-old student-soldiers and was considered an insult to our dignity. It was at that time customary that all antiaircraft gunners receive an extra ration of tobacco products—cigarettes, cigars, pipe tobacco—for every action they had participated in, for every alert. I think it was five cigarettes per alert. But not for Marine-helfer. Naturally, we were waiting impatiently for our first tobacco ration, although most of us did not even smoke at that time. Instead we received several packages of the hard candy which was popular with children. We were enraged and failed to see the humor when our older comrades laughed heartily and dubbed us *Bonbon-Soldaten*, "candy soldiers."

Despite these disappointments and tensions, we performed our duties conscientiously and with enthusiasm. There were two reasons for this: first, we had the burning desire to protect our homeland, our villages, towns, and cities and prevent further devastations similar to the Hamburg one; second, we enjoyed the new feeling of being treated as adults who wore the uniforms of real soldiers and did the work of soldiers. We were immensely flattered when during the final inspection, after the basic training period was over, our battalion commander praised us in a short speech: it had been "refreshing" for him to see recruits once again who carried out all orders smartly and snappily, *zackig*, and performed their jobs quickly, alertly, and intelligently.

Our relationship to the regular emplacement crew was, at first, one of distance and reticence on their part. This initial reaction of our older comrades was understandable, the reasons being twofold. The first was a certain class consciousness, for at that time the less than 6 percent of all young people who attended a Gymnasium were automatically considered members of the present or future upper classes. The second reason for their initially cool attitude toward us was more important. Because of our presence, their war service, hitherto absolved in a remote and relatively safe area, was about to come to an end. Many of them would be transferred to places where they would be potentially exposed to real combat. I know of at least two soldiers of our Leuchtgruppe who were transferred to France and later lost their lives at the Atlantic coast during the Normandy invasion by the Allied forces. But gradually we were accepted by them, and they did not take out their fears and anxieties on us, probably because the fair-minded ones among them realized that we, just like they and all Germans, were following orders, and orders were there to be carried out.

It caused a small sensation when, in the fall of 1943, we appeared for the first time in our school. The students in the lower grades admired us because to them we looked like genuine soldiers. Even our teachers were

My friend Helmut D. and I as navy artillery gunners in dress uniforms, 1944. Helmut D., having just finished basic training, is wearing the Hitler Youth armband, whereas I, a twelve-month "veteran," disregarded this rule of dress.

impressed and had to get used to facing students in blue navy uniforms every morning. I remember one of our classmates, Jürgen K., who had not become Marinehelfer, had been selected by the party and the HJ authorities—perhaps he had volunteered—to supervise all DJ youth activities in the whole county. He was given the relatively high rank of a *DJ-Stammführer* and was in charge of several thousand boys. But that no longer counted among our younger schoolmates, and certainly not among our female classmates. We were soldiers and he was a civilian, and I know how much he suffered from this distinction.

The school routine continued in relatively normal fashion. Sometimes we were tired after our night duties, especially when there had been more than one alert, but our teachers showed much understanding, and they also had been advised to make allowances because of the special circumstances. Even our military superiors had received orders to see to it that we left the emplacement punctually every morning, that we did our homework conscientiously, handed in our papers on time and were prepared for examinations.

The only major row that I remember happened in our mathematics class. Our teacher for mathematics and chemistry was Dr. S., a popular, kind, and not very strict pedagogue. After a few months of service in the Wehrmacht, he had been discharged for health reasons and allowed to return to his teaching position. He especially showed much understanding for the strain of our dual role as soldier-students. A few times, but not often, we took advantage of his tolerance and sympathy and invented fictitious excuses for missing homework assignments or lack of preparation for a test. One day each of us in the class was working independently on solving some assigned mathematical problems. Dr. S. was walking up and down the aisles proctoring our work. By sheer coincidence he stopped at my desk and started leafing through my mathematics copybook, which was sitting there. It was a hefty exercise book, about a hundred and fifty pages, into which we had to enter all our homework assignments. Unfortunately, these were not the only entries. We had used the last thirty or forty pages to record the results of our daily *Skat* games, the most popular card game in Germany.[2] Dr. S. immediately recognized the tables for what they were, and he exploded. We received a severe dressing-down: it was not the war service that interfered with the daily preparation but the miserable card games; this was the way we were paying him back for his sympathetic understanding; he was inclined not to believe any of our excuses about anything anymore. It took weeks and months before calm and friendly relations were reestablished between our teacher and us. Many years after the war when I visited Dr. S.—he was retired by then—and reminded him of this scene, he could not remember, and even then did not find it very amusing. We perpetrators, however, remembered the episode well, including his philippic and his subsequent, frequently pointed innuendoes.

It was also Dr. S. who cringed every time we pronounced certain numbers the way we had learned in the military: *zwo* (two) instead of *zwei*, for example, or *zwozehn* (twelve) instead of *zwölf*. This was standard procedure especially on the telephone, when "zwei" sounded too much like *drei* (three), "zwölf" too much like *elf* (eleven) and could lead to serious misunderstandings. Dr. S., however, told us often that there was a time and a place for everything, and his geometry class was definitely not the place for word monsters like "zwozehn."

Another teacher, our Latin instructor, Herr L., looked at us with a certain amused distance and could well distinguish between justified excuses and sheer goldbricking. When ten months later some of us were promoted to

Marineoberhelfer (two narrow gold stripes on our left sleeves), he gave us a mock lecture that we of superior rank now also had to demonstrate superior achievements in dealing with Latin writers like Livy, Cicero, and Horace. It was sheer sarcasm, and we did not like it at all. He also consistently addressed us as "Obermarinehelfer" which, because of the false designation, also sounded sarcastic to us, and was probably meant to be, and that did not amuse us either.

We were housed in one of the four bunkers of the emplacement, five Marinehelfer in one room, which we naturally had to keep clean and neat ourselves and which was inspected daily. We were also responsible for the immaculate condition of our dress and work uniforms and for our laundry. That was a drastic change for us, because up to then our mothers had taken care of all that. It was made especially difficult because according to navy tradition, our work uniform consisted of white blouses and white trousers, the most impractical color about which my father, thirty years earlier, and many sailor generations before and after him, had grumbled. I remember well how many hours we spent in the laundry room in order to remove especially stubborn tar, grease, and grass stains from our whites. Sometimes we used, against all regulations, a high-grade ammonium detergent that was provided for cleaning floors, sinks, and toilet bowls. This powder certainly removed the spots, but often it removed part of the uniform as well and left holes in trousers and blouses. It took a while before we had learned all the tricks of a garrison soldier.

It was sometimes difficult to find a quiet spot in the afternoons and on weekends for doing our homework. In warm and dry weather we went outside to sit on the grass to write our essays, solve mathematical problems, and prepare for our English and Latin classes. In inclement weather, however, and in our part of the country this was often the case, the situation became problematic. To be sure, we had a large table in our sleeping quarters, but with four roommates present it was almost impossible to concentrate. The large all-purpose room of the emplacement was available to us, but the frequent pointed remarks of our older comrades who had not attended a Gymnasium soon got on our nerves, especially when we had already withdrawn with our books and papers to a quiet corner. ("What are you doing there? Latin? Nobody speaks it anymore. Dead language.") Nevertheless we were usually well prepared for our classes. I do not believe that our education was seriously impaired by our Flak service.

Once a month we got an overnight pass and were allowed to go home, a most welcome interlude, and on those occasions we gladly let ourselves be spoiled by our mothers. After twelve months we were eligible for a regular furlough of two weeks, which my mother and I spent in our beloved Prerow. That was in the summer of 1944. It was my last visit to the village and to the house where I was born. They were two unforgettable weeks of good weather, frequent swims in the Baltic Sea, long walks along the magnificent sand dunes, and, in the evening, the warm security of being a member of a large family.

An event that made an indelible impression on all of us Marinehelfer occurred a few weeks before the Prerow vacation, in the early summer of 1944. It was a Sunday morning and we were off duty and sunbathing on the roof of our bunker. We were watching from a distance several B-17 wings of the Allied bomber command flying past us at 20,000 feet over the middle of the Elbe River. This was nothing new. The big four-engine planes liked to use the river as the approach route for their raids on Hamburg, Berlin, Hannover, and other cities. If they stayed exactly over the center of the Elbe, they were at that altitude practically out of range of the heavy Flak batteries on either side. They were easy to see because each plane was marked by the long white vapor trails behind it. Suddenly, something unusual happened. One formation had already passed Brunsbüttel, as they had done many times before, when all at once they turned around and approached our town. We saw the well-known and feared target markers being dropped right into the town, and then the attack began. We could see and hear the many bomb detonations—after all, we were less than ten miles away and had strong binoculars available. Then everything was covered by a huge, rising cloud of smoke and dust. We just stood there profoundly shaken and horrified. Nobody said anything. We knew that our families were in the middle of this inferno—dead, injured, or alive. All telephone connections had been severed during the attack. A half-hour later an unending stream of ambulances, sirens blaring, raced past our emplacement taking the victims to the hospitals in Marne. We watched them not knowing whether one or more members of our families were inside the ambulances. I have never before and never since felt so much fear, horror, and helplessness.

Only late in the afternoon were the roads to Brunsbüttel open again, and our CO, *Obermaat* O., allowed one of us, my friend and neighbor, Helmut D., to rush home by bicycle to gather information. Helmut came back after a few hours with good news. All our families had survived the raid. Buildings had been hit, but our houses were still standing. The nearest bomb in our neighborhood had fallen into his family's garden and had uprooted an apple tree. Our joy and relief were boundless.

I remember one of my father's remarks during my next overnight stay at home. He shook his head in disbelief and said: "The raid does not make sense. The *Engelsmann* must believe that he cannot win the war. Why else would he attack our locks, which after a victorious war's end he would need for the ship traffic to the countries around the Baltic?" His insight and his logic were correct once again, except that he had not calculated the factor of human error. Many years after the war we learned that the attack on the Brunsbüttel locks had indeed been an error. The raid had been spontaneously initiated by an individual commander, for which, according to the rumors we heard, he was court-martialed.

In the fourteen months of my Marinehelfer time in the searchlight battery, Battalion Brunsbüttel, consisting of fourteen emplacements manned by approximately one hundred fifty soldiers and Marinehelfer, not a single enemy plane was *aufgefasst*, caught in our powerful light beams. Our only useful function was raking the cloud cover from below, when there was one, giving the high-flying German night fighters a more visible target against the illuminated cloud cover when they attacked the Allied bomber formations from above. That at least was the theory. In reality I do not know of a single British plane being shot down due to our elaborate efforts. It is an illustration of the ancient old rhythm in military history which occurs when rapidly advancing offensive (or defensive) technology surpasses conventional defensive (or offensive) strategies and often leaves them far behind. Not until late in 1944 were our successors, the Marinehelfer of Jahrgang 1928, transferred to a heavy gun battery. But even then the Leuchtgruppen were not declared obsolete and dismantled. For a few months these now useless installations were serviced by women soldiers and, toward the end of the war, by physically and mentally handicapped personnel. It is one more example of the inflexibility, the stubbornness, and the longevity of a military bureaucracy.

Our discharge in September 1944 was a very unceremonious affair. We were simply told to hand in our uniforms and all our gear at the supply depot and wait at home for orders for our next assignment.

Toward the end of my tour of duty as a Marinehelfer, an event occurred which today I consider of the greatest importance for the course of modern German history, even though it had no immediate consequences for the political and military situation at the time: the assassination attempt on the Führer on July 20, 1944. There now exists a veritable library of books about this event—memoirs, monographs, historical analyses, diaries, volumes of correspondences, and more. I am familiar with part of this vast literature. I have participated in many formal discussions, conferences, seminars, symposia, and memorial services pertaining to July 20, and I have been involved in innumerable private conversations about the resistance movement in the Third Reich which culminated in the actual attempt to remove Hitler forcibly. I have two basic convictions. They are among the firmest and most unshakable premises of my whole political and historical consciousness.

The first is that the attempt to kill Adolf Hitler, to topple the NS regime and replace it with a new government, was absolutely necessary. The honor of the German nation was at stake—the good name of the German people and the place of Germany in the family of civilized and humane countries. These are high-sounding phrases, but they are appropriate because of the special historical circumstances. The great majority of the conspirators was, as we know now, very much aware of this obligation. They were patriots in the best sense of the word; they loved their country more than their own lives, and they were ready to sacrifice their existence for it. They were true idealists. One of the most moving experiences of my life was my 1967 visit to Berlin-Plötzensee, the memorial for the participants of the July 20 action. I stood in the stark, empty hall which in 1944 had served as the place of execution for many of the conspirators, where they were hanged with piano wires on meat hooks to prolong their agony.

However, I believe it was just as necessary for the attempt to fail. That is a statement that is most difficult to make knowing today of the horrendous and cruel revenge of the NS regime on the conspirators and their families, and in view of the fact that from July 20, 1944, to May 8, 1945, additional hundreds of thousands of people on both sides lost their lives or their health. The insanity and the devastation of the war continued for almost nine more months. As a present-day historical observer and a knowledgeable witness of the conditions and the mood of the German people at the time, as somebody who was present, I am convinced that a successful assassination attempt would have led to a civil war in Germany and most certainly would have given birth to a new Dolchstosslegende. The war had to continue to its bitter end. The total military defeat of Germany was necessary so that after the war's end, on the ruins of the inhumane Third Reich, a totally new German state could be built on the basis of generally accepted moral and ethical principles.

The news of the attempted coup came as a total surprise for everyone in my family and for all our friends, classmates, and neighbors. The resistance movement was by its very nature numerically limited. Only a small number of people actually knew of and participated in the action. It was never a mass movement, as conspiracies never can be. On July 20, 1944, my mother and I were returning from our visit to Prerow. The first indication that something unusual was going on was the great number of extra guards and patrols on the trains and at the stations where we had to change trains. I had to show my papers at least seven or eight times because I was in uniform. After our arrival home we heard the news on the radio and then Hitler himself spoke. His voice sounded rougher than usual and he spoke haltingly, but nobody had any doubts that it was the Führer himself. With strong expressions he condemned *den ganz winzigen Klüngel von ehrgeizigen Offizieren*, "the tiny clique of ambitious officers," and he thanked "destiny," *der Vorsehung*, one of his favorite words, for having spared him so that he could continue to serve the German people *bis zum Endsieg*, "until final victory." One of the reasons why I re-

Last visit at my grandmother's house in July 1944. *Left to right*: My sister-in-law Anni, my grandmother, Hannelore (the first grandchild and my niece), my mother, my cousin Irmgard, and I.

member this speech so well is his use of the word "Klüngel," with which I was not very familiar, and the word *Kamarilla*, later used in the media and which I had to look up.

My own reaction to the sensational events was one of relief and gratitude that the plot had failed, and one of horror and anger directed against the officers who had tried to stab their own soldiers in the back, their comrades who were fighting fiercely on all fronts. Only much later did I learn that not only army officers but also representatives of the churches, the forbidden labor unions, and the suppressed democratic parties were involved. I am sure that many of the German people felt the same as I did. A few days later one of my friends tried to make a joke about the whole affair ("This time the carpet eater almost ate himself to death"). He was told in no uncertain terms by all of us present to refrain once and for all from uttering any more *Quatsch*, "rubbish," especially now in such critical times. Unfortunately, I cannot report anything about my parents' reaction. I presume that the reason for this apparent gap in

My parents on June 22, 1944, their silver wedding anniversary.

my memory is that there was no overt reaction, that they maintained complete silence. In the first place it was much too dangerous to express any criticism in such a highly charged political atmosphere. Secondly, I can well
imagine that my usually well-informed and farsighted father could not decide
whether Hitler's death would have been a blessing or a curse for Germany and
the world. I am certain that it was an inner dilemma for him and for many
other Germans of his generation, not the least because for him, as a former
soldier and loyal civil servant, it must have been nearly impossible to approve
of breaking one's oath of allegiance to the head of state, which in this case was
committed by high-ranking officers of the armed forces. We know today that
this had been a gnawing inner moral conflict, a *Gewissenskonflikt*, for many
of the actual participants of the July 20 action.

The furious propaganda campaign of the regime against the conspirators in
the following weeks and months made no strong impression on us, although
Goebbels's ministry had arranged to show in the newsreels and newspapers
some of the participants in the most humiliating and undignified poses at the
trials. The reasons for our lack of interest were partly the repugnant screaming

style of the president of the people's court, Roland Freisler, but more importantly, because the further course of the military events—the war—far overshadowed these trials. We were certain that the ultimate verdict would be the death penalty for these perpetrators of high treason. About the bestial manner of execution at Plötzensee we knew nothing.

The only reservations and scruples some of my friends and I had, which bothered us to some extent, was the fact that among the conspirators were men whose family names we had learned to idolize—von Moltke, Yorck von Wartenburg, von Bismarck. We did ask ourselves what could have motivated these members of Prussian-German elite families to act the way they did, what could have driven them to undertake such a radical step.

At this point I will temporarily give up the largely chronological narration of events and relate two occurrences that are very relevant. In film language they are "flash forwards," one a national event and the other a personal experience. They illustrate our thinking and feeling and our attitude in 1947 and 1950, respectively, vis-à-vis the then-recent past.

In November 1947 the German premiere of a play by a German author in exile, Carl Zuckmayer, was given in the Hamburger Schauspielhaus, one of the largest and most reputable theaters in Germany. The play was *Des Teufels General* (The Devil's General). It created a tremendous sensation and became immediately part of the repertory programs of all major theaters in what were then the three western occupation zones. Even in many small towns amateur groups ventured to put on performances of this huge theater hit. Later a film version, which was also shown abroad, was produced with the well-known actor Curd Jürgens in the title role. The play was a major cultural event in those bleak years, and the most phenomenal side effect was that a performance often led to spontaneous public discussions, which were frequently very emotional and often bitter. Soon some of these discussions were organized by adult education agencies, book clubs, and even by the embryonic new political parties. There could not have been a single thinking German citizen in the winter of 1947–48 who was not directly or indirectly affected by the play and the discussions about it.

Carl Zuckmayer, a successful playwright during the Weimar years, had escaped from the Third Reich under rather dramatic circumstances and had gone into exile. He had finally settled down on a farm in Vermont and there, during the war, wrote *The Devil's General*. It was based to some extent on the life of German World War I flying ace Ernst Udet. The success of the play, its powerful audience appeal, is in part due to the creation of the three-dimensional role of the protagonist, the air force General Harras. Because of his love of flying he had offered his service to the NS regime, although he fully recognized the diabolical element in it, *das Teuflische*. He continually talks about this, agonizes about it, and finally chooses to escape by committing suicide. General Harras became a major role for every prominent actor in the theater of German-speaking countries, and practically all actors starred in it in the months and years after the premiere.

The play was also produced in our town by some gifted semiprofessional actors and actresses and was repeated several times. In the discussions following each performance, the actions and the motivation of Harras and his inner dilemma were analyzed. The debates became heated and emotional when the figure of Oderbruch and his motivation were mentioned. The figure of Oderbruch in the play is a highly placed technical assistant of the general, a member of the resistance movement who, with some helpers, but without Harras's knowledge, deliberately sabotages the airplane production in his factory. These acts of sabotage inevitably result in the death of many German pilots, including personal friends and comrades of Harras and Oderbruch. This was always the point when discussions became explosive. Among the questions asked repeatedly by the participants in our town and by hundreds of others were: Was the resistance necessary? How could the conspirators and saboteurs justify their actions? Has one human being ever the right to kill another human being? Is there such a thing as a higher moral law? Who is the ultimate judge in questions of high treason?

In the many public and private debates and discussions there were always two extreme groups, one for and one against Oderbruch, and then the large group of people who pensively listened to the arguments, reflected on their own attitudes and actions during the recent past, and cautiously tried to find a plausible and acceptable standpoint. Some of my friends and I belonged to this large middle group. We were groping for a new *Weltanschauung*, "worldview," and for us *The Devil's General* was a powerful vehicle to trigger what was soon to be called *Vergangenheitsbewältigung*, "coping with the past." It goes without saying that long before this we had dealt with similar questions in many conversations at school and with friends, but our arguments became more pointed and well reasoned after having seen and read Zuckmayer's *Des Teufels General*.

The second forward flash is a personal experience I had three years later. In the summer of 1949, after a two-year waiting period, I was finally admitted as a matriculated student at the University of Bonn. One of the lecture courses I enrolled in was a three-semester cycle on Roman history given by Professor P., an internationally known scholar. In his course he surveyed the development of the Roman Empire from its beginning to its end a thousand years later. We knew little or nothing about the individual Professor P. There were some rumors that he had been a member of the resistance movement.

Three times a week for three semesters at nine o'clock in the morning we went to the lecture hall, the *Akademisches Kunstmuseum* of the university, to listen to his lectures and to take copious notes. His classes were informative and proved his vast knowledge of the subject, but they were also quite dry and sometimes soporific. One morning, however, Professor P. was lecturing on the assassination of Julius Caesar in the year 44 B.C. He analyzed in detail the general condition of the Roman state and especially the mood and motivation of the conspirators around Brutus. Then he said, "Under these circumstances there remained only one means of action for the conspirators: political murder. With these words, ladies and gentlemen, I conclude my lecture as I did once before on July 19, 1944." *Mit diesen Worten, meine Damen and Herren, schloss ich meine Vorlesung am 19. Juli 1944.* There was a short pause. We stopped writing and looked up, and when we fully realized the meaning of this statement, a spontaneous and tumultuous burst of applause broke out, the likes of which the venerable Kunstmuseum probably had never experienced. There were about two hundred students in the lecture hall. All of us were either veterans or had at least consciously lived through the events of July 20, 1944. Here now, six years later, we were in the presence of someone who had been an active member of the resistance and had lived to talk about it. It was an unforgettable experience for all of us. There was no discussion afterward about the justification of the assassination attempt; there were only expressions of approval and admiration.

11
They act
as though
the war
will go on
forever

After my discharge from the navy artillery, induction into the *Reichsarbeitsdienst*, "Reich labor service," was imminent. The RAD was a relic from the NS prewar days. At that time, 1935, every male German citizen was drafted to spend six months in this organization before his regular two-year mandatory service in the armed forces. In that RAD capacity he was to serve the people's community *mit dem Spaten in der Hand*, "with the spade in his hand," as the propaganda ministry continuously proclaimed. Another formulation to justify this additional half-year of service was that the gap between *Arbeiter der Faust* and *Arbeiter der Stirn*, between manual laborers and intellectuals, was to be overcome. After the outbreak of the war, the six-month period of RAD service had been quickly reduced so that there would be more recruits available for the Wehrmacht. But the RAD organization was never entirely eliminated, and we all knew that before our regular Wehrmacht service, we had to join the RAD for a period of three months.

My notification was a few weeks late. One after the other of my classmates departed for one of the various RAD camps. I was one of the last of our class who was still at home. I do not know the reasons for this delay, but I do remember how anxiously I waited every morning for the mailman. My impatience was so noticeable that, without meaning to do so, I hurt my mother's feelings. One morning, when I must have looked especially disappointed because the long-expected postcard still had not come, she said sadly, "Heavens, Willy, you really cannot wait to leave home, can you?" That, however, was a misinterpretation on my mother's part. I was not unhappy in our home. My relationship with my parents and with my sister was good and intact. But I felt very strongly that a sheltered existence, the family haven, at this time and under these circumstances, was not the appropriate place for me. A seventeen-year-old civilian did not fit into the German society of September 1944.

The military situation for the Wehrmacht had deteriorated in 1944. The Reich was threatened on all fronts, in the east, the south, in the Atlantic, and, as of June 6, 1944, also in the west. There had been nothing but military reverses, setbacks, defeats, and retreats for our soldiers. Even we young people were aware of this. One look at a map of Europe was sufficient for us to realize that the war was not going well.

For this very reason—and this may sound paradoxical, especially to foreigners who were not present—, we were waiting with much anticipation for the invasion of the Allied forces, Operation Overlord, as it is known today, the large-scale landing somewhere on the Atlantic coast. We took it for granted that the Wehrmacht high command would let enough Allied troops come ashore and then, with a massive counteroffensive, throw them back into the sea. That would have been a great victory in the style of the early war years. After that the Wehrmacht would concentrate on the eastern front and, without the invasion threat at its back, have the strength to drive the Red Army back behind the Volga River and the Ural Mountains. That is how our youthful and amateurish imaginations were working, and it was supported by innumerable reports and documentaries about the "impregnability" of the *Atlantikwall*, the fortifications on the French coast facing England. The famous Desert Fox, Fieldmarshal Erwin Rommel, now one of the commanders of the German forces in the west, was a further guarantee for us that the Allied invasion was bound to fail. Therefore we waited in May and June of that year with great expectation for the news of the landing. When it finally came on June 6, 1944, we were relieved and even happy about it.

The great German victory on the Normandy coast did not materialize. The Red Army continued to push farther and farther west. Allied troops were fighting their way up the Italian peninsula. There was hardly any more news about the submarine warfare, and the air raids on German cities became evermore frequent and devastating. It was therefore all the more urgent for us young people to serve and contribute individually to the war effort and to protect our homeland against the advancing enemies. That is the reason why my classmates and I considered a civilian existence in the fall of 1944, even for a few weeks, singularly inappropriate and even indecent, and why I received my RAD notification with relief and joy. I was to report to the RAD Camp in Ütersen, a town not far from Hamburg with a large military airfield. Thus I started out once again on a trip to the next station of my war service.

Upon our arrival in Ütersen we were confronted again with a camp and everything that it encompassed. This RAD installation was relatively large and looked more attractive than any other camp I had experienced before. The footpaths and the parade ground were lined with whitewashed rocks. Even bushes and hedges had been planted around the wooden barracks. It was easy to see that the raison d'être of the Reichsarbeitsdienst was manual labor. When we entered the buildings, however, the same familiar odor hit us,—the peculiar mixture of green wood that had not air-dried long enough and of dust and sweat—which invariably clung to these structures and which I recognize even today. There were twelve of us per room with a squad leader. Almost everything was an imitation of the regular Wehrmacht service: early rising; inspection; close-order drills. At mid-morning we marched to the construction site, where our job was to lengthen the runway of the neighboring military airfield. There we worked for several hours, filled the small hand lorries which ran on iron tracks with sand, pushed them a few hundred meters, and emptied them. All this was done with our spades and without the help of tractors, graders, and other heavy machinery, probably to stress the importance of manual labor and to deemphasize mechanization. After lunch we worked for a few more hours. Then there was more military training on the firing range, throwing grenades, map reading, and so on. Even the evenings were rarely free. We had to listen to lectures about the "History of the RAD" and "Symbolism of the Spade" and similar topics. Lights-out came at half-past ten.

After a few weeks, all actual manual labor service was canceled for all RAD camps by order from Berlin, so that our instructors could concentrate exclusively on the military training aspects of our units. There were no furloughs in the two-and-a-half months, not even for a few hours on Sunday afternoons. We would have liked to get out of the camp once in a while to visit the town of Ütersen and sit perhaps in a café in civilian surroundings, although we only could have ordered a cup of ersatz coffee or an abominable punch called *Heissgetränk*, "hot drink," since we did not have any ration coupons for a piece of cake or a sandwich. But these restrictions did not faze us much. We considered our time here an interlude between the navy artillery and the real military service in the armed forces.

That must be the explanation for the fact that my memory of these months is unusually pale and sporadic. There are only two aspects of my RAD service that I remember with clarity. One is that for the first time we had close daily contacts with a group of people our age from a different part of the country. About half of the members of our unit hailed from the Rhineland, specifically from Solingen and Wuppertal. They were, collectively speaking, good comrades. They were more loquacious and communicative than most of us from Schleswig-Holstein. They talked faster, sang, and laughed more than most of us did. Even today I entertain a small positive prejudice for the Rhenish people and their soft dialect. Solingen had been for almost a hundred years the industrial center for the production of quality steel needed to manufacture knives, blades, table cutlery, and so on. Indeed, when in a personal conversation with our Solingen friends we asked, "What does your father do?" or "Tell me about your family," the replies were inevitably, "My father works in the blade factory," or "My family owns a small cutlery." I corresponded with some of these friends for years after the war was over. In 1949, when I became a student at the University of Bonn, I immediately enjoyed being exposed again to the Rhineland dialect so familiar from my days in Ütersen.

My second memory of my time in the RAD is the *Spatenkult*, the "cult of the spade." Naturally, immediately upon arrival we were issued uniforms. But instead of the navy-blue tunics, trousers, and caps of my Marinehelfer tour, or the gray-green later in the infantry, here we wore "earth-brown" uniforms. Our equipment was not a rifle, bayonet, cartridge belt, and so on; the main item was the spade. This spade had to be attended to and groomed like the rifle, the "soldier's bride." Every night we sat in our rooms trying to polish our spades and, with the help of sandpaper and steel wool, give them a silvery burnish so as to pass inspection the next morning. Even the tiniest rust spot on the blade could lead to a minor explosion by the inspecting instructor. At close-order drill, at the flag ceremony, while standing guard and, of course, at work, the spade was always with us. During the manual-of-arms drills, instead of the military commands of "Left shoulder-arms," "Order-arms," "Present-arms," our instructors literally shouted *den Spaten-über, Spaten-ab, Präsentiert den-Spaten*—"Left shoulder-spades," "Order-spades," "Present-spades." From a distance, and in retrospect, these commands and the whole spade cult may seem slightly bizarre, and we *Arbeitsmänner,* "Workmen," our official rank, made private jokes about some of these spade exercises. But just as the swastika was the symbol for the party, the Iron Cross the symbol for the armed forces, and the victory rune the symbol for the DJ, the spade was the symbol for the Reich labor service, and we accepted it as part of the new order. Besides, we did not have a choice.

In the middle of December I returned home from RAD camp. My parents and my sister were glad that at least the four of us could enjoy the Christmas holiday together, since my two brothers were doing their war service far away from us. My second brother had not been heard from in months. We could only hope that the reason for this was the general retreat of the Wehrmacht from northern Russia, which had severely interrupted all mail service.

This time I was not waiting impatiently for my notification from the army, as I had done three months earlier. I was looking forward to spending Christmas at home, and my classmates and friends were in the same situation. We were, of course, very anxious to find out where our next orders would take us. I had volunteered, as was customary in our class at the time, partly out of idealism and partly because that way I could select the branch of the armed forces I wanted to serve in. Navy and air force were out of the question for me because I was nearsighted and wore glasses, and with this handicap combat service would be most unlikely. The *Fronterlebnis*, "combat experience," for which we had trained for years and had inwardly prepared ourselves for so long was what the boys of my age were then craving. To be shunted aside in some rear depot or supply office in the navy or the air force was outside the realm of possibility. At the preliminary physical examination I had put down "army" on the questionnaire in the category "preferred branch." I had briefly been interviewed by two young officers who had asked me whether I had a special request as to the subbranch of the army. Without hesitation I had replied "Panzergrenadiere." They exchanged a quick glance, and one of them said smilingly: "Ah, you want to be driven into the war in one of our coffins," *Aha, Sie wollen also mit den Särgen in den Krieg fahren. Särge*, "coffins," was, as I learned later, the in-house term for the armored personnel carriers in which motorized infantry units rolled almost simultaneously with the Panzers into combat. My response was a snappy *Jawohl, Herr Leutnant*. I was at this moment either not aware of the implication of the term "coffin" and of the high casualty rate of the armored infantry units or if I was it certainly did not bother me.

My friends and I discussed and speculated daily where they would send us, what branch, what garrison, what training camp. About one thing we were sure, the date. We would have to report a few days after Christmas, perhaps even after New Year's Day. Even my father, who was experienced in military affairs, shared our opinion. But it turned out differently. Even he had underestimated the rigid and soulless inflexibility of the German military bureaucracy. On December 20 my induction notice came by postcard. I had to report to the replacement battalion of the Panzergrenadier Regiment 76 in the Boehn Barracks in Hamburg-Rahlstedt. When I read the date of arrival I almost dropped the postcard. It read: "Report before or at 1600 hours on December 24, 1944." My first reaction was that it must have been a typing error, but my father only shook his head sadly and said, "Perhaps. But they never take back a date." My sister, who was employed by the German postal service as a long-distance operator, was so upset that she undertook an unusual step, and simply called the barracks of Regiment 76. That was unheard of, a civilian contacting the replacement battalion of a large active Wehrmacht unit. She managed to get through and talked to the battalion adjutant who, as she reported, was very polite but also made it unmistakably clear to her that if the draft notice said "December 24" it meant "December 24, Christmas or no Christmas." He added that the *Wehrbezirkskommando*, "military district command," did not make mistakes. Especially the last remark was sheer nonsense, but now I had no choice. On the morning of December 24, my parents and I stood once again at our small railroad station and said good-bye.

The rail connection from Brunsbüttel to Hamburg was still intact, and in the Hanseatic city itself the *S-Bahn* and *U-Bahn* tracks and tunnels had been repaired.[1] So in the early afternoon of December 24, I arrived with my little suitcase at the big gate of the Boehn Barracks. I went inside, was registered, and thus was now a real soldier,—but under what circumstances! Nobody in the huge barracks complex was prepared for new arrivals at this time on this day. Everybody was furious at me and at the tiny group of other former civilians who had to be processed. We had considerable difficulties in finding rooms and cots, in obtaining eating coupons from the kitchen, in being issued uniforms and boots in the supply depot. Everything was closed and most functionaries had already left the barracks to celebrate Christmas in private. Most certainly no one knew what to do with us for the next few days. On the other hand nobody had the courage to say: "Go home, boys. Come back on December 27 or, even better, on January 2." After the barracks gates had been closed behind us, we were part of the Wehrmacht. It made no difference that during the next few days nobody wanted us for anything, that we sat around uselessly and senselessly in the practically deserted Boehn Barracks. It was a Kafkaesque situation, as I would say today.

The Christmas holiday of 1944 was the saddest and most miserable of my whole life. On December 26, in Germany called the Second Christmas Day, there was an additional complication. Many Hamburg families had invited for dinner soldiers who could not go home to their own families. Officially, I was not allowed to leave the barracks area because I had not been sworn in. Theoretically, I could have disappeared without being legally charged for being absent without leave. The duty officer, a good-natured man who probably felt sorry for me, found a solution, although it involved a slight personal risk for him. He handed an older comrade and me the address of an elderly couple in the city who had asked for two guests. However, he instructed my companion never to let me out of his sight during the train rides, during the dinner, and the entire visit, *nicht einmal, wenn er aufs Klo will*, "not even when he wants to go to the toilet." Thus I was able to spend at least a few hours on Christmas Day in the home of kind people, although at first they were a little taken aback by my appearance and were not sure whether I was really a member of the armed forces. I must have looked rather quixotic in my patched-together uniform made up of the tunic of the old Reichswehr of the Weimar years, trousers and boots of the Serbian army, a black overcoat from the supplies of the Danish army. Only my peaked cap was regular German army issue. But on Christmas Eve and also on New Year's Eve, traditional family get-togethers in Germany, I sat in some large hall with a group of strangers who were just as depressed as I was. We listened, not very attentively, to the *Ringsendungen* of the Greater German radio network, live reports from places in Europe that were still under German occupation, and

to the pep talks by the NS propaganda minister Joseph Goebbels. We felt
very sorry for ourselves.

The Boehn Barracks was a large garrison complex in the northern part of
Hamburg, about forty minutes by S-Bahn from the center of the city. Since
the days of Emperor Wilhelm II it had been the home of the infantry regiment, later Panzergrenadier Regiment 76. The regiment proudly called itself
the *Hausregiment* of the people of Hamburg. Together with the 90th
Regiment in the Von-der-Goltz Barracks at Hamburg-Wandsbek, it formed
the 20th motorized infantry division, renamed Panzergrenadier division well
into the war. It was a very large area with many red brick buildings to house
the soldiers and their vehicles, the depots, the big barracks square, and all the
other facilities that are required for such a large unit. Today it is once again
home for a *Panzerbrigade* of the armed forces, the *Bundeswehr*, of Germany.
Once again it is called the "home brigade" of the city, as I read every now and
then in the local Hamburg newspapers. The Boehn Barracks was to be my
home for the next four months, and, in contrast to my RAD tour in Ütersen,
I have many exact and even photographic memories of these last months of
the war.

We were soldiers now. We were where we thought we belonged, and in
training we performed our duties with enthusiasm to prepare for the great
Feuerprobe, the crucial test (literally "ordeal by fire")—our first real combat
experience. In retrospect it seems to me that we lived as though we were under a large glass bell with little contact with the rest of the world. We did not
read newspapers and barely took notice of general announcements on the bulletin boards on every corridor of our billet. The only radio available was in the
mess hall, which we young recruits rarely entered except for meals. The mail
service was still functioning, but the letters from my mother, the letter writer
in our family, only contained personal and family news. She never mentioned
political or military events, which would have been blacked out by the censors
anyway. On Sunday afternoon leaves we went to the movies, to museums, or
to a bar, but we had little interest in the general military situation of the
Reich, although at this time, in the early months of 1945, it became more
and more alarming. This insular existence, of which we were not conscious at
the time, was largely voluntary and self-inflicted. Our lives, our thoughts and
feelings, our ambitions and plans for the future were, as I see it now, strangely
illusionary and removed from reality.

Two examples may illustrate this. At the end of March, no longer a recruit
but now a member of the *OB-Inspektion*,[2] I happened to run into an old acquaintance from my hometown. He had been a classmate of my sister and
thus was six years older than I. He had been seriously wounded at the beginning of the war and walked with a noticeable limp. In my Gymnasium years
I had seen him a few times when, as a member of the home guards, he was

guarding columns of Polish and Belgian prisoners of war on their way to work on farms around our town. Here now we met again in the middle of the barracks square of the Panzergrenadier Regiment 76, where he had just arrived. There were many questions. I asked him about his experiences and why he was here and no longer with the home guards. He had been transferred from unit to unit, because, despite his handicap, he could still walk and thus was considered capable of "limited combat duty." He was a real veteran who had been around.

Then he began to ask me questions, and one of them was: "Tell me, Willy, what kind of an outfit is this?" *Was für ein Haufen ist denn das hier?* "They act as though the war will go on forever." He, as an old soldier, had observed correctly. Everybody acted as though the situation was normal. The daily garrison routine continued with strict emphasis on discipline and order. All officers and noncommissioned officers had to be saluted snappily inside the barracks area and in public as well. All garrison activities, close-order drills, room inspections, weapons training, and so forth were carried out uninterruptedly. There were no signs of laxness or slackening in the Boehn Barracks, no indication of the disintegration which, as we know now, was fairly common during these last weeks of the war at the front as well as in many garrison units of the Wehrmacht. It was this ostrichlike behavior, this burying one's head in the sand, which my older friend had noticed immediately upon arrival and had identified correctly.

A second illustration of this phenomenon happened even later, sometime in April 1945. Our regiment had been fighting for nearly four years in the northern sector of the Russian front, and since 1944 had been pushed back further and further by the Red Army and was now engaged in heavy combat in the eastern suburbs of Berlin. In this street fighting the last regular commanding officer of our regiment, Colonel I., had been killed. While turning a street corner he was hit squarely in the chest by a Soviet tank grenade. Somehow his staff had managed to ship his body by truck to his home garrison, where he was to be buried with full military honors in a Hamburg cemetery. We were the military honor guard, the OB-Inspektion, since we were by far the best disciplined and uniformed unit of the replacement battalion. Thus we were called out on a Sunday morning to practice the routine of an honor guard, and it took the whole day to prepare us for the elaborate full-scale military burial. On the following day we marched together with the regimental band—it too was still intact—to the cemetery in immaculate dress uniforms. We flawlessly performed our duty upon command: *Hoch legt an-Feuer! Laden.* "Ready-Aim-Fire! Load." We gave the traditional military salute, firing three volleys across the grave of a fallen soldier in the presence of the commander's family and a large gathering of his friends and comrades. It was an impressive military spectacle in the revered tradition of the Prussian-German army. But the point in time, a few days before the end of the war, made the whole ceremony appear unreal. There was no longer a correlation between our activity and the political and military reality.

But back to the early months of 1945 when, on January 2, we were organized and became the new company of recruits of the replacement battalion. For the next ten weeks we were to undergo basic training, a large part of which was becoming familiar with our tools, the light weapons of a Panzergrenadier: rifle and pistol; the new assault rifle; hand and rifle grenades; light machine gun and light mortar; and the relatively new antitank weapon, the bazooka. We obtained regular uniforms and regular equipment and were trained by experienced instructors. Our company was unusual in that only two-thirds of it consisted of seventeen-year-olds; the other third were grown men in their thirties and even forties. They were *Volksdeutsche* who had become victims of the "Heim-ins-Reich" policy of the NS regime.[3] These ethnic Germans had been persuaded to give up their farms in southeastern Europe on the Black Sea and had been resettled at the eastern border of the Greater German Reich. Their new farms were located in what used to be Polish territory, now called "Warthegau," but their homes were in serious danger of being overrun by the advancing Red Army.[4] They were a very depressed and alienated group. They were physically much stronger than we, but they had never had any premilitary training. Their German was rusty or archaic—the language of the eighteenth century, when their ancestors had migrated and settled in the Balkans. Many of them could barely read or write, and I remember many an hour at night when some of us sat with them and wrote their dictated letters to their families. They could only hope that these letters would reach their wives and children in their new "homes." In contrast to us highly motivated and trained youngsters, they were poor soldiers. They were men who had worked hard all their lives but were now uprooted and in danger of being completely overrun by the course of history. We felt very sorry for them. I do not know what eventually became of them.

The training was physically demanding but otherwise no challenge because of our years of premilitary schooling. The only new aspect was the training with the real combat equipment of the German infantry, not with spades or French World War I weapons. We were eager learners. Our instructors, only a few years older than we, all of them wounded and with extensive combat experience, were quite satisfied with our performance. The fact that they shouted not only their commands but also their instructions did not bother us in the least. We were used to it and accepted it as part of the military milieu. With a few exceptions they were reasonable and decent men who did their best, partly, of course, because they did not want to jeopardize their safe jobs away from the front.

We were the second to last company of recruits of the Regiment 76 in World War II, and some experiences and episodes deserve to be recorded to offer some insights into and impressions of life in a German infantry garrison at this time and about the mood and attitude of the soldiers, the training routine, and the general atmosphere.

Every military bureaucracy is slow, rigid, and often not very open to innovations. One of the most glaring and most often quoted examples of this in the German army is the fact that the infantry went to war with a rifle designed and constructed in the year 1898. Nevertheless, after years of war, the army high command realized that although close-order drills, snappy in-step marching, and exact execution of manual-of-arms drill enhanced the discipline of a unit, one could not win battles that way. The officers of our regiment were especially aware of this since our unit had been engaged in combat against the Red Army for nearly four years under the most severe field conditions. Consequently, the recruit training schedule had been modified.

An example was the radical change of the last two weeks of our basic training period. Especially during night exercises we had been told again and again that the "primitive nature boys," the average Russian soldiers, were superior to us because we in Central Europe had grown up in civilized towns and cities, whereas the "culturally backward Ivan" was closer to nature and could adjust better to open-field combat conditions. There was an unmistakable tone of racial superiority (Germans over Slavs) in these remarks, but it was a common concept at the time, and we believed our instructors. Consequently, we did not spend the last two weeks as recruits in the Boehn Barracks but in a *Waldlager*, "forest camp," in Wohldorf-Ohlstedt, a heavily wooded area north of Hamburg. It was a kind of survival camp. We stayed in tiny subterranean bunkers and prepared our own food. There were no showers or other amenities of civilization. The training schedule included field exercises every night. Nevertheless we considered this camp life a welcome change from the barracks routine. We were experienced campers and felt quite at home here. We were soldiers now, but for most of us, all of this was still a game, *Krieg spielen*, "playing war," which we had practiced since childhood.

The return to the barracks was not quite the end of our recruit existence. The climax and summary of our basic training was to be four or five days spent on the huge combat training ground in Munsterlager in Lower Saxony, about a hundred kilometers south of Hamburg. The main purpose of this last part of our training was continuous practice with live ammunition under simulated combat conditions. Thus, after a short stay at the Boehn Barracks to clean up a little, we and several other units rolled south in a long freight train.

Munsterlager looked like a moonscape, but I do not remember many details. I only know that, despite our constant handling of live ammunition and grenades, we had no injuries, which was a great relief for our officers and non-coms. Our return to Hamburg, however, is one of my most vivid memories. We had been told that part of our return trip was to be done on foot. That did not bother us at all, for we were used to long marches. We counted on marching fifteen or twenty kilometers and then going the rest of the way by train. It turned out that the original announcement had been a ruse. From the beginning the plan was to cover the entire distance from the camp to the southernmost S-Bahn station, Hamburg-Harburg, on foot in one day, arriving in our home barracks around midnight—seventy-five to eighty kilometers of marching. This entire exercise was the most exhausting physical ordeal I have ever experienced. The last ten or fifteen kilometers before we got to the Harburg station were sheer torture, but nobody dropped out. All of us stayed the course, an achievement that even our instructors, who rarely praised anything, recognized.

There were two reasons for our passing this endurance test. One was adolescent pride. Dozens of times we told ourselves *Nicht schlappmachen*, "Don't quit." For eight years as children and adolescents, this motto had been hammered into our consciousness. The very term "schlappmachen" and the related "*Schlappschwanz*, "quitter, softie," had become horror words for all of us. We would rather have collapsed or fainted than to become known as a Schlappschwanz. The second reason for this amazing display of stamina of a hundred and twenty young men—our older Romanian-German comrades had been transferred to another unit—was the model performance of our company commander, Lieutenant G. He had been severely wounded when a Russian hand grenade had rolled into his foxhole and exploded. He had miraculously survived but had lost one eye and his left arm and walked with a noticeable limp. This seriously handicapped officer marched—or more accurately, hobbled—the entire distance at the head of his unit. Not even during the rest periods did he sit down; instead he walked from squad to squad to check on our condition and offer words of encouragement. It was the most outstanding display of fortitude and of the superiority of mind over matter I had ever witnessed, and it was unthinkable for any of us to give up before the CO did.

We finally reached the station and staggered into the S-Bahn cars. Though it was late and the train was only half full, we were not allowed to sit down, even though some of us looked green in the face from exhaustion and a few women offered us their seats. We were proud of our accomplishment and, when one of the women whispered to a friend standing next to me, "Well, boys, what part of the front did you come from," I felt indeed like a combat veteran. This was what real soldiering was all about, we thought. Somehow we managed to cover the last stretch from the Rahlstedt train station to the barracks, another three kilometers of marching, and we did arrive at mid-

146

night. The next morning a small miracle happened: we were allowed to sleep until nine o'clock and then were off-duty until noon. I am sure this had not happened in the Boehn Barracks on a weekday in years.

Most members of our former company of recruits were transferred immediately to the so-called *Marschbattalion*, "active replacement battalion," and were shipped east by train to strengthen our regiment, which at this time was already fighting west of the Oder River and was suffering abominable daily casualties. I do not know how many of them survived, how many were killed, wounded, or taken prisoner by the Soviet army. But about twenty-five of us were former Gymnasium students and had been given a temporary diploma, the Notabitur. Thus we were entitled and encouraged to volunteer for officers' candidate school. Most of us did so because even this late in the war we considered it a *Selbstverständlichkeit*, "matter of course," for soldiers with our educational background and years of premilitary training to choose the career of officers.

Since there was a great need for OBs, most of us were accepted, although we had to pass the OB test first. It was a mere formality, and one feature was rather bizarre. The first part simply consisted of having the prospective OB lead the platoon for an hour in close-order drill, and we could do that with our eyes closed. The second part was an oral examination in the form of an individual interview of each candidate with a group of two or three officers. In my case I was first asked by a lieutenant, probably not more than two years older than I, about my interpretation of the end of Goethe's drama *Faust*. My impromptu reply of about ten minutes evidently was satisfactory, and they switched to the next topic, proper conduct in the officers mess hall, *Kasinositten*. Among the questions I had to answer were: "When do you address a lady with '*Gnädige Frau?*' " "Is it proper to kiss a lady's hand outdoors?" "Is hand-kissing appropriate at all with an unmarried woman?" I do not remember whether I was fully aware of the lunacy of this interview at this time and under these circumstances. If my interviewers were conscious of it they certainly did not show it, for they acted as though these questions and answers were perfectly normal and proper.

Of these days of transition from recruit to OB, I have to report an episode that had tragic consequences and shows the vagaries that sometimes determined survival in the critical days at the end of the war. One of my best friends in our company was Gerd F. We had become friends quickly, partly because he and I were among the few non-Hamburg people in our unit. His home was in a town neighboring Brunsbüttel, and he was the cousin of one of my old classmates of the Gymnasium. He was intelligent and levelheaded; he did not say much, but he liked to laugh. He was an excellent athlete (soccer, gymnastics) and a very good soldier. We spent much time together.

One day, toward the end of basic training, he said casually: "Listen, Willy, I will not opt for the OB *Inspektion*. At most I want to become a noncommissioned officer. I'll apply for noncom school." I was completely taken by surprise and shocked. The noncom school was located somewhere in Saxony, which meant that we would have to separate. I remember our last evening together. We had an hour before lights-out and were sitting in the canteen. Almost the whole time I tried to persuade him to change his mind. He just shook his head and kept repeating that all of this fuss in the Inspektion would get on his nerves. He wanted to be a soldier, not a *Kasinohengst*, an "officers' mess lizard," as he phrased it. When I told him about my test interview, he laughed out loud and said: "There you have it. That's what I mean." This decision cost him his life. A few days later he said goodbye and was transferred to the noncom school, which was soon overrun by the advancing Red Army. His parents never heard from him again. Statistically, he is listed as missing in action. Nobody knows whether he was killed in combat or perished in a Soviet prisoner-of-war camp.

For the rest of us, relatively little changed in our daily existence. We remained in the Boehn Barracks and simply moved to a different building down the road. The daily training routine began again, although the days now were even longer and the training more demanding; for example, reveille was now at four-thirty instead of six in the morning. We were thrilled and proud to wear the two silver cloth stripes of the OB on our epaulettes. When we left the barracks on Sunday afternoons, we also added our regimental number, 76, although it was officially forbidden because of the secrecy obsession in the military. Thus in public, in the subway, the movie theaters, or in a café we were often identified as "76ers," especially by children who were proud of their home regiment. We thought we had reached the first rung on the ladder to the cherished rank of lieutenant.

The training schedule had not only become longer and more demanding, but much more emphasis was placed on independent action and thinking, on making decisions and later justifying them, often in writing. One of the favorite methods of our instructors was to appoint one of us as squad leader for a specific exercise or even for a whole day while they did not interfere, limiting their functions to just monitoring our performances. At one of these exercises, I had been appointed squad leader during night exercises, which were becoming more and more frequent. We had been awakened an hour after midnight, driven by truck to a place about thirty kilometers from the barracks, and dropped into the middle of nowhere. My order was to lead the squad back to the barracks by six o'clock in the morning. That sounds more difficult than it actually was. All of us had learned to be prepared for such a situation. It was forbidden to use map and compass, but I had both in my gas mask container. As soon as we were alone—the instructors this time had driven back to the barracks—I had quickly determined with the help of map and compass where we were. Thus I also knew where the nearest town with a train station was. We simply marched there, bought tickets for the earliest train to the city, and arrived in the barracks in plenty of time. The use of public transportation had not been the idea of the exercise, but since we had arrived before six o'clock, I received credit points under the rubric "Adjust, adapt, use your imagination."

While marching through open fields and small woods on the way to the station, I, as squad leader, was walking ahead of the group, rifle in my right hand and the precious map in my left. There was cloud cover—no moonlight, no stars. Only the map enabled me to find the right direction (a small flashlight was also part of my private "skeleton pack"). It was pitch dark and we could not see more than a few feet ahead. We had to cross a shallow stream, which was more like a brook and so small that it did not appear on the map. Its bank, which was about three feet high, could not be seen. Suddenly I lost my balance and stumbled and fell headfirst into the water. Any normal person would have tried to break the fall with outstretched arms and hands, but not the well-trained Panzergrenadier Schümann. For years it had been drummed into our heads to keep the rifle—the soldier's most precious possession, his "bride"—dry and clean. It had become an instinct. Thus I sailed into the brook with arms stretched backward and hit the water face first, but rifle and map remained dry. My comrades burst into laughter about Schümann's "belly-whopper" into the stream, and I too found the whole incident quite funny, although I was very wet. Years later when I began to reflect on our life in the Third Reich and about our soldier training, I remembered this little scene. It became clear to me how thorough our training had been, that this kind of brainwashing had even changed some basic self-protection instincts. My reaction in that little meadow brook was that of a modified Pavlovian dog.

Part of our daily schedule was two hours of theoretical instruction in classrooms. The topics were, among others, "Organization of the Wehrmacht" and "History of Regiment 76," but also more practical subjects like writing clear and precise field messages and even introduction to rudimentary tactics. Least popular was the one hour per week with the NS *Führungsoffizier*, a kind of political commissar. It was a position that late in the war had been forced upon the armed forces by the party. His function was to instruct us in NS ideology. But the "History of the NSDAP" or Hitler's vita had long ago ceased to interest us, certainly under the present circumstances. We were soldiers now and wanted to be nothing but soldiers. Besides, this particular officer was a young, arrogant lieutenant without any decorations. We did not take him seriously, and all of us dozed through the weekly instruction hours.

Only once did we sit up and take notice, when with his jarring voice he proclaimed: "It is the tradition of our regiment that 75 percent of the

149

Offiziersbewerber do not come back from their first combat tour." Our reaction was rather remarkable. We knew that his pompous statement was no exaggeration. After six months in the OB-Inspektion we were to be promoted to the rank of special corporal called *Fahnenjunker-Unteroffizier* and then be transferred to our combat units. It was a matter of course that, as future officers, we would have to volunteer for every dangerous mission. That and the fact that, despite our thorough training, the OBs were completely inexperienced in real combat resulted in the high casualty rates of the OB Inspektion. But here—now—we were confronted by the reality with brutal candor. We were not shocked. We just sat there, looked around quietly and tried to guess who would survive if three out of four of us were to be killed. Our lack of reaction was by no means a secret death wish, but it has to be explained as ignorance, immaturity, and youthful optimism. Besides, we thought that this situation was quite in order. As future officers we considered ourselves members of an elite group, and every elite group has to make sacrifices. That had been our ideology for years, and we thoroughly believed in it. It was simply part of the new order and of our view of life and the world. Therefore, this monstrous statement of the NS commissar did not faze us in the least.

It was now April 1945. The war in Europe was inevitably grinding to a halt, but we refused to accept this. I remember a scene which took place on April 20, Hitler's birthday. We were out on the regimental outdoor training ground and had practiced assault on fortified positions. At noon we were called together and ordered to fall in. Then came the order *Stillgestanden!* "Attention!" and the last *Tagesbefehl des Führers*, "special bulletin of the Führer," was read to us. I can still hear the voice of our *Inspektions-Kommandeur*, Captain H., who read: *Prag ist deutsch. Berlin bleibt deutsch. Wien wird wieder deutsch*, "Prague is German. Berlin will remain German. Vienna will become German again." And we believed it, at least we seventeen-year-old officer candidates did.

How is this blindness to be explained? Even I who was present and who was one of the diehard believers have difficulties today coming up with a satisfactory explanation for this incredible phenomenon, to offer a reason or a set of reasons that would be comprehensible for people who were not there, especially for non-Germans. I have been asked about this again and again in the last forty years. My answers can only be a partial explanation, but I can vouch for their validity at the time.

First, there was the aforementioned insular existence in the barracks. It was this head-in-the-sand attitude which consciously or semiconsciously made us close our eyes so as not to recognize the full extent of reality and face the consequences, although we knew approximately where the front lines were. The fact that we were members of a regiment in which strict discipline was upheld to the last day contributed to this.

The second reason was the propaganda campaign conducted by Goebbels and his ministry to the very end. Much has been written about this in the relevant literature. I can testify to its effectiveness for myself and my comrades of the same age. There was the claim that the new weapons which were being developed, or were ready to be deployed immediately, would turn the course of the war around in favor of the Reich. I remember almost verbatim the formulation in one of Goebbels's earlier speeches: "I have just returned from a weapons testing ground. I have seen weapons that did not make my heart beat faster but almost made my heartbeat stop." The message was clear. It was officially stated that the Wehrmacht had available to them instruments of war of such devastating effectiveness that the Allied forces could not match them and that they would decide the outcome of the war in our favor. It was just a question of holding out until "five minutes past twelve" and not quit "five minutes before twelve," as allegedly imperial Germany had done in November 1918. That was sheer mendacity, but officially the idea of final victory, *Endsieg*, was maintained to the very end.

We believed in the existence of secret weapons. In these last days in April 1945, the OB-Inspektion spent much of the time on the open-field training ground. It may have been the same day of the reading of the last Tagesbefehl when we were suddenly startled by an ear-splitting screech and thunderous noise that we had never heard before. It was made by two low-flying planes that roared with incredible speed across the area. They were jet planes of which we had heard rumors but had never actually seen. They were definitely German planes because the black and white markers were clearly visible on the fuselage. That was a relief, because the Luftwaffe had nearly disappeared from the sky at this time. Much more important was the psychological effect. We enthusiastically told ourselves that if we had superplanes like that then there must be other secret weapons about which so much had been written. The "new weapons" claim suddenly was very plausible indeed.

Finally, there is the third and perhaps the most important attempted explanation for our ostrichlike behavior. It was simply not possible for us to believe that the war was lost. We were psychologically not capable of accepting the reality that the nearly five-year-long gigantic effort of the German people, the millions of victims, the devastated cities should have been in vain, that all of this should result in a second and probably even harsher Treaty of Versailles. Such a vision of the future was simply beyond our imagination. We could not yet take that psychological step. A few days later Allied ground forces were approaching the city of Hamburg.

12

Every person
for himself

The order came from above, that is to say, from the commanding officer of the replacement battalion: "The OB-Inspektion has to stand ready to move out with full battle gear, weapons, and ammunition." We were, with the exception of some administrative personnel, the last intact combat unit in the huge and now empty complex of the Boehn Barracks. In the previous days and weeks all other units, including the regimental band and the lightly wounded in the convalescent company, had disappeared. They had been ordered to join hastily formed combat units and had moved to the front. I do not know how many of them actually saw action. Considering what we know today about the collapse of the Wehrmacht in the last weeks of the war, it is more than likely that most of these prospective combatants found a way to desert, to "crumble away," *sich verkrümeln,* as it was called in our slang expression at the time.

Thus there was the somewhat unreal and slightly bizarre spectacle of a company of about eighty young soldiers who, at the end of April 1945, were marching aimlessly back and forth on the huge barracks square practicing, among other things, rifle drills and close-order drills and who had endless rifle inspections. We were probably the best trained and most disciplined army unit in all of north Hamburg at the time. More importantly, we wanted to go to the front; we wanted to see combat action. For eight years we had been prepared mentally, physically, and ideologically for this moment. Now it had finally arrived, and what did we do? We were practicing "Attention!" "At ease!" "Eyes left!" "Eyes right!" "Left shoulder-arms!" "Order-arms!" and so on. We were totally frustrated, and if we had not been German soldiers there would have been mutiny.

I learned and realized much later that the personal initiative of the commanding officer of the OB-Inspektion, his foresight and his courage, had saved the lives of many of us. He knew very well what kind of mood we were in, that we finally wanted to prove that we were elite soldiers. He was aware of our impatience and our èlan. But he also knew that, in spite of our long and arduous training, we were absolutely green when it came to actual combat action. It was clear to him, although certainly not to us, that under the circumstances the last OB-Inspektion of the Panzergrenadier Regiment 76 would have been wiped out in a matter of days. Courage and idealism are not factors in combat when facing a superior enemy, in this case British and Canadian armored attack units with enormous fire power. There is no doubt in my mind that we would have given a good account of ourselves, but I am equally certain that most of us would not have survived.

Our CO, a highly decorated and experienced combat officer, knew all this, and he must have used his official connections, and perhaps some not-so-official tricks, to keep our unit as long as possible in our barracks in Hamburg-Rahlstedt, thus avoiding a last and totally senseless bloodbath. I do not know what became of Captain H., but his bold and imaginative initiative deserves to be mentioned here.

"The OB-Inspektion is ready to move out." It goes without saying that the preparations were done in a matter of hours. But then it became known that we were to move north, not south where the action was and where we thought we were needed. We could not remain in our home barracks. *Gauleiter* Koch,[1] the highest NS functionary, wanted to declare Hamburg an "open city." He also did not want to blow up the huge bridges across the Elbe River, although all preparation for demolition had been made by the combat engineers stationed in Harburg. There are many people today who think that these decisions were the only sensible orders ever issued by the Gauleiter. Because of these measures, the heavily damaged city of Hamburg was spared from becoming a battlefield with street fighting, artillery shelling, and more air raids, as was the fate of Berlin.

When I learned of the new destination of our unit, I made a quick decision. The prospect of long exhausting marches with full equipment and ammunition was so depressing to me that I went on sick call. My imaginary illness was "footsoreness," which I knew was always taken seriously in an infantry unit. I also knew that there was no time for a thorough medical examination. Thus our platoon leader simply decided to assign me to a squad that, led by a corporal, was to stay behind and guard the regimental supply and ammunition train sitting in the big freight yard at Hamburg-Barmbek. I reported to my new squad leader there. Our main unit moved out and later got as far as the Schleswig area, some ninety kilometers north of Hamburg. On May 8, 1945, they became prisoners of war like hundreds of thousands of German soldiers in the province of Schleswig-Holstein, and then were discharged in July and August, as was I.

But for the time being I had achieved what I wanted: I was allowed to remain in Hamburg. Our duties were light—rather, they did not exist. We reported every morning at eight o'clock to our squad leader "to see whether the train was still there," as we joked among ourselves, received our food rations for the day, and then each of us was on his own. We visited friends and acquaintances, went to the movies, or just took long walks, always trying to catch the latest news on the radio about the position of the Allied forces and how far they had advanced in their drive toward Hamburg. We were still hoping that their advance could be stopped somehow, although there was no serious battle action anymore in Lower Saxony, the province south of Hamburg. But that was hidden from the population in the last bulletins issued by the high command of the armed forces.

Then came the day, April 30, 1945. Several members of our squad and I and our corporal happened to be in a boxcar of our train and had access to a radio when we heard the special news bulletin of the *Grossdeutscher Rundfunk*, the official state radio corporation: "The Führer and Chancellor of the Greater German Reich has fallen today leading an assault unit against the Soviet army in the city of Berlin." After this bulletin all stations played funeral music by Beethoven and Chopin. Today we know, of course, that this was one more official lie of the government. The Führer had not been killed in action but had committed suicide in his safe bunker ten meters below the streets of Berlin while hundreds of young soldiers, many of whom were of my generation and younger, paid with their lives to protect him in his last hours.

I have often been asked in later years what our reaction to this news was. After all, our world was collapsing with the death of our idol, a world whose values and splendid future achievements we had believed in to the very end. I have often tried to reconstruct our feelings, sentiments, and mood on that day. Neither in our small squad, nor in the streets, nor with our acquaintances did I observe any emotional outbursts of despair, any tears, any nervous collapses. There prevailed a general numbness among the population which now affected us young soldiers also. It was a natural reaction to the enormous tension and stress of the previous few months which had brought us one crisis after the other. An even more important and plausible explanation is that for every one of us the most essential activity at this point was simply to survive. We were no longer part of the Volksgemeinschaft, the national community; we no longer felt that we were members of an organization like the army or any other group, as we had been indoctrinated so effectively to believe for ten or more years. From then on we only acted and reacted as individuals. *Sauve qui peut*, "Every person for himself," suddenly became the slogan of the day. It certainly was the motivation for our small group of train guards. This survival at any price became the main impulse in the following weeks, months, and years for all Germans. There had been an abundance of altruistic and

Der Führer gefallen

Führerhauptquartier, 1. Mai 1945

Der Führer Adolf Hitler ist heute nachmittag auf seinem Befehlsstand in der Reichskanzlei, bis zum letzten Atemzuge gegen den Bolschewismus kämpfend, für Deutschland gefallen.

The headline "The Führer has fallen" was one of the last mendacious announcements of the NS propaganda machine concerning Hitler. In reality, he had committed suicide in the relative safety of his bunker.

idealistic slogans in the Third Reich—*Gemeinnutz geht vor Eigennutz*, "the public weal comes first," *Du bist nichts, Dein Volk ist Alles*, "you are nothing, your nation is everything"—but all of this was discarded in this moment of crisis. All we wanted to do was stay alive.

This was certainly true for our squad at the freight depot in Hamburg-Barmbek. Our squad leader was a mature, experienced, and highly decorated NCO (EK I, Purple Heart, Bronze Combat Badge) for whom we had the greatest respect. He called us together for the last time and said in his relaxed manner with his soft Hessian dialect: "That's it, boys. The war is over. Nobody needs ammunition anymore. I'm going home. Good luck." In this most unceremonious manner, the squad was dissolved, the last unit in Hamburg of the once-famous Regiment 76. In spite of our young age and our lack of experience we were smart enough to know that even in these chaotic days we would be risking our lives to walk around the city without valid identification papers. Some military police units were still patrolling the streets. Their first order would be, "Your ID papers." The consequences of being identified as a deserter could have been fatal. All of us remembered the horrible pictures of hanged German soldiers on the eastern front with signs around their necks reading, "I am a coward." Therefore, I asked our corporal to make an entry in my ID papers to the effect that our squad had been officially disbanded. He was very willing to do so and wrote with pencil: "This is to certify that Panzergrenadier Willy Schümann has been discharged on April 30, 1945, from a special unit of the OB-Inspektion of the

155

Panzergrenadier Regiment 76. Name. Corporal." This was a friendly and humane gesture on his part, but he knew and I did too that it was totally useless because he had no official stamp. But I probably thought "better than nothing." I saluted him for the last time and departed.

My closest friend in Hamburg was Gerda S., a good friend of my older sister. She came from our hometown and was working as a telephone operator in the postal service. I had visited her a number of times at her place, not with any romantic hopes—she was six years older than I and thus out of my league—but to escape the barracks milieu, to relax and be a civilian for a few hours. Gerda lived in a small attractive apartment on the Rothenbaumchaussee close to the center of Hamburg. She was exceptionally hospitable and always had something good to eat—(her parents had a small farm near Brunsbüttel). I remember one evening in February or March when we were having supper, and I was enjoying myself just sitting on a regular chair eating at a table with a tablecloth, and chatting about mutual friends in our hometown. This idyll was suddenly interrupted when the doorbell rang, and a sergeant in infantry uniform stood in the door. He was an old friend of Gerda's from Brunsbüttel who was just passing through Hamburg and came to pay her a short visit. I was enormously impressed by his decorations, among them two tank destruction badges, which indicated that he had destroyed two Soviet tanks in combat. This situation could have become awkward, but he soon realized that I was no competition for him with the attractive Gerda. The three of us spent a pleasant evening together, although I never knew whether I should address him as "Herr Feldwebel," "Sergeant" or just "Peter." Around midnight Gerda prepared her couch for me to sleep on—I had an overnight pass—and the two older ones disappeared into the bedroom.

So she was the friend I went to see on April 30. The Rothenbaumchaussee had been one of the grand boulevards of Hamburg with many trees, wide sidewalks, good restaurants and stores, and many expensive private homes. I took the train to the Dammtor railroad station—some subway lines were still functioning—and then had to walk for about twenty-five minutes along the Rothenbaumchaussee to get to her house. Streetcars had stopped running days or weeks before.

On my way I had to pass the Hotel-Pension Impala located not far from the railroad station. It would take the flight of fancy of a science fiction writer to imagine that eighteen years later the former Panzergrenadier Schümann would live for a year in this building as an American citizen and professor at Smith College, but that is exactly what happened. In 1963–64 I spent a year as director of the Smith College junior-year program at the University of Hamburg. My duties were to guide a group of young American students who had enrolled in the university to learn German and to introduce them to the academic life at a German university and to German society in general. The former Hotel Impala had been purchased by the foundation *Weltweite Wissenschaft*, affiliated with Hamburg University, and it served now as the *Gästehaus* of the university. In the fall of 1963 I was one of the first "foreign" visitors in the renovated building.

On this day in April 1945, however, I marched down the street past the Impala to see my friend, to ask for advice, and perhaps to borrow some civilian clothes, if possible. The Rothenbaumchaussee had lost much of its former luster. To be sure, it had been spared the monstrous fire storm of July 1943, but many houses on both sides of the street lay in ruins. In many cases the rubble of the destroyed buildings had not been cleared away.

I arrived at Gerda's house late that morning. She was still asleep since she had worked the night shift in her office. But when I rang her doorbell and identified myself, she was immediately wide awake. When she heard about my predicament, she jumped out of bed and began to look through her closet and drawers for some fitting clothes. She found some ski pants, a shirt, and a dark jacket, which might be considered a piece of men's clothing. Everything was a little short and tight, but they might do as a disguise in this emergency situation. Nevertheless, after some deliberation we came to the conclusion that it was too risky for me to play the role of civilian noncombatant without any valid identification papers and wait for the arrival of the enemy. We both thought it would be better for me to go where I felt I belonged,—Brunsbüttel. Grateful for everything she had done for me, I said good-bye to my friend. It was not until years later that I saw her again. She was married then and was a frequent guest in my sister's house, and we celebrated a spectacular reunion.

Once more I took the train back to our boxcar in Barmbek to pick up my few belongings and, more importantly, to attend to a very special matter. I wanted to arm myself. Of course we all had our rifles and plenty of ammunition, but carrying a rifle on my journey northwest was too awkward, too visible, and not advisable in general. What I thought I needed was a pistol, preferably an officer's side arm, caliber 7.65 mm, which I could easily carry and conceal in the side pocket of my uniform jacket. Even the heavier and bulkier Luger would have been welcome. For days rumors had circulated in Hamburg that prisoners of war—Poles, Belgians, Frenchmen, and Italians— had broken out of their camps and, together with the many displaced persons, were ravaging the countryside in Schleswig-Holstein, plundering farms and taking revenge for the injustices of the past.

Two of my comrades were still at the freight yard because they could not decide what to do next. The three of us searched all of the cars that we were able to open. They contained enough weapons, gear, and ammunition to equip whole infantry companies: rifles, machine guns, mortars, landmines, hand grenades, and ammunition in abundance, but no pistols. For two years we had become used to having weapons with us at all times. It seemed too risky to start out on our uncertain and potentially life-threatening journeys under such unstable and chaotic circumstances without being armed in some fashion. Therefore we opened a box of hand grenades, and each of us took five of these projectiles, including fuses and fuse cords. They were not the unwieldy "potato mashers," the well-known stick grenades, but the smaller egg-shaped grenades—we actually called them *Eierhandgranaten*, "egg hand grenades"—which fit nicely in our knapsacks. I am sure we had only the vaguest notion of situations in which these grenades actually could become useful. Very unceremoniously we tossed our rifles into a corner of the boxcar, and each of us went his own way.

Nothing, it seems to me, symbolizes better the collapse of all soldierly values than this careless abandonment of our rifles. For years it had been hammered into our consciousness that the rifle was our best friend, that it was absolutely essential for survival, that it had to be cared for constantly, that it had to be kept in superb working order by cleaning and oiling it for hours every day, that we had to take it apart and reassemble it literally with our eyes closed. Rifle inspection had been a daily routine as common as brushing our teeth. Now, without giving it a second thought, we nonchalantly left our "brides" behind and departed. My worldly possessions at that point were my uniform and my knapsack, in it half a loaf of bread, a piece of sausage, a pair of socks, and five hand grenades.

The first stretch of my journey was easily covered. In addition to the subway trains, some of the suburban trains were still running, in irregular intervals to be sure, but they were running. I was lucky and had enough savvy to get on one of the hopelessly overcrowded trains—standing room only—which took me to Elmshorn, about twenty kilometers closer to my destination. At the Elmshorn railroad station I was forced to join the gigantic column of soldiers that was moving away from Hamburg, now an "open city," in a north-western direction into Schleswig-Holstein, the last German province not yet occupied by Allied forces. I had a definite destination, but the great majority of my comrades acted as irrationally as refugees of all countries at such times do. Their motivation was to get away from the enemy; put as much distance between themselves and the threatening unknown; remain as long as possible with familiar people, one's own people. It seems that in such situations simple physical movement—marching, driving, or being driven—is preferable to gloomy, lethargic resignation and just waiting.

Thus I was marching after all, just like my old unit, the OB-Inspektion, but I was alone and did not have to carry any arms and equipment. "Alone," however, is a relative term, because on the road I was one of tens of thousands of soldiers wearing the uniforms of all colors of all the branches of the Wehrmacht. Many moving vehicles were part of this column, from heavy trucks to bicycles and pushcarts. Once or twice one of the truck drivers gave me a ride. They had, as was customary in these last months of the war, a soldier sitting on the left fender. He was the lookout, and his task was essential, for at any moment, within seconds and without warning, Allied fighter planes could appear strafing the column. A new slang word had been coined for this lookout; *Lucki-Lucki*, after the English word "to look." A truck without a Lucki-Lucki was a suicide vehicle. As soon as the lookout began hammering on the fender, the truck braked sharply, and drivers and passengers disappeared with lightning speed into the ditches.

At one point we passed a place where only minutes before the strafing planes had caught several vehicles and destroyed them. The sight of the dead and wounded, who were just then being cared for by medics, was sobering enough for me to jump off the truck and rely again on my own legs and my own hearing and power of observation, not on those of a Lucki-Lucki. Thus I myself could hear the roar of the approaching planes and, since they were always enemy planes—the German air force had ceased to exist—I would quickly seek cover in the closest ditches or bushes.

After hours spent in this manner, I found myself close to the town of Itzehoe. More than half the distance was done. I was tired, and my legs and feet were sore. To be sure, I was a trained foot soldier, and we had learned to march long distances according to the famous Tempo 90 (Prussian general staff officers in the nineteenth century had determined that an infantry soldier became least tired by doing forty-five double steps per minute and thus could cover the greatest distance), but it had been a long day.

Not far from the road I saw a woman's bicycle leaning against a hedge. The girl or woman had carelessly not locked it. I quickly looked around; nobody seemed to pay attention. I got on the bicycle and pedaled away. Now I knew that I would get home before the end of the day. It is characteristic of the time and the moral disintegration that I felt only relief at this point. I had no guilty feelings about stealing even though I had been brought up in a very middle-class family in which theft was considered a criminal offense. Sauve qui peut. Even my parents protested only mildly when I told them later under what circumstances I had acquired the bicycle. On the other hand, nobody in our family was very upset when a few months later this same bike was stolen from our backyard.

I covered the last twenty-five kilometers from Itzehoe to Brunsbüttel in less than two hours. The huge column of soldiers and vehicles had diminished to a trickle because Brunsbüttel is located somewhat off the main road. Shortly before reaching my hometown, there was a sight that struck me as especially absurd and incongruous under the circumstances. Some desk warrior or NS functionary had ordered foxholes to be dug at the town periphery to be occupied by the *Volkssturm*, the last reserves.[2] There I saw fourteen- and fifteen-year-olds and old men in these primitive foxholes, most of them in

159

civilian clothes, only with the white Volkssturm arm band for identification. They were equipped with French World War I rifles for which they probably did not even have enough ammunition. This pathetic handful of "soldiers" was to stop British tank columns. Several times somebody shouted to me, "Where are the Tommies?" And I could see the relief on their faces when I replied, "Don't worry. They are still south of Hamburg." Fortunately, an encounter between such unequal forces never took place. The old men and the children of the Volkssturm probably "crumbled away" shortly thereafter, like the rest of the once so formidable Wehrmacht.

The last obstacle of my odyssey of this day was the Kiel Canal. Since my parents lived on the north side of Brunsbüttel, one could get there only via the big locks or by ferry (a bridge was not to be built until thirty years later). The canal locks, as a high priority military target, were still heavily guarded, and it was out of the question for me to use them. I had either heard or knew by instinct that military roadblocks had been set up at the ferry landings. Thus I approached the ferry ramps very cautiously. This was my hometown, after all, and I knew every street and street corner. I was right! From afar I could see bright metal disks blinking in the sunlight. They were the badges of the feared *Kettenhunde*, the "chained dogs," in soldier slang, the military policemen. They wore large and heavy metal shields on chains around their necks to identify them as MPs, a two-hundred-year-old tradition going back to the army of Frederick the Great. Suddenly the knowledge of my stampless identification papers weighed heavily on my mind. From a distance I observed the busy scene at the ferry ramps for some time, and I soon noticed that the Kettenhunde paid much closer attention to vehicles than to individual soldiers. I waited until there were several heavy trucks lined up by the ferry gates to be inspected. While the MPs were checking the papers of every vehicle, I simply pedaled past the inspection site on the other side of the trucks and got safely on the ferry. Once again my luck held out. Nobody had noticed me. We crossed the canal and ten minutes later I was home. I can still hear the joyful outcry of my mother, who happened to be gardening in our yard. "Willy is back!" For weeks my family had no knowledge of my whereabouts because the postal service had become very irregular. Now at least their youngest son was home safely.

After some happy confusion and many questions and answers, my mother said in her typically practical manner: "You must be hungry. Let's go into the kitchen. I'll fix you something to eat." In the kitchen I finally took off my knapsack and emptied it, and there on the kitchen table of my very civilian mother lay five hand grenades. This moment has become part of our family lore and was to be told and retold many times in later years.

My mother was a very typical German Hausfrau who knew a great deal about running a household and bringing up children, but she knew next to nothing about military weapons and ammunition. She showed this splendid ignorance by at first not reacting at all to the sight of the five dark green metal objects which, even to me, seemed totally incongruous and out of place among the pots and pans and plates and cups of our kitchen table. At that moment my sister's fiancé entered the room. He was a combat officer in a parachute unit, had been wounded on the eastern front, and had illegally extended his medical furlough to wait at home for the end of the war. He immediately spotted the war utensils on the table and asked. "Willy, where are the fuses?" I calmed him down by assuring him that they were not in the grenades but in the side pocket of my uniform tunic. There was no danger of blowing up our apartment. But now my mother became quite excited. She wanted "those things" out of the house at once. Thus my first activity after returning to my parents' house was, together with my father and future brother-in-law, to dig a deep hole in our backyard and bury "those things." I am sure that the remnants are still there.

My father had served for almost six years before and during the First World War in the Imperial Navy. He knew the military and especially the long arm of the military bureaucracy, and he insisted that I report immediately to the nearest assembly point, a school building a few blocks down the road, for stragglers of the Wehrmacht. I had to agree with him. The word "deserter" still had a dangerous and sinister ring for us at that time. Thus I was not able to spend my first night at home in my own familiar bed, but had to sleep on a straw mattress on the floor of a former classroom. Early the next morning, however, I went back home anyway, since at this so-called assembly post nobody seemed to be interested in us. Nobody registered us. It was all part of the general chaos.

A few days later my two older brothers arrived. Hans had been the first mate on a German merchant vessel and had participated in the last large-scale operation of the German navy, the evacuation of thousands of refugees from East Prussia to Denmark and north Germany. Rudi had served in the ground crews on a German airfield near Leningrad. He had been transferred to an air force infantry unit and had been wounded in combat near Danzig. Both of them had made their way home under much more adventurous circumstances than my own, although both of them had better—that is, "safer"—papers than my brother-in-law and I.

A small miracle had happened. All members of our family were home by the end of the war. Our house had been spared by the bombing raids. There were not too many families in Germany at the time for whom this was true. My mother was not a particularly religious person, but, I am sure, she said many a prayer of thanks to God in those days.

I did, however, become a real prisoner of war a few days later under circumstances that were very undramatic, quite humane, and slightly funny. It was the first Sunday after the general armistice had been declared in the European theater of war. We were having supper at the family table in our dining room when the doorbell rang. My father got up to answer it. He opened the door and was confronted by a British military patrol—a sergeant, two privates, and a German lieutenant who served as interpreter. From the dining room we could hear the question: *Sind deutsche Soldaten im Haus?* "Are there German soldiers in the house?" My father's reply, spoken in his beloved Low German, has also become part of our family history: *Jo, veer Stück. Nu koom Se man rin*, "Yes, four of them. Why don't you come in?" All four of us—my two brothers, my brother-in-law, and I—wore civilian clothes, our Sunday best, of course. The British soldiers wore light-brown khaki uniforms. It was the first time that I got a good, close-up look at our former enemies. All of us were well aware of the strange and unusual fact that this first face-to-face encounter took place in my mother's kitchen and not on the battlefield.

The formalities were quickly taken care of. Our names were entered on a list, and we had to hand over our identification papers. Nobody seemed to be interested in the fact that my brother-in-law and I had no valid discharge stamp. We were instructed to report at 0800 the next morning at the closest assembly point, a soccer field just around the corner from our house. Ten minutes later the patrol left, and we returned to our supper table. That is the saga of my being taken a prisoner of war. It was two days after my birthday; I had just turned eighteen.

13
The bad
years

The next morning I reported as ordered at the assembly location, and we "prisoners" were driven by trucks to the prison camp. But this term is misleading. At the place where we were dropped off, there were no tents or barracks, no watchtowers, guards, or barbed wire, all of which are usually associated with this term. We were simply ordered to get off the trucks at one of the farms surrounding our town. The farmer, Herr S., had been ordered to make his largest barn available for the housing of about sixty to seventy soldiers. This rather unusual conversion of an ordinary farm to a prison camp by the Allied military authorities was justified. During the last weeks of the war hundreds of thousands of German soldiers had fled into the northwest corner of the Reich to the last unoccupied province, Schleswig-Holstein. Now the entire area of the province north of the Kiel Canal and south of the Danish border was declared a restricted area, *Sperrgebiet*. It was one huge prison camp. Within the demarcation lines the population, including the soldiers, could move around with relative freedom, although during the first weeks and months certain restrictions were enforced; for example, curfew was set at nine o'clock at night. It meant that after dark no German civilians or soldiers were allowed to be outside their homes or camps.

This designation of half of the province as a restricted but relatively open area was no risk for the Allied authorities. The Third Reich had ceased to exist and with it the once powerful and all-intrusive Wehrmacht. I know of no one who ever thought of, let alone talked about, rendering active resistance as hidden snipers, for example, or through acts of sabotage. As military units we were totally demoralized and ineffective. The defeat was absolute and complete. Not at the time, nor in later years, was there even the slightest attempt made by anyone to create a new Dolchstosslegende. Instead of the NSDAP and the Wehrmacht and their many suborganizations, there were now only thousands of individuals trying to adapt to the new situation in order to survive. It was necessary to maintain a certain degree of discipline to prevent total chaos, such as wholesale looting and plundering. Therefore, in each "camp" (farms, schools, youth hostels, hotels) a *Lagerältester* was appointed as a kind of camp speaker.

We on Herr S's farm had the misfortune of having as camp leader an army captain who was a caricature of what an officer should be. He was the proverbial desk warrior. This man tried to treat us as though we still were a regular garrison company. In addition to the daily roll call, he literally wanted to conduct close-order drills, uniform inspection, and even regular checking of our sleeping area, *Bettenappell*. The latter was especially nonsensical because we did not have any beds; we slept in the barn on piles of straw, which for reasons of hygiene and health we kept reasonably clean anyway.

I was one of the youngest in this mixed and motley unit, and one day I was involved in a minor altercation. One morning we lined up for inspection, and the captain slowly moved from soldier to soldier criticizing almost everyone. One man had not shaved closely enough; the next one's uniform jacket had a button missing; a third had not polished his boots. After a while this whole bizarre and silly spectacle seemed so incredibly out of place to me that I burst out in a loud and audible tone of voice: *So ein Quatsch!* "What rubbish! He hasn't noticed that the war is over." Our officer whirled around, glared at me, and screamed: "You, an OB of all people, are undermining the unit's discipline. Your punishment is three days in a military jail," *drei Tage verschärften Arrest.* This struck me as so funny under the circumstances that I laughed out loud, infuriating him even more. He was indeed ready to put me in a pigsty or a toolshed, either of which were to serve as improvised jail cells. But then I got some help. Two of our noncoms, both of them decorated sergeants with years of combat experience—the captain had never been close to real combat—knew me. Gustav N. and Otto C. were classmates and friends of my older siblings. Both of them were reasonable and level-headed men, and after the inspection was over they simply approached the superdisciplinarian and made clear to him that his methods of maintaining order and discipline at this time and under these circumstances were passé, inappropriate, and quite counterproductive. The captain surprisingly yielded to the arguments of the serious and experienced soldiers who, because of their achievements, were men with real authority, and my sentence was revoked. Thus I did not have to serve my three days of *verschärften Arrest.* Without my friends' intervention, however, my career as an officer in the German army would have ended in a Schleswig-Holstein pigpen. After we all had been discharged, every time Gustav N., Otto C., and I met again at a soccer game or in our local dance hall, we liked to recall this mad episode of June 1945.

How did we spend the next few weeks and months? Some of the group were asked by Herr S. to help with the farm work. He urgently needed workers on his fields and in the stables because the Belgian and Polish prisoners of war who had been assigned to him during the war were not there anymore. He rewarded our work with good food, meat, eggs, butter, and cheese, and therefore there always were enough volunteers. Most of us, however, sat around the whole day and played cards. I have a very vivid memory of these endless Skat games which were indicative of our boredom. But the general mood was remarkably good, all things considered. The older comrades, the real veterans especially, were relieved to be in a rather idyllic and safe place where there was no more shooting, where no life-threatening attack airplanes would suddenly appear, where no sudden reassignment to a hot spot at the front was imminent. The worst aspect of our captivity was the lack of food. We received only a few slices of bread per day, almost never any meat or cheese. We lived mainly on a tasteless soup of cabbage and beans, of which there was an abundant supply on the farm. We were constantly hungry. But we soon found a remedy for this misery.

It became apparent to us very quickly that neither the British nor what was left of any German authorities exercised any control over our presence on the farm in the daytime. The crazy captain had for some reason disappeared after a few weeks. Therefore, since we were located not far from our hometown, a routine developed: after the usual roll call in the morning, we simply got on our bicycles, which a family member had delivered to the farm, pedaled home, slipped into our civilian clothes, and spent the day with our families. Every evening the reverse procedure was followed. We put on our uniforms and rode back to the camp. It was important not to be on the road after curfew because the British military patrols, particularly during the first weeks after the armistice, were likely to be strict and could become unpleasant. Even our non-Brunsbüttel comrades benefited from this arrangement. In addition to Gustav M., Otto C., and me, there were several other soldiers whose homes were close enough that they too could go home every day. The rest of the unit divided our very modest food rations among themselves.

The big question in these summer months of 1945 was when we would be discharged. "Discharge," *Entlassung,* now became the magic word for all of us. It was the main topic of our conversations, and a hundred latrine rumors made the rounds. For example, we heard that it was dangerous to put down "coal miner" or "metal worker" on the questionnaire in the category of job training. Examples were cited where comrades in these categories were suddenly rounded up to be transported to France or Belgium to do reparations work there in coal mines or factories. On the other hand, all jobs in food production were highly desirable. The occupation government had quickly realized that one of its most urgent tasks was to improve the food supply situation in order to prevent catastrophic shortages and large-scale starvation. The soldiers who in civilian life had been farmers or farm workers could count on being among the first to be discharged. My brother Rudi, for example, who was a trained electrician, wrote down "fisherman" as his vocation, although he had never been on a fishing smack and could not distinguish between the upper and lower end of a fishing net. He got away with it, though, and obtained his precious discharge papers months earlier than most of us. As a student, I was at the bottom of the priority list, since all schools and universities were closed. My friends and protectors were in the same boat. Gustav N. was a music teacher and Otto C.'s family owned a furniture store, certainly not high priority categories. But in the middle of August 1945 it was finally our turn.

We were to be driven by truck to the discharge camp. At the assembly point an incident occurred which at that time shocked me considerably. There were not enough vehicles available, so some of our group had to stay behind and wait for the next transport convoy, which probably arrived a few days later. We were already on our trucks when suddenly a naval officer in the group of those rejected ran up to the British officer in charge. I knew him; he was the father of one of my classmates in elementary school. He was crying and kept repeating: "Please, take me along. Don't leave me behind. Please! Please!" The Englishman just turned away without a word of reply, but I can still see his expression of disgust about this undignified spectacle. I was very much ashamed having to witness this lack of self-control and decorum by an officer of the once so-proud German navy.

The discharge camp was a huge improvised installation in Bad Segeberg not far from Lübeck. There we were to be processed within three or four days, which meant filling out the inevitable questionnaires and undergoing a rather cursory medical examination. But most of the time was spent waiting, which was nothing new to us, according to the old, rhymed army saying: *Die Hälfte seines Lebens Wartet der Soldat vergebens*, "A soldier spends half of his life waiting for nothing." There were no barracks or tents. We slept in a field enclosed with barbed wire. Since it was summertime, this inconvenience did not bother us very much.

I have two clear memories of our short stay in Bad Segeberg. The first is of a kind of interrogation, one on one, by a man in a British uniform who spoke fluent German with a slight Berlin accent, obviously a German emigrant. He was polite but very cool and distant. It was my first encounter with a member of the large group of German emigrants; in the following decades I was to meet many others. The whole interview lasted about five minutes. He wanted to know about my Hitler Youth years, my service in the armed forces, the number of our regiment, and my rank. Since I was only eighteen years old, there was not much to check and to report. They were looking for much larger fish.

The second memory is of us prisoners lining up and removing our jackets and shirts. Then in single file with our left arms raised we had to pass a small group of British officers. The reason for this did not become clear to me until later. They were looking for members of the *Waffen-SS*.[1] All soldiers of this elite organization had their blood type not only marked on their identification tags but also tattooed in their armpits. During the war this had been a prudent measure, taken to prevent mistakes during a blood transfusion. Now it was used to identify all members of the SS, which was to be declared a criminal organization, and these soldiers were to be isolated in special camps. I remember a small group of them sitting in one corner of the camp surrounded by extra guards. They seemed to be very depressed and full of apprehension about their future. But most of us were "clean," and we finally received our discharge papers, which consisted of just a single six-by-four-inch slip of poor-quality paper. Since it was properly signed and stamped, however, it was enormously important for every one of us. I still have this document.

We were driven back on British army trucks not to our respective hometowns but to the relevant county seat. For us it meant Meldorf, a town about twenty-five kilometers distant from Brunsbüttel. Since the whole public transportation system had collapsed—no buses or trains were running—it meant a substantial hike for us from Meldorf to Brunsbüttel. There were approximately fifteen to twenty Brunsbüttelers on our truck, and some of the old soldiers for whom improvisation had become second nature had an idea. They said to me: "Listen, Willy. You have had many years of English in school. Sit with the English drivers, make friends with the Tommies, and offer them two hundred cigarettes if from Meldorf they do not return directly to Segeberg, but go by way of Brunsbüttel. It's hardly any detour." Here was my first real chance to use my knowledge of English, to understand and speak the language in a practical situation.

It failed miserably. After seven years of school English, I was not able to communicate on the simplest level. I lacked all practical vocabulary, such as "do a favor," "detour," "hometown," and a hundred other words. The speech of the drivers was just an incomprehensible torrent of words. They might just as well have spoken Greek. I understood nothing. Upon our arrival at the Meldorf town square, I had to admit the failure of my mission to my comrades. They did not hold it against me. Within ten minutes, using sign language and a few English words and by showing them a carton of cigarettes, they had persuaded the two young Englishmen to make their return trip by way of Brunsbüttel. This pathetic shortcoming of my communicative skill in a foreign language gave me considerable food for thought, among other things, about the methods of language teaching at that time. We were able to read Shakespeare's *Julius Caesar* in the original, but I could not barter for a ride. An hour later we arrived in Brunsbüttel, and I was once again a legitimate civilian.

In our family and in our neighborhood some drastic changes began taking place in the summer, fall, and winter of 1945 and 1946. Our household was growing in numbers. Several close relatives fled the Soviet-occupied zone and appeared on our doorstep one day, including my sister-in-law and my two nieces, one of whom I had never seen. My sister had recently married, and the newlyweds also moved in with us. There were too many people in our medium-sized apartment with six rooms, but with good will and talent for improvisation everybody found a place to sleep, though privacy was in short supply during the next few years. The food situation had not become critical. That was yet to come.

For my mother especially, there began now a period of extreme hardship. She was responsible for a household that sometimes consisted of as many as thirteen people, and she faced up to this task with a certain innate stoicism and considerable courage. There were crises and some inevitable tensions, but on the whole she managed to see us through these difficult years and hold the family together in admirable fashion. Her life had not been easy up to then, not on account of her own doing but because of political and historical circumstances. In many ways her life was typical of her generation. She was born in 1896. As an adolescent she had experienced the First World War and had lost two brothers, and the sudden death of her father from heart failure meant the loss of the family fortune. As a young wife and mother she had to cope with the devastating consequences of the 1923 inflation. Then came the Third Reich and the Second World War, during which her very life was threatened by bombing raids; she experienced rationing for the second time, and she was constantly worried about the well-being of her sons. And now came "the bad years," *die schlechten Jahre,* from 1945 to 1948.

Despite all this, my mother was very much aware of the fact that she was much better off than millions of other women in Germany. My parents had lost none of their children, and they had not been bombed out of their home. They were grateful for this, and my mother sometimes said so. But the deterioration of the living conditions and the deprivation of the next few years— the extreme housing crisis, the shortage of all foodstuffs and absence of all consumer goods, the black market, the second total collapse of the currency in twenty-five years—made extreme demands on her. It is no wonder that during the last years of her life (she died in 1969) I noticed in her a certain fatalistic view of life which certainly was not atypical for the German women of her generation and background.

Our family's greatest worry in the summer and early fall of 1945 was the very real possibility of being forcibly removed from our apartment. The British occupation forces had, as was the case in all four zones, selected the towns' and cities' most attractive homes and apartments in which to house their troops. Since in our town the civil servants' quarters were among the better living areas, a number of our closest friends and neighbors were ordered by the occupation forces to vacate their homes within twenty-four hours. We helped these unfortunate people as much as we could by moving some of their furniture and providing storage space. It was bitter for them and for all of us, but refusal to move or even active resistance was out of the question.

This pervasive feeling of bitterness and anger was intensified by a coincidental factor. In our neighborhood, parts of a British tank unit were garrisoned, and the Tommies simply drove their vehicles into the front yards and parked them right at our front doors. For decades the gardens of tended flower beds, clipped hedges, and carefully manicured lawns had been the pride and showpieces of their owners. Now all this was simply crushed under heavy steel tank tracks. The expression *vae victis*, "woe to the vanquished," was illustrated to us every day. At that time, and under the circumstances of the fall of 1945, very few people faced up to the question that today's observers would ask immediately—namely, how did all this happen? To what extent were the German people themselves responsible for the fact that British tanks were parked in the front yards of the German middle class? Most certainly we young Germans were at the time far from willing to find answers to these questions.

Our attitude toward the Allied occupation soldiers can easily be summarized with one word: distance. It was not hard to maintain distance, since on the other side there existed the order of nonfraternization that, at least in the beginning, was strictly enforced. In general the conduct of the British soldiers was correct. There were no humiliating incidents like the ones our neighbor Frau D. recalled from the days of the Ruhr occupation by French troops in 1923.[2] As a young woman she had witnessed German civilians being forced off the sidewalks when they encountered French officers, and she had often told us about it. We did not have any similar experiences, but our attitude vis-à-vis our former enemies was neither friendly nor respectful. How often I heard the derisive phrase, and thought and expressed it myself, *Und die haben den Krieg gewonnen?* ("and they won the war?") when we heard of or saw examples of lack of discipline and general sloppy behavior among the occupiers.

One night around midnight, a small group of us were on our way home from a party—curfew had been lifted by then—and we passed a hotel that served as headquarters for the British regional commander. There was a sentry by the main entrance. The soldier was obviously bored and had leaned his rifle against the wall, lit a cigarette, and tried to flirt with any passing girls or young women. We were genuinely shocked by this unmilitary behavior and for days discussed it. These discussions inevitably led to the question of what it takes to win a war, and it was a minor revelation to us that strict adherence to the discipline we were used to did not seem to be a prerequisite. We were still unreconstructed soldiers in civilian clothes. For us eighteen- and nineteen-year-olds especially, it took years to change our attitude concerning the military and arrive at a more normal, reasonable, civilian, and civil position.

Another remembrance of these first postwar months is of the early fall of 1945. The first movie theaters reopened at that time and offered their programs. Almost all of the films were British. One Sunday night two friends and I went to the movie house. Before the main feature, a newsreel was shown, and we saw for the first time the horrendous scenes of the liberation of the Bergen-Belsen concentration camp. We saw the piles of corpses which, for sanitary reasons, had to be buried quickly by military bulldozers; the skeleton-like survivors staring apathetically at the camera; the piles of cut-off human hair; and all the other unspeakable scenes the liberators found and which have been shown since then in innumerable documentary programs about the Third Reich. Our reaction? We sat there silently, hardly shocked at all, and observed the horror scenes in a detached manner. We did not believe them. We were of the unanimous opinion that all of these were simulated scenes. After the film was over we talked about what we had seen. Then, and also in similar later discussions, everybody declared with absolute conviction that for twelve years we had been fed one-sided NS propaganda; now the Allies come and use similar methods. I also remember one remark that was constantly repeated in these discussions, and I used it myself: *Deutsche können das nicht gemacht haben,* "Germans could not have done this."

Once again it took years before the full truth sank in, was recognized by us, and became part of our historical consciousness. The Holocaust—the word in the modern sense had not yet come into use—was not a reality at that time. We had served a criminal regime. The awareness of that spread only very slowly, perhaps because the crimes were so monstrous that it was quite beyond our comprehension at the time and surpassed all dimension of human understanding.

In the fall of 1945, in November, the first of the Nuremberg trials opened; the International Military Tribunal began its hearings in Nürnberg, the *Stadt der Reichsparteitage,* the city of the NS party rallies.[3] We followed the proceedings of these trials with some interest. Our main sources of information were the radio and, to a lesser degree, the newsreels in the movie theaters. Newspapers and magazines had not really begun to appear. When we did discuss the trials, our attitude was one of uncertainty and ambiguity. Hitler, Goebbels, and Himmler were dead, and we were quite sure of that despite many lingering rumors that, for example, the Führer had managed to escape

The arrival of a group of Jews at an extermination camp. The yellow star with the word "Jude" can be seen on each person. Courtesy of the Bundesarchiv Koblenz.

by submarine and had been seen in Argentina, in the Near East, and other places of refuge in the world. In the newsreels we saw the former high-ranking members of the NS government and of the party who were still living—Göring, von Ribbentrop, Hess, and others—minus their flashy uniforms and looking old. We heard their familiar voices as they sat day after day for many months on the defendants' benches while their lawyers tried to defend them and, finally, when they rose and spoke in their own defense. It was very difficult for us to identify these very ordinary looking men as the same people who had for years dazzled us with their celebrity, their glamor, their ever-present large retinues, and their effective rhetoric.

This was especially true for Hermann Göring, former Reichsmarschall, commander in chief of the German air force, Reich air minister, prime minister of Prussia, Reich minister of the hunt, president of the Reichstag[4] to name only the most important of his many duties. He had been by far the most popular figure among the high-ranking members of the regime, and there was still a residue of this popularity despite the miserable failure of his

The first Nuremberg trial, 1945–46. The most prominent defendants were (from left) Hermann Göring and Rudolf Hess. Courtesy of the Bundesarchiv Koblenz.

Luftwaffe to protect the German cities. We were not surprised when he and some of his codefendants were sentenced to death, but we felt a certain gloating joy when he outfoxed the tribunal by committing suicide, thus denying the victors the satisfaction of seeing one of the most powerful men of the Third Reich hang.

For many of us young people this first of several trials of the International Military Tribunal was not much more than a show trial staged by the winners. Despite our relatively aloof stance, we sometimes did discuss them, and I remember two main reservations about the trials that were brought up in our debates. One was based on strictly juridical grounds and, despite our lack of any legal knowledge, impressed us as quite convincing: new laws cannot be made post-factum to fit a particular crime. To do so was taking an untenable legal position. We were also highly skeptical of the fact that judges and prosecutors were provided by the same party. If, we argued, it could be proven that Göring, von Ribbentrop, Hess, Speer, Dönitz, von Schirach, and other prominent representatives of the Third Reich participated in or actively supported mass murder, they should be judged and sentenced according to the existing German penal code, the *Strafgesetzbuch*. And "crime against peace"? We had learned enough history to know that wars of aggression had occurred since the Stone Age.

Our second argument that may explain our detached attitude vis-à-vis the Nuremberg trials concerned the participation of the Soviet Union. We were at the time, of course, still infected by the vicious anti-Soviet NS propaganda. Although we were beginning to realize how one-sided, exaggerated, and often mendacious the propaganda had been, there were historical facts that could not simply be explained away as products of Goebbels's imagination: the mass execution of four thousand Polish officers at Katyn; the Soviet invasion of Finland; the millions of victims of the enforced collectivization of Russian agriculture; the many show trials of Stalin's regime. Nevertheless Soviet judges and prosecutors actively participated in the proceedings at Nuremberg, which for us meant that hangmen were made judges, and thus the trials became a farce.

Today, more than forty years later, after having read extensively about the Nuremberg trials, I recognize many valid reasons which caused the Allied governments and especially the United States and the British public to insist on punishing the NS leaders in this way. But I also realize that some of our arguments against them, immaturely presented and crudely formulated, are still being used today in the ongoing debates in legal circles about their validity.

Today there exists an abundance of descriptions, narrations, memoirs, and analyses of the general situation of the destroyed Reich, as well as the serious literature which soon was to be apostrophized as *Trümmerliteratur*, "rubble literature."[5] It would be redundant to report in detail about the life in the four occupation zones—about the lack of all consumer goods, especially of food and fuel; the total collapse of the transportation system; the grim situation in the devastated cities; the various waves of refugees who had been expelled from the eastern provinces, East Prussia, Farther Pomerania, Silesia, and the Sudetenland, and who had to be absorbed; the success or failure of the so-called denazification; the dismantling policy; the black market; the cigarette currency. All this was later, and even today, simply called by the population die schlechten Jahre. But a few remarks about the general mood of the people during these "bad years" are appropriate here, particularly how we very young people—the eighteen-, nineteen-, and twenty-year-olds—thought, felt, and coped.

Our entire philosophy of life and our political ideology had collapsed. Our contemporary idols had fallen. They were already dead, or they sat on the defendants' benches waiting to be sentenced for having committed horrendous crimes. All manifestations of the Third Reich and all memories of it were to be eradicated, thus prompting the ban on almost all films and on many books produced during the previous twelve years, the removal of all NS symbols, and the renaming of streets and squares. Even the brown-yellow uniforms of the NSDAP and the gray-green and air-force blue of the Wehrmacht had to be redyed, so for years large parts of the population walked around in dark blue, dark brown, or black jackets and trousers.

I remember vividly a very strong and comprehensive feeling of fear and uncertainty with all people in my family and in my circle of friends and acquaintances concerning the future. Questions like *Was wird werden?* "What is to come?" "What will the next few years and the future in general have in store for us?" were asked a thousand times. And the people were afraid. This general fear and uncertainty prevailed on two levels, the national and the individual. Everybody asked what a future Germany would look like, or even more elementary, would there be a future Germany. The Morgenthau Plan, named after the U.S. treasury secretary, Henry Morgenthau, Sr., the abstruse idea to transform a modern industrial country into a pastoral dairy land that had briefly been approved by Roosevelt and Churchill, was well known. During the last months of the war it had been presented to us as a deterrent and as a motivational factor to strengthen the willingness of the people to hold out until "five minutes past twelve." Would that plan now be implemented? What would be the consequences? Nobody could imagine that in a few years there would be two separate Germanys, certainly not we young people.

The second component of this prevalent feeling of fear and uncertainty concerned our individual futures, our professional and career plans for the next few years. At first we had none. After a bearable summer and early fall of 1945, the daily food rations were reduced to eight hundred calories per person, which was below subsistence level. There was no coal or firewood available to heat the homes and apartments. It meant that all Germans began the daily struggle for survival, and this struggle was to last for the next three years, until the currency reform of June 1948. Survival was possible only through barter and the black market. Thus we funneled much of our energy and effort into these daily survival activities. In our household we had the advantage that it consisted of a relatively large number of adults, and most of us had, during the war, gathered considerable experience in improvisation. All contributed their special talents and connections, *Beziehungen*, so that at least one room and the kitchen could be heated and, even more importantly, so that for the noon and evening meals my mother could put something edible on the table, usually a vegetable soup consisting of cabbage, beans, and a few potatoes to satisfy the worst hunger. Another great advantage was the fact that we lived in an agricultural area where it was easy to obtain from the farmers a sack of beans, potatoes, or flour in exchange for other goods like tobacco products and discarded children's clothes. For the people in the big cities, these years were much harder than they were for us.

In our large family there grew a feeling of togetherness which we had never before felt so strongly, and it is among my best memories of these years. I know from many conversations with friends and acquaintances, and also from literature, that these altruistic sentiments were prevalent in many other families as well, so much so that some people today think of the "bad years" as the "better years," a time when people cared for one another. Thus even these bitter postwar years are, for some people, gilded by nostalgic memories, especially when compared with the allegedly unabashed egotism and hedonism of the following decades of the 1960s, 1970s, and 1980s.

There were two seemingly insignificant episodes that illustrate some aspects of our family's everyday life at the time. We had been fortunate in being able to rent a few large pieces of garden land in various parts of the town in order to plant vegetables and potatoes. On a Saturday afternoon my second brother and my brother-in-law were busy working on one of our fields turning the soil with spades to prepare it for planting. It was a warm day, the work was hard, and they had taken off their jackets and shirts. Both of them were fairly tall, over six feet, and were rather emaciated. Nobody in those days had a weight problem. For passersby it must have looked as though their bodies consisted only of skin and bones. Among the people walking by was a group of three or four British soldiers. They stopped for a moment and observed the two farm workers. Then they put something on the edge of the field, waved briefly, and walked on. They did not speak because the nonfraternization order had not been lifted. Even if they had, it would have been useless since my family members did not understand English. What the Tommies had left as presents for their former enemies, both of whom, although unknown to the Englishmen, had been combat soldiers, were their box lunches. Obviously, the two young Germans appeared so starved to them that they spontaneously made this small humane gesture. It is characteristic that my brother and brother-in-law did not immediately wolf down the precious sandwiches, but brought them home so that all of us could share. This little gesture made an enormous, positive impression on all of us, even on my father, who was not an Anglophile, and it has become part of our family lore.

The other incident has also become family history. It must have been on a weekend—Saturday or Sunday, because my brothers and my brother-in-law who had returned to their old jobs were not at work but at home—that the four of us were keeping my mother company in the kitchen. Two of us were helping her with the dishes after the main midday meal, and we were all chatting. Suddenly a dinner plate slipped out of my mother's hands, dropped to the floor, and broke, and she exclaimed with some annoyance, *Oh, Scheisse,* "Oh, shit." She then asked one of us to get a broom from the closet to remove the pieces. We four young men looked at each other and were quite taken aback by this outburst of our otherwise proper mother. We laughed, of course, because the situation was comical. We were not only amused but also shocked. As long as we could remember our mother had been the embodiment of many middle-class virtues, of good behavior, proper manners, and most certainly clean language. To hear coming from her mouth this mildly vulgar expletive was so incongruous that it had the double effect of amusement and shock on us. And we knew the reason for it. In this little scene it suddenly became clear to us that we had brought home from our time in the military a language that was, to say the least, quite inappropriate for a bourgeois household. My brother-in-law had spent six years in a military milieu, my older brother five, my second brother four, and I two. Without really being aware of it, we had acquired a camp-and-barracks language, which now came to the fore in the vocabulary of my mother, who most probably had never in her life used such words and expressions. We did not like that at all. At the next occasion when the four of us were together and my mother was not present, the incident came up immediately. My older brother formulated it quite succinctly: "This won't do. Let's clean up our language." And we did. It was one more tiny step in our journey back to civilian life.

14
The need
to catch up

Jn late winter and early spring of 1946, all schools reopened. We of the Jahrgänge 1926 and 1927 had been awarded the Notabitur, the temporary diploma that theoretically entitled us to matriculate at a university. But actually we had attended the Gymnasium for only seven years, and there had been many interruptions. Therefore the school authorities and the universities recommended strongly that we go back to school and make up for the lost twelfth grade, thus acquiring a "real" Abitur diploma, officially called *Zeugnis der Reife*, "certificate of maturity."

The decision to return to the Gymnasium was not a hard one to make for my parents and me. In the first place, we knew very well that my preparation for serious studies at the university had been fragmentary because of external circumstances. Secondly, there was such a rush on the universities, which, just like the rest of the schools, were in the process of reopening at this time, that long waiting periods of up to several years for the younger applicants were common. After all, there were to be admitted the survivors of six or seven Jahrgänge, who had been decimated in the war but were still numerous enough to overload the capacities of the existing universities. (New universities were not founded until much later.) Thus, long waiting periods were inevitable. Almost immediately a point system was introduced. All applicants were given a number of points considering age, length of military service, nature of service-connected injuries, and the like. Soon points were also awarded for manual labor in helping to rebuild the many demolished university buildings. Only after obtaining a certain number of points could one count on being admitted for matriculation.

For these reasons it was almost a matter of course for me to return to my old school and complete my Gymnasium education there. The pleasant aspect about it was that since military auxiliary hospitals were no longer needed our regular school buildings were available again. In general, however, the external circumstances were abominable and not conducive to learning and teaching. Just getting to school, for example, was very difficult and sometimes adventurous for us commuting students. Often we had to rely on hitchhiking, and there were awkward detours and long delays. We had almost no textbooks, since the ones we had last used in 1944 were *verboten* because they were NS infected. Our teachers tried to make do with pre-1933 books, if they were available, or with laboriously typed texts, though there was also a shortage of typing paper. Teachers and students often had to rely on lecturing, reading out loud, and taking notes, for which, again, there was no paper. There are many reports of students in these days writing their homework on newspaper margins or wrapping paper, when available. Doing our homework for an average of five to six hours per day presented other problems. Consumption of electricity was, like everything else, strictly rationed. During the winter months there were frequent blackouts from five o'clock to eleven o'clock at night, the peak consumption periods. It meant that many times I had to get up at three o'clock in the morning to do my homework while the electricity was on. The winter of 1946–47 was unusually severe in Northern Europe, and the fuel crisis became so acute that most schools had to close for what came to be called the *Kohleferien*, "coal vacation." Only for us twelfth graders, since we were only a few months from our Abitur examinations, was a single room in the main building heated with an iron stove, and all of our school activities took place in this room.

We were a class of about twenty young men and women, most of us born in 1926, 1927, and 1928, but a few belonged to the Jahrgänge 1924 and 1925. Many of our older schoolmates had been killed in the war. There was one class, Jahrgang 1923, of which out of the fifteen or sixteen original male members only three had returned from the war; of the three, two had been seriously wounded. In our new class several of the students also had been injured, and the most seriously injured was our class speaker, Herbert N., who had crashed as a fighter pilot and lost a leg.

Despite the differences in age and the apparent variety of experiences there soon developed a good and relatively harmonious class spirit. Our first class discussions and especially our recess conversations were vivid and incessant. One aspect is very clear in my memory. After the initial informational questions of "How did you get home? What happened to Fritz M. or Hans W.?" we rarely talked about our experiences of the previous two or three years, the combat veterans least of all. But this silence must not be misunderstood. The war and the NS years were not taboo subjects. None of us had reached the point in our thinking at which *Kollektivschuld* and *Kollektivscham*, "collective guilt" and "collective shame," over the crimes of the Hitler years had become relevant to us.[1] These emotions were to haunt us all, young and old, through the coming years. It was simply that at this point in our lives we quickly lost interest in these topics because everyone had their own personal experiences which were basically similar and often almost identical.

Of our former teachers, some had not returned from the war. A few had been declared *belastet*, "incriminated," by the denazification panels and were not (yet) allowed to teach again. Some of the teachers were new, refugees from East Prussia and Silesia, but the majority of them were familiar to us. They had been our mentors, and we had last seen them in the summer of 1944. I was fortunate that my strong subjects, German and English, were taught by our familiar Miss J. Our popular history teacher, Herr W., soon returned from prison camp, and he was our instructor in the subject during this last year. The professional task they and their colleagues were facing was new, unheard of, difficult, and a real challenge even for dedicated peda-gogues. With a few exceptions, they courageously and imaginatively met the challenge. One of their main tasks was to make up for all the subjects, areas of knowledge, and intellectual approaches in our curriculum that had been neglected or totally omitted during the war. They continuously had to fill gaps that were all too apparent to all of us, and thus our curriculum looked rather checkered. In our German class, for instance, we read, discussed, and interpreted works from some of the high points of German literature, the High Middle Ages (about A.D. 1200) and the *Goethezeit*, the decades before and after 1800—the Enlightenment, Sturm und Drang, German classicism, and romanticism. Works of the nineteenth century, especially the latter half of it, the so-called poetic realism, and some poetry of the twentieth century, that of Rilke, were also part of our improvised reading list.

Several questions immediately arise in the mind of a present-day observer: How was the literature that had been forbidden in the Third Reich covered? Was the exile literature—that is, works of authors who had fled Hitler's Germany—known? Was the new, very contemporary postwar literature rec-ognized at all? As to the question of *verbotene Literatur*, we now were per-mitted to read Lessing's play *Nathan der Weise*, hitherto *unerwünscht*, "undesirable," because of its message of religious tolerance characteristic of the Age of Reason and also because of the Jewish protagonist. We became acquainted with some of Heinrich Heine's poetry, which had completely been excluded from all NS anthologies. We also read one or two novellas by Thomas Mann and some modern poems by Annette Kolb.[2] I cannot join the chorus of accusatory attacks on the entire German teaching profession launched in the 1950s and 1960s both in Germany itself and abroad. The core of this collective criticism was that the teachers in Germany after 1945 de-liberately excluded any discussion and treatment in general of the Hitler years, that the Third Reich was passed over in silence, mostly by never quite "getting to the NS years" in their courses on literature, general history, art, and music, by stopping well before 1933 or even before 1914. The main reason given by these critics was that so many teachers who had served the regime with enthusiasm did not want to be reminded of their own guilt and sins. Undoubtedly, this was true for some, but in my own experience many of them, and certainly the best among them, did not shirk their moral responsibility. They responded well to this challenge as conscientious and professional pedagogues.

As for the exile literature, I am sure that most of the representative literary works written from 1933 to 1945 outside the Reich were still unknown to our teachers in these early months and years after the war had ended. I am certain, for example, that they were unfamiliar with Bertolt Brecht's best plays like *Mutter Courage und ihre Kinder* (1941), *Der gute Mensch von Sezuan* (1943), or *Leben des Galilei* (1943). The same was true for Anna Seghers's *Das siebte Kreuz* (1942), for Hermann Hesse's *Das Glasperlenspiel* (1943), and for many other novels, novellas, plays, and poems of writers in exile which have since become classics of world literature.[3]

As far as the new postwar literature was concerned, it had barely begun to become known and stir a wider reading public. We graduated in the spring of 1947, but most of the best-known and successful works of the new literature were published after that date. Carl Zuckmayer's stage sensation *Des Teufels General*, with its main conflict of "serve the regime or actively resist it," had its German premiere in November 1947. Wolfgang Borchert's radio play and then stage drama *Draussen vor der Tür*, with the soldier coming home from the war who, literally and metaphorically, finds no home anywhere, was also produced in the late fall of 1947. Heinrich Böll, the 1972 Nobel Prize winner, published his first short novel in 1949 and his first collection of short stories, *Wanderer, kommst du nach Spa*, in 1950. I read them for the first time only after I had been in the United States for several years. Böll at that time, 1953, was heralded in a lecture at Columbia University as "The New Voice of Germany." I also did not read the first poems of Paul Celan until 1952, when his second volume of poetry, *Mohn und Gedächtnis*, containing the poem *Todesfuge*, was published. Even today it is for me the most powerful and harrowing poetic formulation of the topic of the Germans and the Holocaust.

In our history class our instructor, Herr W., was faced with the same problems as our German literature teacher. He had to fill large gaps. Whole epochs of world history and also specifically of German history had before hardly been covered either because of time constraints or for reasons of ideological selectivity. I remember, for example, our very sporadic knowledge of the effects of the Reformation and the Counter-Reformation and of the essence and the spirit of the baroque age. On the other hand, periods like Prussia's rise to *Grossmacht*, big power status, the Napoleonic wars, or the founding of the Second Reich had in the past been presented in such a distorted and one-sided manner that Herr W. often had to do Herculean work to at least lay the foundation of an acceptable objective understanding of the dynamics of historical forces and events. He was just the right person for this. He had not been a member of the NSDAP. As a student he had sympathized with one of the moderate political parties of the Weimar Republic. After the war he became one of the founding members of the newly created center party, the Christian Democratic Party (CDU), in our school town and was for years its county chairman. One of his favorite subjects in class was the Weimar Republic (1919–33), its origins, the flourishing years, and its downfall, and he lucidly analyzed the reasons for its short duration. The very nature of the subject often led him to lecturing and discussing the NSDAP, Hitler, and the Reich's domestic and foreign policy. Our teacher's presentations were for all of us the first elements of an entirely new understanding of and approach to history: for example, what dictatorship in general entailed and the Hitler party-state in particular. For us these history lessons became real eye-openers and formed at the very least the rudiments of our understanding of the essence of a participatory democracy. Nobody, I believe, can reproach a scholar and teacher like Herr W. for not yet being able at that time to offer a thorough, valid, and comprehensive portrait of the Third Reich, its total moral depravity, and its inherent ethical nihilism. Not even he, nor most Germans of his generation, had then, a few months after the collapse of the Hitler regime, the necessary inner distance, the general historical overview, the personal objectivity, or even the concrete factual knowledge to do that. But the idealism of Herr W. and the best among his colleagues and their dedication to their very difficult task were exemplary.

We spent many hours not only in our classroom but also in our teachers' private homes. We read plays with assigned parts, recited poems, viewed reproductions of paintings and sculptures previously designated as *entartete Kunst,* "decadent art." Above all we talked, asked questions, expressed our views, and articulated our concerns. In retrospect it seems to me that we learned almost as much in these semiprivate sessions as in our regular classroom lessons. Historical, literary, and artistic topics were dominant in these meetings, which were extraordinarily lively and intense.

What specifically were these topics? It is almost more fruitful to answer the question "Which subjects did we not discuss?" The scope was enormous: Prussia's role in the history of Germany; which nations were mainly responsible for the two wars; cultural egalitarianism and elitism (Ortega y Gasset's *The Revolt of the Masses* was one of our favorite books); abstract *versus* objective art; the question of "decadent" art; dictatorship and democracy; the new ecumenism, the rapprochement of the Christian churches. There were innumerable topics of a very broad and comprehensive nature. We also became excited in our discussions about such specific and current subjects as the Nuremberg trials and the existence of concentration camps during the Hitler years; we talked about serious films we had just seen and about certain measures of the military government—for example, the dismantling of German industry and its motivation, the Treaty of Versailles and its causal connection with the rise of the NSDAP in the 1920s, the war and why we had lost.

Naturally, very individual and personal questions and problems were aired, our future professional goals, university studies, which careers were open to us, and much, much more. They were unforgettable hours and most valuable to us, in part because there were always one or two mature and experienced teachers present who would moderate and steer our often extreme and abstruse opinions and views in a more reasonable, comprehensible, and objective direction. At the same time, they could in this informal manner convey to us more concrete knowledge in their various fields of expertise, which we happily accepted. For all of us there existed an intellectual *Nachholbedarf,* "need to catch up," which is almost incomprehensible for present-day observers. We were, without really being aware of it, intellectually and culturally starved.

Since all of us had grown up in small towns, most of us had never seen a legitimate theater performance. Therefore, two of our teachers organized a theater excursion to the nearest large city, Hamburg, where the theaters had just opened in their first postwar season. Our whole class participated. By using "connections" and black market means (gasoline), an old truck was rented and we were off to the big city. Since we wanted to see two plays, an overnight stay in the destroyed city was necessary and lodging had to be secured. For two of my classmates and me it meant that we had to sleep in a hotel room where the window panes had not yet been replaced. It was February, and the temperature outside and inside was below zero. We ate in a *Volksküche,* a soup kitchen, and mostly lived on the sandwiches we had brought along. But we gladly suffered these inconveniences, and it was worth it. We saw outstanding productions of Goethe's *Torquato Tasso* and Shakespeare's *The Tempest* with celebrated actors and actresses in the main roles. They were unforgettable theater experiences and provided us for weeks afterward with subjects for discussion and critique.

April 1947 was the date of our big event, the Abitur examination, which with its written and oral parts lasted about a week. Most members of our class passed and we were now faced with the question of "What next?" Only two of our classmates were able to begin their university studies immediately in the summer semester of 1947. Herbert N., because of his age and his serious war injury, was admitted at once for matriculation into the department of agriculture at the University of Kiel. My childhood friend, Helmut D., had decided to study theology and was also admitted to Kiel University, since the school of theology, in contrast to most other departments at that time, had openings for first-year students. The rest of us had to wait.

I was now most anxious to become a university student and, despite the minimal chances for success, had applied for matriculation at several universities. The University of Göttingen invited me to come for a short admissions interview and a brief written examination, but the final decision was negative, as expected, because I had not nearly enough admission points. My disappointment was alleviated by the fact that I was encouraged to participate in their *Akademischer Kursus* in the summer semester of 1947. It was an ad hoc program set up for prospective students for whom there were not yet any openings. By offering us this option, they assured us that we were entitled to admission as regular students, but because of shortage of space we would have to wait one or two semesters before we could matriculate. In modern parlance, we were "wait-listed," and we simply called the Akademischer Kursus our *Vorsemester,* "presemester."

In early May I left for Göttingen with great expectations. I was not yet a real *studiosus philosophiae,* but at least I had been allowed to enter the vestibule of the academy, the alma mater. The general living conditions were most trying: traveling in overcrowded trains which often were several hours late, only semisuccessfully finding lodging. After days of looking and ringing doorbells, an elderly lady, a pastor's widow, out of sheer compassion allowed me to sleep on the couch in her living room. The most critical part was the food situation. Fortunately, it was almost summertime and once in a while one could obtain some fruit or vegetables. With the help of a few small packages from home, I made it through the three months of the summer semester in fairly good condition and with no damage to my health. Two years after the war people were still scrambling to obtain the minimum means of survival, above all food and fuel. Rebuilding of the destroyed country was proceeding only very slowly. The *Wirtschaftswunder,* the economic miracle in the three western occupation zones often praised and admired in later years, had not yet begun.

The course offering of the Vorsemester was outstanding. Some of the best and best-known professors had volunteered to teach in the Akademischer Kursus. For example, Nicolai Hartmann read philosophy, Wolfgang Wittram modern history, Hermann Heimpel medieval history. The latter even made himself available for a Saturday afternoon excursion, a long hike into the scenic surrounding hills of Göttingen, and he made it a point to talk with every one of us, which impressed us greatly since we were not even regular students. Two years later Hermann Heimpel was one of the most frequently mentioned candidates for the office of president of the newly founded Federal Republic of Germany that ultimately, in September 1949, was won by his colleague, fellow professor Theodor Heuss.

We studied hard and for long hours because we wanted to learn, and nobody knew better than we and our teachers how much we still had to make up for. I remember a little scene in Professor Heimpel's class. He sometimes tried to break up the strict lecture format, which was customary at the time, by asking questions leading often to real discussions. On this occasion he was speaking about certain aspects of biblical writing, and he casually asked who the first prophet in the Old Testament was, looking without much expectation into the audience. But one of my fellow students raised his hand and gave the correct answer, Amos. Professor Heimpel applauded with delighted surprise and without sarcasm and said: "Bravo. Your educational preparation seems to be not nearly as fragmentary as some people would have us believe."

We spent much time in the seminar libraries,[4] since absolutely no new books could be purchased, and when we tried to obtain a volume from the general university library, the card almost always came back with the notation: "Not available until three [four, five] months from today." At the end of the semester final examinations were given in each class, and I passed all of them with good marks. Nevertheless, my application for admission to the winter semester 1947–48 was rejected again for the same reason as before: not enough points. I was advised, however, to participate in a second Akademischer Kursus, which would considerably improve my chances for matriculation in the summer of 1948.

After discussing it with my parents and after consulting my former Gymnasium teachers, I decided to follow the advice of the Göttingen University authorities and enroll in a second Vorsemester. In October I returned to Göttingen, but it very soon became apparent that this decision had been a mistake. I had overestimated my physical and psychological strength and resilience. My lodging in the summer semester had been only temporary, and the only place I could find to stay was on the floor of a tiny attic room that was occupied by an acquaintance from the summer semester. Much more critical, however, was the food situation. The food in the *Mensa*, the university cafeteria, deteriorated rapidly and soon consisted only of the daily, watery spinach soup. What foodstuffs were available on ration coupons were totally insufficient, especially for a single person without cooking facilities. I had no connections to the black market in the city and had nothing to barter with anyway. The rare packages from my mother did not help much either, and I had to entertain the idea of giving up, even though it appeared at the time that it would mean the end of my academic career. I saw no way of making it through the four months of the winter semester. I tried to hold out for five or six weeks, but then I began to notice that I was unable to concentrate on my lectures and my reading and writing. My mind wandered more and more to the subject of obtaining something to eat. I felt that I had failed, that this giving up was a kind of a capitulation, an escape back to the secure haven of my family. But under the circumstances, I could not think of any other solution. At the end of November I packed my suitcase and returned home. My parents were, of course, happy to see me, but the concerns and worries about my professional future and career plans overshadowed our good mood the following winter and spring of 1947–48. They were depressing and unhappy months.

It was my father who urged me to review and revise my ambitious plans for an academic career and to consider other options. After some deliberation, I decided to become an elementary schoolteacher. The training period was much shorter and at that time was not university connected. Future teachers were educated at the *Pädagogische Hochschulen* (PH), "pedagogical academies," and admission to these institutions was considerably easier to obtain than to the universities. In preparation for this new career, I contacted the principal of my former grade school, with whom I had always had a good personal relationship, which now became a real friendship. Wilhelm W. was a World War I veteran and had served as a naval officer in World War II. He had not been a member of the NSDAP and had been appointed *Rektor* of the Volksschule immediately after its reopening.[5] He proposed that I join his staff as a kind of teaching assistant without salary in preparation for my entrance into the PH. I was grateful to my older friend and accepted his suggestion eagerly. Thus I went back to my former grammar school from eight to one o'clock every day, audited various classes, was occasionally asked to conduct a class myself, and relieved the real teachers of many of the chores connected with their jobs. In the spring of 1948 I applied for admission to the PH Flensburg and was asked to report for an entrance examination, which I passed with high marks; thus, I could count on beginning in the fall of 1948 as a first semester student at the Pädagogische Hochschule there. I was glad that my unstructured and slightly vagabond existence would soon be over, and I prepared myself psychologically to become a PH student in Flensburg and later to work with young children as an elementary schoolteacher.

But this was not to be. Due to several coincidental circumstances, my professional career was to take a very different direction. My friend and mentor Wilhelm W. had become extraordinarily active in the public life and civic affairs of our town. He held a number of honorary positions, among them directorship of the *Volkshochschule*. The Volkshochschule, an old, traditional institution of the pre-Hitler era, was now beginning to flourish in all cities and towns of the western occupation zones. This adult education program offered the culturally and educationally starved citizens the opportunities to improve their professional preparation, to acquire new skills, to widen their intellectual horizon, and also to make new social contacts. It is not an exaggeration to state that almost the entire cultural life of our town in these first postwar years was in some form connected with the Volkshochschule. An astounding number and variety of courses and events were offered, more than a hundred per year. They were practical courses like typing, shorthand, and technical drafting; hobby courses like creative painting, sculpturing, and pottery; general education courses like essay writing, historical surveys, music appreciation, and many others. Numerous concerts, exhibitions, and lectures were arranged and sponsored, and the *niveau* was always remarkably high. The lecturers and performers, who were experts in their respective fields, were recruited in the town or neighboring cities and offered their skills and talents for a small honorarium. Especially popular were language courses, and among them, for obvious reasons, was English. English courses on all levels were always in great demand, and often there were long waiting lists.

One day Principal W. asked me whether I felt ready to teach one of the English courses in the Volkschochschule, at least on the elementary level. I was flattered and the prospect of a small honorarium also was attractive, but I told him immediately that in the first place I had almost no pedagogical experience and, secondly, despite my eight years of school English at the Gymnasium, I still felt very insecure in the active use of the language. My dismal failure on my return trip from the discharge camp was still fresh in my memory. With a quick hand gesture he swept my reservations aside and said: "We can change that." He had been asked to nominate one of his prospective or active lecturers for a three-week workshop in Rendsburg, a small city located fifty kilometers north of us. The workshop was organized and sponsored by the British Council. In the notification letter to him it was indicated that one or two workshop participants might be offered the opportunity to visit England for a longer stay of two or three months. *So was brauchst du doch,* "That's just what you need," Principal W. said. I accepted his suggestion enthusiastically and spent three pleasant and very instructive weeks in this bilingual workshop in attractive surroundings outside Rendsburg. I made some friends there, among them one of the British lecturers, Dennis E., whom I have mentioned elsewhere in these memoirs. (He was the English lieutenant who, as a prisoner of war in North Africa, had by mistake been given gasoline instead of water to drink.) Dennis E. represented the WEA, the Workers Education Association, on the teaching staff of the Rendsburg workshop. His regular job was lecturer of history in the extra-mural department at the University of Manchester. He was mainly responsible for my being selected to spend three months in England in the fall of 1948.

This opportunity was too enticing to reject in order to begin my studies at the PH Flensburg. With the exception of two short visits to Sweden and Denmark as a child, I had never been abroad for any length of time. Thus I sent a letter to Flensburg requesting permission to postpone my entrance at the academy for a semester. In the beginning of October, I sat in a train of the military government taking me from Hamburg, by way of Hoek van Holland, Harwich, and London, to Manchester to spend three months there as a guest of the WEA at one of their residential institutes.

It was a memorable experience. In these three months I became an Anglophile and fell in love with the English language. There were five of us—two professors from Berlin and Bonn, two teachers from Hamburg and Kiel who were active in the Volkshochschulen in their respective cities, and I. I was by far the youngest in this small group. We were lodged in what was for us a luxurious villa called Holly Royde located in one of the more elegant suburbs of Manchester. It was then the property of the WEA and was used for holding two-week workshops mostly for members and former members of the British armed forces—that is to say, for people my age, almost all of whom at that time sympathized with the governing Labor Party. For us and especially for me, everything was new and exciting: the seemingly intact society with its flourishing cultural and social life; the relaxed and informal style of lectures and discussions; the shops filled with consumer goods, although there still was some rationing; the cities which, despite some visible bombing damage in Manchester, Liverpool, and London, appeared whole and functioning to us because we naturally compared them with Hamburg, Kiel, and Berlin.

We were most impressed by the open and friendly reception and hospitality shown by the many English people with whom we came in contact in our classes, visits, and excursions. After all, the five of us represented a nation with which only three years earlier the United Kingdom had been engaged in a grim struggle for life or death. This uniformly displayed friendliness and fairness toward us as individuals I find repeatedly mentioned in a diary which I kept at that time and which is still in my possession. It also shows our concern over possible manifestations of the Germanophobia we thought we would encounter frequently at this time. I did not record a single incident of openly expressed hostility toward me during the entire stay.

After six or seven weeks I experienced the linguistic "breakthrough" familiar to all language teachers and advanced language students. It occurred almost overnight. I did not hear an incomprehensible torrent of words coming from a conversation partner or a lecturer; I suddenly recognized words and whole sentences. It is a deeply satisfying experience for all language learners. I also had the exciting experience of dreaming in a different language for the first time. I made rapid progress in my English language development and especially in the active speaking of English. It went from timid and clumsy attempts at the beginning—one day I approached an unsuspecting Englishman at a bus stop, holding a cigarette in my hand, and asked him, "Have you fire, please," the literal translation of the German, *Haben Sie Feuer, bitte*—to a lecture in English which I gave with only a few notes about two and a half months later on "The Contemporary Situation in West Germany." According to Dennis E., in whose course this happened, the lecture was quite passable, and I also was able to understand and answer most of the many questions in the subsequent discussion period.

I had told Professor C. of the University of Bonn, the person closest to me in our group in Holly Royde, about my lamentable situation—namely, wanting to study at a university and not being able to be admitted. Shortly before our departure from England, he said to me: "I fully understand your situation and sympathize with you and your fellow students. If you want to apply at Bonn for the summer semester of 1949, I may be able to help you. Besides, you will be old enough by then." That, of course, was music to my ears. It was the break I had been looking for, and I immediately decided to follow up on this lead.

With many presents in my suitcase, splendid memories, and a feeling of profound gratitude to the British Council, the WEA, and all those who had made my stay in England so memorable, pleasant, and exciting, in November I went back to my hometown with a firm resolve to return to hospitable England as soon as possible and for a longer period of time. One of my first acts after I was back in Brunsbüttel was to apply for matriculation at the University of Bonn. The small miracle happened. I was admitted as a regular student for the summer semester of 1949. I was elated, to say the least, and I was very grateful to all the people who had set the chain of events in motion—my parents, my Gymnasium teachers, Principal W., my English lecturer friend Dennis E., and Professor C.—all of whom in one way or another had with their understanding, sympathy, and moral and practical support made it possible for me to reach this decisive turning point for my future career and my future life in general.

In the winter of 1948–49 I gave an oral report to the lecturers of the Volkshochschule about my stay in England. I also taught one of the evening classes in elementary English, an exciting and, at first, nerve-wrenching experience. After all, it was the first time for me to face as a teacher a group of adults who were eager to learn but who came with the most varied educational backgrounds imaginable. But the course went well. A remarkably good class spirit developed, and most importantly for me, I gained considerable self-confidence and was then more than ever convinced that I wanted to become a teacher.

15
In the
wrong army

At the end of April 1949, I set out for the third time in two years to begin my academic career, this time at the University of Bonn, in a city I had never visited. But what a difference in comparison with my first two attempts in Göttingen! Most importantly, I was now in my first semester as a fully matriculated, regular student who could legitimately select those lectures and seminars that were of interest to me. Most of them were in the fields of German literature and European history, and now also in English language and literature because of my new fascination with the English-speaking world.

Almost as important was the second factor that made my third attempt at entering academic life so much more promising: the economic miracle of West Germany had begun. In June of the previous year the currency reform had been carried out and had opened the way for the operation of the *soziale Marktwirtschaft*, the social market economy, a mildly regulated free enterprise economic policy.[1] It meant that for us and for all citizens in the western occupation zones the external circumstances of our lives began to approach normalcy. The new money, the *Deutsche Mark* (DM), was a hard currency of solid and stable value. The shops were rapidly filling up with consumer goods. Food rationing was reduced step by step. A variety of foods was becoming available. People were not starving anymore.

To be sure, there still were some difficulties and inconveniences in our everyday living. Only after considerable searching did I find a small unheated room in Poppelsdorf, a small suburb of Bonn. The main building of the university, formerly the palace of the elector archbishop of Cologne, had been badly damaged by air raids and was in the process of being rebuilt. Many books of the main library and the seminar libraries had been destroyed by fire, and there were huge gaps in their holdings. The public transportation system—streetcars and buses—was far from functioning regularly and on time, so my personal mobility became better only after I brought my bicycle from home during the second semester. But all in all, my semesters in Bonn were constructive and exciting, and I remember them with pleasure.

As to the available courses, I soon found a number of lectures and seminars that appealed to me as relevant and useful. A real advising system for new students did not exist at the time, for the slogan *akademische Freiheit*, "academic freedom,"[2] was still taken very seriously and it included absolute *Lernfreiheit*, "freedom of learning." I made rapid progress, especially in the field of English language and literature. For example, I was admitted in my second semester to an advanced English seminar *(Hauptseminar)* on English and Scottish popular ballads; at that time it was most unusual for a second-semester student to be accepted into such a high-level seminar. In German literature and in history I discovered several courses taught by highly competent and dynamic professors. In the bookstores the first newly printed books were available and could be purchased by students. Some of these acquisitions are still in my possession today. It was also a most pleasant relief that we could now buy newspapers and magazines, or read them in the periodical room of the university library.

Another exciting and enriching experience was the opportunity to go to the opera and the theater in Bonn and Cologne. Most of the time we purchased standing-room tickets on the third balcony, which, despite the location, did not diminish our enthusiasm. I met many new fellow students and became friends with some of them. A few of these close relationships have endured for forty years and are still significant friendships today. We took excursions, for instance, to the spectacular ruin of the Drachenfels castle overlooking the Rhine and to the magnificent Benedictine abbey at Maria Laach. We swam in the Rhine River, which was still possible because it was relatively unpolluted. In February we participated with amazement and enthusiasm in the Rhenish Carnival, that "most splendid party in all of Europe," as *Life* phrased it a few years later. Overall, it was an existence that to some extent could be compared to the legendary happy and carefree student life of the Wilhelmian-Victorian days of the nineteenth century.

We became interested in the new political life of the country, and Bonn was a most favorable location in which to foster our new engagement. The former British, American, and French occupation zones were transformed into the *Bundesrepublik Deutschland* (BRD), the Federal Republic of Germany (FRG). The *Grundgesetz*, the constitution of the new state, was completed in May 1949, and the first general elections for the new parliament, the *Bundestag*, were held in August of that year. The names of the new politicians became familiar: Konrad Adenauer, the first federal chancellor; Theodor Heuss, the first federal president; Kurt Schumacher, the first leader of the opposition party; Ludwig Erhard, the first economics minister and soon called

The opening ceremony of the new Parliament of the Federal Republic of Germany, the *Bundestag,* on September 15, 1949, in Bonn. Courtesy of the Bundesarchiv Koblenz.

"the father of the economic miracle." We saw and heard them often in the new Bundestag as they gave lectures and speeches at the university or at political rallies in the city, or we caught a glimpse of them passing in their black Mercedes limousines. Because Bonn had been selected to become the "provisionary" capital of the new republic, we were witnessing the rebirth of our country, or at least the western part of it.

As is often true with the younger, student generation, our sympathies were with the political Left, in our case with the Socialists, the SPD *(Sozial-demokratische Partei Deutschlands).* It required a radical shift in our political views. After all, we had grown up in a one-party state where all political left-wingers, especially members of the SPD and the KPD *(Kommunistische Partei Deutschlands)* had been maligned and persecuted as enemies of the state.

191

This profound alteration of our ideological position was relatively painless. The distance in time from the Hitler years was slowly becoming greater. It was then over four years since May 1945, the time of the collapse of the Third Reich. We had studied and learned a great deal since then. We had been exposed to objective presentations and evaluations of the events that led to the founding of the Third Reich, and we were beginning to believe in the revelations of the crimes of the regime. Even then, however, we were far from realizing the full extent of these disclosures, from accepting the monstrous aberration of the German people, who for twelve years had transferred absolute power and responsibility to a criminal regime and had supported it.

The *Vergangenheitsbewältigung*, "coping with the past," to use a slogan that became popular in the late 1950s, the 1960s, and 1970s, was a process of decades for the generation of my parents, who had been responsible for the *Irrweg*, "wrong turn," of German history, as well as for my own generation and even for the generations born after 1945. An example of the longevity of this coping process is a scholarly dispute that broke out in the mid-1980s, the *Historikerstreit*, "historians' quarrel." This had to do with the interpretation of recent German history, specifically as to what the underlying and concrete immediate causes that led to the NS dictatorship were. This controversy erupted more than four decades after the demise of the NS state. It would be unreasonable to expect us as students to have developed a similar historic awareness in the year 1950.

My love affair with the English language and my interest in the English-speaking cultures had scarcely diminished, and my desire to return to England and relive the glorious Holly Royde days was still very strong. I applied to various programs that would lead to a second visit to the United Kingdom. Once, in the summer of 1950, I almost succeeded in being admitted to one. There was a program at the time that invited hundreds of German students to England to help in bringing in the potato crop. The compensation for these *Kartoffelhelfer,* was payment of the round trip to England and a short tourist stay after the six weeks of actual labor in the potato fields. I was accepted, but because of a communication failure—I received the notification only after the program had already started—it came to naught, and I was greatly disappointed. This setback, however, was more than compensated for by a scholarship offered to me by St. Andrews University near Edinburgh for the fall semester of 1950. It was a sensational opportunity, and mentally I was already on my way to Scotland. But then I received an even more sensational letter. I had been selected as one of five from the University of Bonn to study for one year at an American university—in my case—Southern Methodist University (SMU) in Dallas, Texas. What was I to do? Edinburgh or Dallas? Scotland or Texas? Actually, however, it was not a hard decision for me to make. It was true that I did not know exactly where Dallas was located, and

I had only a vague concept of Methodism, but the idea of crossing the Atlantic Ocean and spending a whole year in the United States—on a different continent, in a country totally unknown to me—was so enticing that I accepted the American offer immediately. I spent my third semester at Bonn and the following vacation time in a state of exalted expectation and euphoria.

It is appropriate here to say a few words about the origin and the intention of this generous program which is now part of history and which not many people today remember. It was a product of the U.S. State Department, conceived and implemented in the late 1940s. We were quite officially called State Department stipendiaries, and the purpose of granting the stipends was also very openly stated: "for the reeducation of the German youth." In a way it was an offshoot of the European Recovery Program (ERP), the Marshall Plan, which had been announced in June 1947. Some farseeing people in the State Department and in Congress realized that it was not enough to pour into a devastated Europe massive economic aid and hundreds of shiploads of consumer goods and to offer financial aid. In the case of Germany, it was essential to instill a new understanding of a working democracy among the young. What better way than to bring some of them across the Atlantic in order to illustrate to them how a genuine democratic system really functions, and had done so rather successfully for nearly two hundred years! Thus a few million dollars were made available in order to invite university students, young teachers, theologians, scientists, and engineers to the United States. Many American colleges and universities were asked to offer one-year scholarships to these visitors, and the response of American higher education was most gratifying. In my future alma mater, Southern Methodist University, for example, there were in my year three of us State Department stipendiaries.

The reality of the program was that, as of 1948, every year hundreds of young German academics crossed the Atlantic and fanned out all over the country to spend two semesters at a college or a university. This generous, sensible, and, in its pragmatism, typically American program was continued for a number of years. The effectiveness and the ultimate success of the program cannot be completely measured statistically. In my own mind, however, I have no doubt that it was immensely beneficial and profitable for both countries. The political stability of the Federal Republic and the unbroken cordial and mutually supportive relationship between the United States and the new German democracy is due in no small measure to the very frequent and lively exchange of people in both countries through the many short and long programs organized and sponsored by a variety of means: official and unofficial agencies; churches and educational institutions; and, of course, private initiative. Among them the State Department scholarship program of the late forties and fifties holds a very honorable place. For the thousands of

stipendiaries it represents a high point of pragmatic and unbureaucratic thinking in the United States government.

At the end of August I set off in a train to Frankfurt, where the first brief-
ings and a preparatory workshop for our big adventure were to be held. One
of the many events during our three days in Frankfurt throws light on the positive and optimistic thinking of our hosts. One morning we spent about three
hours filling out a set of questionnaires. For all of us it was the first encounter
with multiple-choice tests. Initially, we thought that it was a final examination to determine who would actually be selected for the program. In reality
it was an attempt by an American team of sociologists and historians to determine empirically and statistically whether a one-year stay in a democratic
country could influence and, as was hoped, alter the political views of a large
group of young people who had grown up in a dictatorship. Thus it was necessary to give the same tests a year later to the same group, and that was indeed done in August 1951 in New York City. Almost all the questions related
to the fields of political science, literature, sociology, psychology, and history.
What form of government do you consider the most desirable? Which authors
of American literature appeal most to you? What should be the role of parents
in the education of children? Which events in the last one hundred years of
German history do you consider most consequential? A few of the questions
were fatuous and even silly—one of the yes-or-no questions was "Did Hitler
have any scruples?"—but I am far from ridiculing this method of obtaining
concrete data concerning the general attitude of a large test group. It was a
legitimate and imaginative experiment in the area of behavioral science, and
I am sure it yielded some useful results, although I am not aware of these
results ever having been made available to the general public.

From Frankfurt our group traveled by special train via Strassburg to Cannes
on the French Riviera, where we swam for the first time in the Mediterranean
Sea—which was too warm for us North Europeans and very salty. Close to
midnight we embarked on the ship, the old passenger liner SS *Argentina* of
the Home Lines, which was to take us to the New World through the Strait
of Gibralter, past the Azores, to Halifax, and then to New York. The thirteen-
day voyage was long and relatively strenuous because the *Argentina* was a slow
ship and the weather was miserable, which is unusual for the North Atlantic
in the summer, and the food, prepared by a Greek galley staff, was not easily
digestible for many of us. The shipboard situation was not improved by the
fact that the vessel, in addition to transporting eight hundred students, had in
its hold six hundred crates of garlic. The penetrating odor prompted us to call
the ship *der alte Knoblauchkasten,* "the old garlic bucket." When I told my
father about this later, he smiled, shook his head and said: *Een Musikdamper
mit ne Lodung Knoblauch? Dat heff ik noch nie hört,* "A passenger ship with

a cargo of garlic? Who ever heard of that?" But these small inconveniences were soon to be forgotten in our memories of our voyage to the land of unlimited opportunities.

Our arrival in the New York harbor—all of us were up at six o'clock in the morning to see the Statue of Liberty—and the following three-day stay in the city were a whirlwind of events and first impressions. The Institute of International Education (IIE), which was in charge of the everyday operation of the program, had placed many of us in the Shelton Hotel across the street from the world-famous Waldorf-Astoria. I stayed with three other students in a room on the thirtieth floor, and we were overwhelmed on our first night by the fairy-tale-like view of the Manhattan skyline after dark. There was a television set in our room, and after dropping our suitcases we immediately turned it on. The very first American TV program for us newcomers was a baseball game. We stood in front of the set and laughed about these athletes clad in, for us, strange pajama-like uniforms trying to hit a small ball with a club. The only team sports we were familiar with from home were soccer, field handball, and field hockey, and the participants wore shorts and jerseys.

The IIE staff guided us from reception to reception and took us on visits and excursions. Many speeches were delivered and much advice was given, but we also had some free time in which to explore the metropolitan area on our own and to absorb as many new impressions as possible: Times Square, Rockefeller Center, the Empire State Building, a jazz cellar, Yorkville (the German quarter), Chinatown, and much, much more. Late at night I tried to jot down all the day's impressions in a furiously scribbled diary that I kept, as I had done during my England stay, and which I still have today.

Three days later we were on our way to our various ultimate destinations. About twenty of our group boarded a train of the Baltimore and Ohio Railroad and headed south. In St. Louis there were five of us left, and for the last stretch of the journey to Dallas I was by myself. I was alone now, and despite the great expectations, the adventurous spirit, and a certain bravado, I felt insecure and also quite lonely. Besides, I was exhausted after the turmoil of the last days and weeks and, in addition, I had trouble coping with the temperature of over eighty degrees, which I encountered on my arrival at Union Station in Dallas. This temperature was, as I soon learned, not unusual for Texas in September, but for me in my heavy woolen traveling clothes and with my unwieldy suitcase, it seemed like an unbearable heat wave.

Unfortunately, somebody at the SMU dean's office had missed his assignment, and there was no one to meet me at the train station. I waited for some time for someone to appear, but after many questions I managed to find the right streetcar, called "the green dragon" by the SMU students. It was a forty-minute ride from Union Station to the SMU campus. I reported to the dean in charge and was received most cordially. He apologized for the slip-up of not having sent anyone to the station and then assigned a student to escort me to my room and to help me with my monster suitcase.

On the way from the administration building to my new living quarters, we had to walk across the whole campus. I admired the manicured lawns with several working fountains and the attractive buildings of red brick and white Georgian architecture. After all, I had never seen an American campus. I was curious as to which one of these handsome dormitories my companion was to take me. But I was in for a shock! He steered me in the direction of a large open field with five long one-story wooden structures. They were former army barracks. In the hallway I was immediately hit by the peculiar and unpleasant barracks odor, that mixture of dust and wood that I knew all too well. The buildings did not even have names. I was assigned to Dorm T, Room 5, and this T5 was to be my domicile for the next eleven months. I sat down on my bunk bed, and at once I heard loud talking and radio music from the adjacent room. Because of the thin walls, it sounded as though my neighbors on the left and right were in my room. The barracks had been erected by the university to cope with the flood of new postwar students who were studying under the GI bill. For me the circumstances of my arrival, after all my great expectations, were most sobering and depressing. In my diary I wrote of this day: *Und dafür bist du nun 5000 km gereist, um wieder in einer Mistbaracke zu sitzen,* "And you have traveled five thousand kilometers only to sit again in a rotten barracks." That moment, however, was the low point in my time in Dallas and at SMU. From then on matters improved by leaps and bounds. I spent an enormously enriching year in this new and continuously fascinating environment, made many friends, and also explored other parts of the country, including a bus trip to San Francisco. My first two semesters in the United States made for a tremendous learning experience.

At the end of the academic year I returned to Germany, as was required, and spent another semester at the University of Bonn. But I had already made up my mind. I wanted to become a citizen of the United States. In the spring of 1952 I returned to SMU, was awarded the Bachelor of Arts degree and, one year later, the degree of Master of Arts. From there I moved to New York City and fulfilled the requirements for the degree of Doctor of Philosophy at Columbia University. Today I am a professor in the Department of German Language and Literature at Smith College in Northampton, Massachusetts.

In those first few days at SMU, I, like all students, had to go through the tedious process of registration. It took me almost a whole day wandering from office to office, from one desk to another, and I had some difficulties in filling out the many forms and cards. At one of the last stations there were two lines, one short and one longer. Upon my question as to which line I should join, I received an answer I did not understand. Undoubtedly, my informant used

Photograph of myself after the year at Southern Methodist University, 1951, before I returned to the United States in 1952.

the word "GI," a term with which I was not familiar. When he saw the blank expression on my face, he tried to paraphrase and said that the short line was for veterans. That word I knew because "veteran" also exists in German as a rather old-fashioned term for former soldiers. Since I was that, I asked for the necessary forms and filled them out conscientiously: name, place of birth, and so on; then, length of service; two years; last unit; 20. Panzergrenadier-division, Regiment 76, Offiziersbewerberinspektion Hamburg-Rahlstedt; date

197

of discharge; August 14, 1945. Then I lined up again and slowly moved forward. Finally I was at the desk. The secretary briefly looked at my document, initialed it, and was about to stamp it to make it official when she stopped short, looked at me, and said with a friendly smile; "Well, Mr. Schümann. You are in the wrong line. You were in the wrong army." In later years I have often retold this little scene, but always with a small addendum to myself: "Right you are, Ms. Unknown Secretary, but you could have added, 'and in the wrong country at the wrong time.' "

It seems appropriate to conclude this book of memories by engaging in a brief discourse in which I clarify my reflections on a time long past. All of my remembrances are now of course colored for me by the political ramifications of methodical mind control, of youthful allegiance to the dictator and the party, of the willingness at that time to give our lives for the Third Reich. What happened during those years cannot be altered. What has changed is my acceptance of what was done and my understanding of it all. The life of a graduate student and, later, of a teacher and scholar provided me with the opportunities of confirming my attitude toward the past, seeing those years for what they truly were and moving forward in my own more mature thought. My abhorrence for the pure evil of the Hitler years has affected my understanding of history and underscores my need as an educator to be very clear in my view of the early years of the 1930s and 1940s. I am now a naturalized citizen of my country of choice and have been for more than thirty years. My own firm belief in democracy, in individual liberty and responsibility, and in tolerance is mirrored in the recent revolutionary changes in Eastern Europe. The end of the cold war era brings the democratic experiment more fully to life in the country I once knew well and still love. For I remain even today a divided person: at one with my adopted country and at the same time recalling the memories of my homeland, of being present.

Notes

1. The "unloved republic," is a term widely used by historians to indicate that large segments of the population were reluctant to accept the new republic as the successor state to Imperial Germany. In 1980 a book of documents appeared under the title *Die ungeliebte Republik*, edited by Wolfgang Michalka and Gottfried Niedhart.

2. *Der Jahrgang* is a difficult word to translate: age group, class, vintage (for wines). It means all people born in one specific calendar year. The white Jahrgang implies an intact age group. There is even a generational novel, written in 1928 by Ernst Glaeser, under the title *Jahrgang 1902*.

3. The Jena Burschenschaft was a patriotic student fraternity founded at the University of Jena in 1815. They selected black-red-gold as their colors after the Lützow Jäger, a *Freikorps* volunteer corps, formed in 1813, which gained national fame through the poems of Theodor Körner, one of its members who was killed in battle. The corps uniform was black with red lapels and gold braiding.

4. SA-Standartenführer was a rank in the paramilitary organization of the NSDAP, the SA *(Sturmabteilung)*. It was the equivalent of a colonel in the army.

5. He had read that the German submarine commander observed through his periscope the suffering and the drowning of hundreds of passengers and crew members and had enjoyed it.

6. SA-Scharführer, a rank in the SA, was the equivalent of a corporal or a sergeant in the army.

7. Since no portraits of Frederick I existed, the artist had simply used the head of the famous statue of the Bamberg Rider and had added the superimposed crown.

"Der Alte Fritz," a term of endearment for Frederick II, king of Prussia (1740–86), was coined during the last years of his reign. There are dozens of anecdotes about "Old Fred."

8. The Gymnasium, a type of school in the German educational system, was founded in 1788 in Prussia and still exists today. Students normally attend the Gymnasium from the ages of ten to nineteen. Successful passing of the final set of examinations entitles the student to matriculate at a university.

9. *"Schleswig-Holstein meerumschlungen,"* "Schleswig-Holstein embraced by the sea," is the name and first line of the hymn of the province of Schleswig-Holstein written in the nineteenth century.

2 / Young people must be guided by young people

1. *Der Pimpf* was originally a disparaging dialectical term for immature beginners in a trade—"he who cannot make a Pumpf-Pumpernickel." After 1920 it was used to designate young members in the Youth Movement without any derogatory connotation. The Youth Movement, *die Jugendbewegung*, was an organization founded at the turn of the century in Berlin. It was a rebellion of the adolescents against the rigid adult class structure of the Wilhelmian society, an attempt to create a life-style more appropriate for the young. Special features were the *Fahrten*, excursions into the countryside, always on foot, to achieve closer contact with primitive nature; revival of century-old folk songs; adoption of dress and uniforms emphasizing informality, such as open shirt collars and short pants; celebration of old "Germanic" annual events like winter and summer solstices.

2. Thomas Mann (1875–1955) was one of the most prominent German writers in the twentieth century and was a Nobel Prize winner in 1929. His novels *Buddenbrooks, The Magic Mountain, Dr. Faustus*, and his novellas *Tonio Kröger* and *Death in Venice* are classics of world literature today. Heinrich Mann (1871–1950) was the older brother of Thomas Mann. His best-known satirical novel, *Professor Unrat*, was made into the film classic *The Blue Angel*.

3. Günter Grass (1927–), a prominent postwar writer, has immortalized these ceremonies in his novella *Katz und Maus* (1961). His best-known work is the novel *Die Blechtrommel, The Tin Drum* (1959).

4. For *Dienst*, the English "service," or "work" is an inadequate translation. In the Hitler Youth and all other NS organizations it implied all activities connected with the organization. The ideological implication is service to the state or party. Even today it is customary for civil servants to say *Ich muss zum Dienst* for the English phrase "I have to go to work."

5. In NS terminology the word "system" was consistently used for the political structure of the Weimar Republic, and it was meant to be derogatory. It implied a corrupt and decadent pluralistic multiparty system that was unable to govern effectively, in contrast to the centralized one-party structure of the NS regime.

6. The Polish Corridor was the area south of Danzig (today Gdansk) carved out of former German provinces in the Versailles treaty. It was created to provide the newly founded Polish state with access to the Baltic Sea. It separated the province of East Prussia from the rest of Germany.

7. The full text of the first stanza of the song is quoted from memory. The prose translation is my own.

Es zittern die morschen Knochen
Der Welt vor dem grossen Krieg.
Wir haben den Schrecken gebrochen,
Für uns war's ein grosser Sieg
Wir werden weiter marschieren,
Wenn alles in Scherben fällt.
Denn heute da hört uns Deutschland
Und morgen die ganze Welt.

The rotten bones of the world tremble facing the great war. We have conquered this terror. It was a great victory for us. We will go on marching even though everything will go to pieces. Because today Germany will hear us and tomorrow the whole world.

8. *Kristallnacht* was the centrally organized assault of SA units on Jewish stores and synagogues on November 8, 1938, although the NS propaganda ministry immediately called it a "spontaneous expression of the free will of the German population." With the grim humor characteristic of Berliners, these pogroms were named "Crystal Night," because the morning after the attacks the streets were covered with glittering splinters from the smashed windows and glass doors.

9. Today there exists a vast literature on German public opinion and the Jewish question, and I am familiar with some of these studies, such as Herbert A. Strauss and Norbert Kampe, eds., *Antisemitismus: Von der Judenfeindschaft zum Holocaust* (Frankfurt a. Main and New York: Campus Verlag, 1985).

3 / The flag rates higher than death

1. KLV, *Kinderlandverschickung*, was a program to evacuate children from the larger industrial centers to the less threatened areas in central and southern Germany. The program was initiated in 1941 just before the first massive air raids on German cities. See chapter 9.
2. *Der Wandervogel*, literally "migrant bird," was the name of the core organization of the Youth Movement.

4 / As it actually happened

1. The term *Mark* was artificially revived. In medieval times it was a "boundary land." A *Markgraf* was a nobleman commissioned by the emperor to protect the Reich by strengthening his border province, the "Mark." In NS terminology Schleswig-Holstein was sometimes called *Nordmark*.
Memelland was a territory named after the river Memel (Njemen in Russian) and the port city Memel and until 1919 was part of Prussia. The Sudetenland, an area named after the Sudeten mountain range separating Bohemia and Silesia, soon became the term for all border territories of the newly founded CSSR, Germany, and Austria, where many ethnic Germans lived. According to the Munich Agreement (September 29, 1938) between Germany, Italy, France, and Great Britain, Germany was entitled to the border territories of the Sudetenland. Czechoslovakia was only informed of this four-power agreement, but peace in Europe appeared to have been saved. Today the Munich Agreement has become synonymous with appeasement.
2. The English word "polder" is of Dutch origin. It is a tract of low land reclaimed from a body of water, usually the sea. The German is *der Koog* or *Kog*.
3. Albert Speer was an architectural adviser to Hitler and the choreographer of the NS mass rallies. During the war he became Reichsminister for armament and ammunition. At the Nuremberg trials he was sentenced to twenty years imprisonment.
4. Leopold von Ranke (1795–1886) was dean of nineteenth-century historians in Germany. Among his major works were *Die römischen Päpste; Deutsche Geschichte im Zeitalter der Reformation; Weltgeschichte*. His world-famous quote, *wie es eigentlich gewesen*, indicates an approach of utmost objectivity in historical writing and research for generations of historians in the nineteenth and early twentieth centuries.
5. During the war an album with cigarette pictures was published with the title *Raubstaat England*, "Robber-Nation England," which attempted to prove with maps, pictures, cartoons, and a long essay that the British had acquired all their possessions by shamelessly oppressing and exploiting the native population.
6. Gleiwitz was a former German city in Upper Silesia. The raid of the radio station in August 1939 was staged by the SS using concentration camp inmates dressed in Polish uniforms.

5 / Many enemies, much honor

1. A system of fortification on France's eastern border, the Maginot line was begun in 1930 to protect against a potential German invasion like the ones in 1870 and 1914. It was named after the French defense minister. The Westwall, a similar system of fortification, was on the German side of the French-German border. Construction began in 1938.

2. The "fourth division of Poland" was an analogy to the three previous divisions: in 1772 Poland lost half of its territory and a third of its population to Russia and Prussia and Austria; in 1793 Russia and Prussia forced further cession of territory; and in 1795 Russia, Prussia, and Austria divided the rest of the country. This final division meant the end of Poland as a nation, and it was not resurrected until 1919.

3. The Panzergrenadiere historically were elite infantry soldiers trained to throw grenades. During the war the older title *Schütze* was replaced by the new term *Grenadier* in recognition of the outstanding achievements of the German infantry. Panzergrenadiere were motorized infantry units following Panzer spearheads into battle, usually in half-tracks.

4. Johann Wolfgang Goethe (1749–1832) is generally recognized as the greatest German poet and is ranked with Dante and Shakespeare. His lyric poetry, his *Faust* drama, the novels *Die Leiden des jungen Werthers* and *Wilhelm Meisters Lehrjahre* are classics of world literature. The decades of 1770 to 1830 are often referred to as "the Age of Goethe."

5. Heinrich von Kleist (1777–1811) was a writer of novellas *(Michael Kohlhaas)* and plays *(Prinz Friedrich von Homburg)*.

6. Theodor Storm (1817–33) was a poet and novella writer *(Der Schimmelreiter)*. Wilhelm Raabe (1831–1910) was a novelist *(Die Schwarze Galeere;* the trilogy *Der Hungerpastor, Abu Telfan, Der Schüdderump)*. Both Storm and Raabe are considered representative of poetic realism.

Friedrich Schiller (1757–1805), a dramatist, poet, historian, and philosopher, is often called one of the greatest German literary figures, second only to Goethe. His dramatic masterpiece is the trilogy *Wallenstein*. His "Ode to Joy" was used by Beethoven for the finale of the Ninth Symphony. Rainer Maria Rilke (1875–1926) is considered by many to be the greatest modern German poet *(Duineser Elegien)*. Theodor Fontane (1819–98) was a writer of ballads and realistic novels *(Effi Briest)*.

7. Karl May (1842–1912) was an immensely popular writer of adventure and travel stories.

6 / Something exciting was going on again

1. In April 1915 Churchill had conceived the plan for an amphibious operation to conquer Gallipoli, a peninsula west of the Dardanelles, and open the way for Allied forces to Constantinople, thus eliminating Turkey as an ally of the Central Powers, and then to push north to threaten Austria-Hungary. It was a military catastrophe for the Allied forces, and they were withdrawn eight months later.

2. Flieger-HJ was a special branch of the Hitler Youth for boys aged fourteen to eighteen who were interested in airplanes and flying. Other special branches were the *Marine-HJ* and the *Motor-HJ*.

3. The Gestapo, an acronym for *Geheime Staatspolizei*, "secret state police," was administratively part of the SS and became a notoriously inhumane and feared government agency for the protection of the NS regime; it was allowed to operate without any restraint by the judiciary.

7 / My Lord, doesn't this ever stop!

1. Caspar David Friedrich (1774–1840) was a German romantic landscape painter.

2. Tobruk, port city in northeast Libya on the Mediterranean Sea, was fiercely contested during the war in Africa and changed hands several times.

3. "Landser" was a colloquial term for soldier, like the American "GI" in World War II and "grunt" in the Vietnam War. It was used only in the Wehrmacht of the Second World War. Its derivation is unclear, though it could be based on *Landsmann*, "countryman" or "comrade."

8 / *Amerikabild*

1. Rum grog, a popular drink in northern Germany, especially among sailors, consists of rum, sugar, and hot water. Wine grog is a similar drink, but instead of rum, red wine is used for the preparation.

2. Instead of absolving the mandatory two years of military service, a group of draftees was allowed to serve only one year. They were mostly young men who had attended the Gymnasium for at least six years. My father qualified for this dispensation because he had obtained his mate's license, the A5 diploma, from the merchant marine school.

3. BDM, *Bund deutscher Mädel*, was the youth organization for girls and young women aged ten to eighteen. JM, *Jungmädelbund*, the organization for the younger girls, aged ten to fourteen, was a subbranch of the BDM and the equivalent to the DJ for boys.

9 / What must not be, does not exist

1. *Nibelungenlied*, a German epic of the early thirteenth century written in Middle High German by a southern German poet, recounts the story of Siegfried and Kriemhild and the annihilation of the Burgundians at Attila's court. *Gudrunsage*, another thirteenth-century German epic, was influenced by the *Nibelungenlied*.

2. The Feldherrnhalle is a memorial hall in the center of Munich. During the putsch on November 9, 1923, Hitler's march to the Feldherrnhalle was stopped forcibly by police and army units loyal to the Bavarian state government.

3. Barbarossa was the name given Frederick I, emperor of the Holy Roman Empire (1155–90). Prinz Eugen was the best-known military commander of the Holy Roman Empire in the eighteenth century (1663–1736). Seydlitz was a famous Prussian general under Frederick the Great (1721–73). Blücher was a popular Prussian military commander during the Napoleonic wars (1742–1819). Moltke was the master strategist of the Prussian army in the wars against Denmark (1864), Austria (1866), and France (1870–71).

4. The famous battlefields are: Belgrade, the war of Spanish succession; Leuthen, the Seven Years' War; Waterloo, the Napoleonic wars; Königgrätz, the Prussian-Austrian war; Sedan, the Franco-German War; the Somme, World War I.

5. U-boat wolf packs were groups of German submarines which attacked Allied convoys in World War II. This new tactic was called *Rudeltaktik (Rudel,* "wolf pack") and was very successful from 1940 to 1943.

10 / Tough times—tough people (and soft heads)

1. The collective term for both groups was *Flakhelfer* (Flak, an abbreviation for *Flugzeugabwehrkanone,* "antiaircraft gun").

2. Skat, a popular card game in Germany, is nearly two hundred years old. Three players participate. The deck consists of thirty-two cards, the lowest cards being the four sevens.

11 / They act as though the war will go on forever

1. The *Stadt-Bahn,* "city train," connected the center of the city with Hamburg's suburbs and outer regions. *U-Bahn* is the abbreviation for *Untergrund-Bahn,* subway.

2. After basic training, future officers were trained in the OB-Inspektion for six months and were called *Offiziersbewerber,* OB. They were then sent to the front with the rank of special corporal, *Fahnenjunker-Unteroffizier.*

3. *Heim-ins-Reich Bewegung,* literally "home-to-the-Reich movement," was the attempt by the NS regime started in the thirties to persuade or lure "ethnic Germans" back to Germany. Most of the families of these ethnic Germans, Volksdeutsche, had lived for generations in other parts of the world—for example, in the Balkans, along the Volga River, or in Brazil.

4. Warthegau was one of the administrative units created after Poland had been carved up following its defeat in 1939. Warthegau means "Warthe province"; the Warthe River (in Polish *Warta*) is a large tributary of the Oder River.

12 / Every person for himself

1. Gauleiter was a relatively high rank in the NS hierarchy. A *Gau* corresponded often to the older German provinces. A Gauleiter can be compared to today's prime ministers in Germany or to a governor in the United States.

2. Der Volkssturm, literally "people's storm" or "people's assault," was an analogy to the *Landsturm*, units of untrained volunteers fighting against French hegemony during the Napoleonic wars. The NS propaganda announced the Volkssturm's formation with much fanfare during the last months of the war as a spontaneously created resistance movement against the Allied forces once they had entered German territory. There was nothing spontaneous about these last reserves, and they were of no military significance.

13 / The bad years

1. The Waffen-SS was the armed branch of the notorious SS organization. SS divisions were considered elite units because of their modern equipment and their alleged fierce fighting spirit. There existed considerable rivalry between regular army units and Waffen-SS units.

2. In January 1923 French troops occupied the Ruhr area, where the German coal and steel industry was concentrated. The reason for this drastic step was the claim that the German government had been deliberately tardy in delivering the coal reparation payments which had been stipulated in the Versailles treaty. The last French soldiers did not leave until August 1925.

3. From 1923 to 1938 nine *Parteitage*, literally "party days," were held in Nuremberg. The city was chosen by Hitler because it seemed to represent *das Altdeutsche*, the specific, splendid German elements of the late Middle Ages and the Renaissance, especially as described by the German romantic writers. The outstanding representative of this period was Albrecht Dürer, one of Germany's greatest painters (1471–1528), whose home city was Nürnberg. The Allied tribunal selected the city for the trials because it symbolized to them the NSDAP spirit.

4. The Reichstag, historically the diet of the Holy Roman Empire, from 1871 to 1933 was the lower chamber of the legislature in Imperial Germany and the Weimar Republic. After March 1933, it was just a forum for pro forma approval of all measures of the NS executive government.

5. The term "Trümmerliteratur" was coined by the 1972 Nobel Prize winner Heinrich Böll. His early writings, short stories, and novels, deal primarily with the survival efforts of ordinary people among the "rubble" of destroyed Germany toward the end of the war and during the immediate postwar years. Another writer of Trümmerliteratur was Wolfgang Borchert (1921–47) with his enormously successful play *Draussen vor der Tür, The Man Outside*.

14 / The need to catch up

1. In the 1950s there raged a continuous debate in Germany and abroad as to whether the whole German nation should be held responsible for the crimes of the Hitler regime. Professor Theodor Heuss, president of the newly founded Federal Republic of Germany, rejected the concept of collective guilt for any nation and suggested the term "collective shame" for the German people.

2. Gotthold Ephraim Lessing (1729–81), dramatist, essayist, and critic, was the outstanding thinker of the German Enlightenment. In addition to *Nathan der Weise* (1779), his best-known plays are *Mina von Barnhelm* (1767) and *Emilia Galotti* (1772). Heinrich Heine (1797–1856) was a poet, essayist, and writer of verse satires (*Deutschland. Ein Wintermärchen*, 1844). His lyrics were used in some three thousand compositions by Robert Schumann, Franz Schubert, and many others. His best-known song, "Die Lorelei," has become a German folk song. Virtually all his work has been translated into English. Annette Kolb (1870–1967) was another German novelist, essayist, and poet who fled Nazi Germany.

3. Bertolt Brecht (1898–1956) was a dramatist, poet, and essayist. His *Die Dreigroschenoper* (1928), in collaboration with Kurt Weill, became an international success. In his theoretical writings on the theater, his concept of the revolutionary "epic theater" had far-reaching effects. It was designed to create—through the use of techniques such as bright lights, films, and mottoes displayed on cards—a politically conscious distance between the spectator and the stage.

Hermann Hesse (1877–1962), novelist and poet, wrote, in addition to *Das Glasperlenspiel (The Glass Bead Game)*, the novels *Siddharta* (1922) and *Steppenwolf* (1927), among his best-known works. He was awarded the Nobel Prize in 1946.

4. Each department and institute at a German university has its own seminar library where books are to be used in situ and can only be checked out overnight.

5. Today the Volksschule is called Hauptschule which the majority of all school-age children attend for nine years (formerly eight years).

15 / In the wrong army

1. On June 20, 1948, the old Reichsmark (RM) currency was declared invalid and was replaced by the Deutsche Mark (DM). The exchange rate for RM and DM was set at 10:1. In the Soviet occupation zone a similar reform was carried out four days later, on June 24, 1948.

2. Akademische Freiheit was the concept of absolute freedom for scholars and students to study, teach, research, and publish—*Freiheit des Forschens, Lehrens, und Lernens*. It was first formulated and implemented by the writer, educator, and statesman Wilhelm von Humboldt (1767–1835) at the founding of the University of Berlin, 1810.

Index

WITHDRAWN

BEING PRESENT
was composed in 10/12 Electra on a Xyvision system
with Linotron 202 output
by BookMasters, Inc.;
with initial capitals and book title set in Fraktur
by Reporter Typographics;
printed by sheet-fed offset on 60-pound, acid-free,
Glatfelter Natural stock
by Braun-Brumfiled, Inc.;
text designed by Will Underwood;
jacket designed by Diana Gordy;
and published by
KENT STATE UNIVERSITY PRESS
Kent, Ohio 44242